PAPER TO FLIGHT

The Design Story of India's Carrier Borne Fighter

PAPER TO FLIGHT

The Design Story of India's Carrier Borne Fighter

Cmde. CD Balaji (Retd)
Distinguished Scientist
Former Director ADA

Foreword by

Admiral Arun Prakash, PVSM, AVSM, VrC, VSM (Retd)
Former Chief of the Naval Staff

PENTAGON PRESS LLP

First published in 2024 by
PENTAGON PRESS LLP
206, Peacock Lane, Shahpur Jat
New Delhi-110049, India
Contact: 011-26490600

Printed by Aegean Offset Printers, Greater Noida
Cover Illustration by Ms. Sonali K Balaji

ISBN 978-81-971986-7-0

www.pentagonpress.in

CONTENTS

	Foreword	*vii*
	Preface	*xiii*
1.	Recap of LCA Air Force Version (Tejas)	1
2.	Background & Summary of LCA Naval Version	13
3.	The Beginning: LCA AF, Project Definition & Pre-Project Phase of LCA Navy	20
4.	Carrier-Borne Fighter Aircraft	30
5.	Commonality & Differences with LCA AF and Major Challenges	42
6.	Design & Development Cycle of LCA Navy	58
	Colour Picture Sheets	81
7.	Shore Based Test Facility (SBTF)	89
8.	Arrester Hook System (AHS)	112
9.	Landing Gear (LG)	133
10.	Leading Edge Vortex Control (LEVCON)	147
11.	Other Specialised Test Facilities	156
12.	Carrier Compatibility Test (CCT) or Carrier Suitability Demonstration (CSD)	171
13.	Control Law (CLAW) Development	183

14. LCA Navy Mk2 – As of Mar 2017 199

15. My Experiences as Director ADA 212

16. Conclusions & Lessons Learnt 227

In Gratitude 232

Tables – For details 234

Glossary 245

Index 255

FOREWORD

This book provides an absorbing account of a bold and audacious technological initiative, successfully undertaken by India's Aeronautical Development Agency (ADA), to transform a combat aircraft, designed purely for land-based operations, into a platform, compatible with the extreme demands of operations from an aircraft carrier. Underpinning the narrative is the remarkable journey of the author, Commodore CD Balaji himself, from the position of aeronautical engineer in a carrier-borne naval air squadron, to the Project Director LCA Navy, in the grade of Scientist-H and then the prestigious post of Director, ADA, in the grade of a Distinguished Scientist.

Not many recall that the first combat aircraft, designed and built in India, albeit with foreign assistance, the HF-24, Marut, took flight in mid-1961. After building 167 Maruts, Hindustan Aeronautics Ltd (HAL), shut shop, and for the next few decades, India imported or license-built a few hundred combat aircraft, of Soviet and western origin. It was only in the mid-1980s that we embarked, once again, upon a project to design and develop an indigenous combat aircraft, designated the Light Combat Aircraft or LCA, meant to replace over 300 MiG-21s, in IAF service since the 1960s.

Technologically ambitious in scope, the LCA faced early scepticism, both from the government and the IAF. The early 1990s, thus, saw the project languishing for want of funds. At this juncture, Naval Headquarters (NHQ) was in the process of examining various design options for its projected Indigenous Aircraft Carrier (designated, IAC-1). The dimensions as well as configuration of this ship would be influenced by the choice of aircraft selected, but this had become a vexed issue.

Availability of carrier capable fighters was, at that point, limited to just a handful of aircraft of US and French origin, all of them requiring a steam catapult for ship launch. Catapults were, however, manufactured only in America, and given the uncertain state of India-US relationship, this option had been discounted by NHQ. The only ship-borne aircraft which did not need a catapult (because it used a ski-jump) was the vertical take-off/landing, Sea Harrier fighter, already in IN service. The Sea Harrier was, however, a sub-sonic aircraft, and the navy wanted a more advanced fighter. This is where the USSR opened new vistas by pioneering a novel technique for carrier operations.

In the mid-1980s, Soviet engineers, in the face of much scepticism, embarked on a bold experiment. Using the ski-jump - a recent British innovation – they proved that it was possible for land-based fighters to get airborne after a very short take-off run, and could, therefore, undertake ship launch, without a catapult. A heavily modified Sukhoi-27 and MiG-29, fitted with a tail-hook, were launched from a ski-jump equipped aircraft carrier, and recovered, on board, using arrester wires. The Soviets, thus, evolved a new mode of carrier operations, termed STOBAR, for "short take-off but arrested recovery".

Against this backdrop, NHQ felt that a STOBAR version of the LCA could offer an attractive indigenous option for the new aircraft carrier. A tentative query was sent out to ADA, about the feasibility of evolving a ship-borne version of the LCA. On receiving a positive response, I as the Assistant Chief of Naval Staff (Air), initiated discussions with ADA. While Dr Kota Harinarayana, leader of the LCA design team, was enthusiastic about the prospect, he did not underestimate the challenges involved, in converting the LCA into a carrier capable aircraft, and sought to undertake a detailed examination. Consequently, in 1993, NHQ accorded formal approval, and a sanction of Rs. 4 crores for ADA to initiate a project-definition study.

While the study confirmed feasibility of the project, and ADA scientists expressed willingness to take on all challenges, the low-speed characteristics of a tail-less, delta-wing aircraft, especially, in the context of stability post-ski jump exit and pilot visibility on landing approach, were areas of major concern. Other issues that would need in-depth examination were:

- Overall structural robustness to withstand the stress of high vertical and horizontal forces involved in carrier-borne operations.

- Landing gear re-design which could absorb the high sink-rates required for arrested landings.
- Design and position of an arrester-hook which would have to withstand immense loading.
- Need for lift-augmentation devices, due to lower ski-jump exit and landing speeds.
- Development of special digital flight-control laws for ski-jump take-offs and pinpoint deck-landings.

The navy re-affirmed its faith in the concept by initiating a jointly-funded engineering development programme and contributing Rs. 400 crores as well as personnel to ADA for the development of a carrier-borne version of the aircraft, dubbed, LCA Navy, which would operate in the STOBAR mode.

At this juncture, CD Balaji, then a young Captain in the Navy, was deputed by NHQ to ADA in 2002, as the Navy's representative in ADA. He was tasked to draw up a note for the Cabinet according approval for a full-scale engineering development of LCA Navy. Balaji went on to play a pivotal role from the earliest phases of the project, acquiring comprehensive insights and understanding of the challenges of the program, that have enabled him to write this book.

The LCA Navy project was seen by the IN as a pioneering initiative, whose success would not only provide a boost to our defence-technology base, but also place India in a select list of just three countries which could design and produce carrier-borne aircraft. However, it is important to point out, that both NHQ and ADA were cognizant of the possibility that this project may, either not succeed, or fail to meet the performance-criteria/timelines stipulated. NHQ had, therefore, recorded a decision, that in parallel with the LCA Navy development, it would identify an alternative aircraft for its new carriers. As the LCA Navy programme kept slipping, this alternative turned out to be the MiG-29K, acquired, along with INS *Vikramaditya*, in 2010, and which now also equips INS *Vikrant* (IAC-1).

Having surmounted design and engineering challenges and suffered delays due to internal and external factors, the prototype LCA Navy took its first flight in April 2012. After an intense flight-test campaign in Goa, the LCA

Navy made its historic first landing on INS *Vikramaditya* on 11 January 2020, by naval test pilot, Cmde JA Maolankar, and therefore demonstrated deck operations. This was followed the very next day by a successful ski-jump launch. Yet another, historic, milestone was the February 2023 landing of India's indigenous LCA Navy, by another naval test pilot, Cmde Shivnath Dahiya, on board the indigenous aircraft carrier, INS *Vikrant.*

The LCA Navy project was unique in many respects. Conversion of a shore-based aircraft into a carrier variant was, an undertaking, fraught with risk and uncertainty, and its ultimate success demonstrated the confidence and ingenuity of our scientists. Excellent IN-ADA/DRDO synergy was evident in the process of continuous consultation between the two, as well as funding and personnel support provided by NHQ. Notable was the ADA/DRDO's nomination of Cmde Balaji, a naval aeronautical engineer, as Director ADA, and Cmde Maolankar, a naval aviator, as project test pilot. The creation of a sophisticated, shore-based test facility, along with a telemetry station, in Goa, where ski-jump launches and arrested landings can be actually undertaken is another valuable fall-out of this project.

The LCA Navy, has not met the navy's operational requirements, and will not be inducted into service, either in its current version, or as Mark 2. This has caused much disappointment, not only for ADA, but also for those of us, who had supported the project for decades. The IN has, however, drawn satisfaction from the fact that its investment in a "technological experiment" has paid such rich dividends in terms of experience gained. This bold leap into the unknown, has served as a huge confidence-building exercise for everyone involved: ADA scientists and flight-test personnel as well as HAL production engineers and the naval staff. There should be no doubt that the huge amount of flight-test data generated by the LCA Navy project will form an invaluable basis of ADA's other aeronautical ventures: the navy's Twin-engine Deck-based Fighter (TEDBF), as well as the IAF's advanced medium combat aircraft (AMCA).

This book is a valuable compendium of information, which describes the unique journey from conceptualization to actual flight, of an aircraft, emphasizing the importance of innovation and collaboration in the aerospace field. It highlights the technological challenges, project phases, and collaborative efforts of various organizations involved in the design and development of the LCA Navy. Seldom will the Indian reader find such detailed coverage of aspects such as the aircraft requirements, technology development, testing, and integration of systems, as well as the experiences and lessons – typical to India - learned throughout the project.

Cmde Balaji is to be commended for having painstakingly recorded his 15-year long experience in the LCA project - India's pioneering venture in the field of aeronautical design, production and flight-testing. I have no doubt that this book will find readership and appreciation; not just amongst the aeronautical fraternity, but also amongst the larger military aviation community as well as analysts, and laypersons, alike.

Goa
03 August 2024

Admiral Arun Prakash, PVSM, AVSM, VrC, VSM (Retd)
Former Chief of the Naval Staff

PREFACE

'Paper to Flight' is an attempt to chronicle both the evolution of aircraft development and my personal journey in it. I graduated in Mechanical Engineering and was commissioned into the Indian Navy in September 1978, where I specialised in naval aviation and gained experience in operation and maintenance of aircraft, and operating from an aircraft carrier. I later pursued a Master's degree in Aerospace Engineering from the Indian Institute of Science, Bengaluru. This combination of hands-on carrier operations and academic expertise led to a golden opportunity: developing a carrier-borne fighter aircraft for India.

In 2002, I joined the Aeronautical Development Agency (ADA) on deputation to work on the development of a Naval Version of the Light Combat Aircraft (LCA Navy). My involvement began with securing government approval in March 2003 and continued through to the designing, developing, building, and flight testing of the LCA Navy prototypes. In a nutshell, as project director, I oversaw this comprehensive process, capturing the essence of '*From paper to flight*'.

A milestone was achieved with the historic maiden flight of the first naval variant (NP1) on 27 April 2012, followed by the maiden ski-jump launch on 20 December 2014. History was made in January 2020 when the aircraft landed and took-off from *INS Vikramaditya*.

On 1 December 2006, I gave up my uniform and was permanently absorbed into the ADA, where I rose to the grade of Distinguished Scientist and was appointed as Programme Director (Combat Aircraft) and Director, ADA, from July 2015. I superannuated from this position on 31 March 2017. It is to the credit of the Department of Defence (R&D) that they accepted and reposed faith in an erstwhile uniformed person to head this prestigious organisation. Let me briefly describe the entire journey of 'paper to flight' of the Naval Version of the Light Combat Aircraft (LCA Navy).

The LCA Navy is the first-of-its-kind carrier-based fighter aircraft developed by the country. The original requirement for a single-engine light aircraft was to replace the Sea Harrier, which was in operation with the Indian Navy (IN). The top-level operational concept of the LCA Navy was to develop it for Ski-jump Take-off But Arrested Recovery (STOBAR) aircraft carriers. *INS Viraat,* on which Sea Harriers operated, is Ski-jump Take-off and Vertical Landing (STOVL) based. The LCA Navy had to be adapted for operating on *INS Vikramaditya,* which was under upgrading and refitting primarily for MiG-29K operations in Russia, as well as for the future indigenous carrier, *INS Vikrant.* The requirements sought the development of a single-seat fighter as well as a two-seat trainer variant of the LCA Navy.

Carrier interface details are critical inputs for the design of deck-based aircraft. The design of the LCA Navy was initiated with broad-based inputs on the carriers with which the aircraft was to be made compatible.

The main constraint imposed on the design was to convert the land-based LCA with deck interface features to make it compatible with Indian Navy carriers. Along with this requirement from the Indian Navy, the design of a trainer variant for the Indian Air Force had yet to be undertaken. Therefore, a decision was made to design a fuselage shape that would be common to both the LCA Air Force trainer as well as the LCA Navy fighter and trainer variants. This would incorporate an additional nose droop required to achieve higher over-the-nose vision angle, allowing the naval variant to approach the carrier at a higher angle of attack and, hence, reduced speed. Inherently, commonality became a necessity considering the challenges of resources available for this programme.

As previously mentioned, the land-based aircraft with the engine selected to suit its requirements was adapted for the naval version also. However, high sink rate landing and arrested landing loads associated with the STOBAR configuration necessitated a higher strength landing gear, inclusion of an arrester hook, and associated structural reinforcements. To reduce approach speed during the landing phase, an aerodynamic solution in the form of LEVCON, a flight control surface at the leading edge apex of the wing, was introduced.

The dry empty mass of the aircraft was originally estimated to increase by around 600 kg, and design studies indicated that this would still permit the aircraft to remain within the hook-to-wire engagement speed limits of the carriers.

The landing gear design posed a tough challenge in terms of interfacing it as a fuselage-mounted configuration. The requirement for a wider track to utilise the Restraining Gear System (RGS) on the carriers and larger shock absorbers increased stowage volume, resulting in large fairings that contributed to drag.

The arrester hook interface in the rear fuselage of a single-engine configuration had associated challenges that required extra structural reinforcement for load transfer during arrested landing on a carrier. In the case of the LCA Navy, the rear fuselage bottom zone was completely covered by the engine bay door, which lacked the rigidity required for interfacing the arrester hook with the large load transfer demands. A separate platform had to be added for this purpose. This external structure increased drag, and the additional mass also had to be compensated for with ballast in the nose section.

As the design effort progressed and mission performance targets were clearly defined by the user, an evaluation of the attained configuration was carried out. The mass of the aircraft exceeded the original estimate by around 500 kg.

Design optimisation efforts, with the objectives to enhance installed thrust and reduce mass, were prioritised, and a multi-disciplinary committee was formed to define the way ahead. Based on deliberations, activities to identify weight reduction in the fuselage and landing gear were undertaken. An aerodynamic solution to improve the air intake pressure recovery was implemented, resulting in the incorporation of a three-door auxiliary intake feature with an incremental intake pressure gain on the second LCA Navy prototype, NP2.

The 'commonality' with the LCA AF version, which was imposed as a constraint, resulted in a sub-optimal solution even for the available engine option. However, as a first-time development of naval aircraft, this approach covered the risks involved in the 'up and away' flight control characteristics while focusing on the 'launch and recovery' aspects of the flight regime.

The engineering effort towards the design and development of the naval variant derived from the LCA AF aircraft culminated in successfully demonstrating carrier suitability testing on the *INS Vikramaditya* and *INS Vikrant*, even with resource constraints as compared to other peer programmes. Phase-1 of Full-Scale Engineering Development of the Naval Version of the Light Combat Aircraft (FSED Navy Phase-1) thus established a path for future naval combat aircraft development in the country. It is understood that the venture aims to develop a Twin-Engine Deck-Based Fighter aircraft (TEDBF) on the lessons learnt from the development of the LCA Navy.

High-strength landing gear of the LCA Navy was a completely new design, requiring fresh sourcing of indigenous maraging steel raw material from Midhani. This was followed by forging large components of landing gear, which required a high-tonnage press identified after considerable effort. Machining the large landing gear parts of maraging steel was challenging due to frequent cutting tool failures. Wire cutting processes were used to realise the parts through identified vendors with special-purpose machines.

The rotary-geared LEVCON actuator integration on the stub wing and the moving flight control surface presented unprecedented precision manufacturing challenges for a part about 1,600 mm long. This was overcome with process improvisations during machining.

Specific requirements for the qualification of the airframe and systems, due to the high sink rate recovery onboard the carrier and the shocks from the Arresting Gear System (AGS), had to be pioneered in this programme as a first-time naval aircraft development effort.

Carrier Compatibility Testing (CCT) is an elaborate process for making the aircraft operational on a carrier. The Shore Based Test Facility (SBTF) built at the Naval Air Station in Goa was specially set up for CCT. The SBTF replicates launch and recovery features onboard the carrier. The aircraft was cleared for flight trials onboard the carrier after successful trials on the SBTF.

A hardware-in-loop simulator, the 'Iron Bird', specific to the LCA Navy, was built. Simulation in this facility, with naval aircraft-specific launch and recovery simulations, was carried out towards certification.

The design of the landing gear for the LCA Navy was validated to withstand high sink rate landing loads in carrier operations landing gear drop test rig at a vertical sink velocity of 7.1 m/sec. The arrester hook, being a new introduction for the naval aircraft, was tested in a dedicated test facility.

All system equipment was separately qualified to withstand the significantly larger arrested landing shock loads. This was successfully completed with specially designed fixtures and the utilisation of test facilities in the country.

All in all, it was an exciting and challenging journey of 'paper to flight' that I was able to participate in. The crowning glory were the flights that I undertook in both the LCA Air Force trainer and the LCA Navy trainer that gave me a first-hand experience of the wonderful machine.

Bengaluru
21 September 2024

Cmde. CD Balaji (Retd)
Distinguished Scientist
Former Director ADA

Emotional Moments after Maiden Ski-Jump of LCA Navy NP1

1

RECAP OF LCA AIR FORCE VERSION (TEJAS)

In the 1980s, the aviation landscape of India looked sparse. Taking a commercial flight between two cities in India was a once-in-a-lifetime aspiration for most middle-class Indians. Airports were few and far between, and their presence usually meant that the city was either a metro, an international tourist destination, inaccessible by other means or, a military air base with restricted access.

It is true that the Indian Air Force (IAF) and Indian Navy (IN) have a fleet of helicopters (choppers), fighter aircraft, transport aircraft, reconnaissance aircraft and Unmanned Air Vehicles (UAVs). However, they were largely procured from countries like Russia, France, the UK, and USA. In some cases, these have been built under licence in India. The challenges in this have been high cost, maintenance-intensive, a strong dependence on foreign vendors for spares and service support, etc. Further, invariably, we would end up with outdated technologies, limited access to software, and other such constraints.

In such circumstances, it was almost audacious for India to envision developing a 4th-generation fighter aircraft that would meet the operational needs of the IAF. Remember, it had been over two decades since the HF-24 (Marut) project by Hindustan Aeronautics Limited (HAL). In the meantime, technologies and processes involved in developing an aircraft had leapfrogged into the future.

The team that took it upon themselves to commence the Light Combat Aircraft (LCA) project did not need to just develop the aircraft – they had to first build the ecosystem within which to develop it. This involved, firstly, identifying and pooling human resources. The logical next step involved identifying the technologies envisaged for contemporary fighter aircraft and the gaps in the country. It then involved building up the infrastructure for designing, building, and testing the aircraft.

It has to be pointed out that it was an extremely progressive and far-sighted decision to leap forward from the 2nd generation to 4th generation technologies at the very beginning. People may wonder at this step. It was the tough road to take but a necessary one; otherwise, we would have spent decades trying to build an aircraft that would have become obsolete when ready.

Dr. VS Arunachalam, former Scientific Advisor to the Defence Minister, catalysed the need to develop aeronautics in the country and hence the seeds of the Aeronautical Development Agency (ADA) were sown in the early 1980s.

The first step in this development journey was to understand the magnitude of the design and development gaps that existed in terms of human resources, Technology Readiness Levels (TRLs), and other infrastructure to handle this massive task. *(Definitions of TRLs are tabulated in the section on tables at the end of this book at page 234).*

The next step was to pull together a small band of dedicated scientists, engineers, technologists, academicians and others to take stock of the envisaged dream and see how it could be realised. There was a need to develop advanced technologies necessary for a contemporary aircraft, and the resources and strengths dispersed in the country had to be brought together by an agency acting as a nodal point. Accordingly, the ADA was formed as an autonomous body in 1984 to undertake coordinated development of an LCA, and it started functioning in 1985. The Indian Air Force (IAF) issued Air Staff Requirements (ASR) for the LCA in October 1985 indicating a requirement of 200 LCA fighters and 20 LCA trainers.

Dr. APJ Abdul Kalam, former President of India, was the Secretary, Dept. of Defence R&D and the Chief of the DRDO from July 1992 to December 1999. He has famously quoted "*You have to dream before your dreams come true.*" This was so true in the context of dreaming to develop a fighter aircraft in the country. He was closely followed by Dr. VK Aatre under whose watch the historic maiden flight of the LCA took place on 4 January 2001. It was also during his tenure that the Cabinet approval for full-scale engineering development of the Naval version of the LCA was accorded in March 2003. These pioneers shaped the history of fighter aircraft development in the country.

Dedicated personnel came together from various established and stable organisations like HAL, ISRO, DRDO, academia, certifying agencies, and quality assurance agencies, among others. They left their comfort zone and plunged to achieve something extremely important for the country. In the initial stages, major contributions from the Indian Air Force and the Indian Navy were in terms of test pilots and flight test engineers. These persons would play a pivotal role not just in flight testing but also in participating actively in the design and development process. Dr. Kota Harinarayana, a young scientist then, was appointed to spearhead this band of enthusiastic scientists/engineers and other administrative staff.

One of the critical objectives was to bridge the technology divide in the country and in the LCA programme. Accordingly, a number of critical technologies were developed, including unstable aerodynamics, reliable Control Law (CLAW) development for unstable aircraft, digital fly-by-wire flight control system, lightweight carbon-carbon composite structures, open system architecture for avionics, glass cockpit, various mechanical systems, digital design, analysis technologies, etc. The development process led to the creation of substantial design support, testing, and evaluation facilities within the country.

Let us start with unstable aerodynamics as the first technology challenge. Normally, aircraft are inherently stable and conventionally controlled by the pilot in the three rotary degrees of freedom of roll, pitch, and yaw by three corresponding control surfaces - namely, aileron, elevator, and rudder. When we move to the unstable domain, it is not physically possible for the pilot to control the aircraft by himself. There is a need for artificial stabilisation that can be obtained by a complex control system built into the aircraft to support pilot control. This would be akin to a bicycle, where, left on its own, the cycle will fall on its side, but the rider provides the artificial stabilisation to maintain it erect and enable it to be ridden.

Aircraft structures in the 1970s and 1980s were largely built of metal, predominantly high-grade aluminium. However, a decision was taken to leapfrog in technology to use composites to enable a lighter aircraft with a reduced radar cross section. This was an entirely new technology area, and much was learnt in aspects of design, material sourcing, fabrication technologies, curing technologies, testing, etc. As a result, a stupendous 90 per cent of surface area and 42 per cent by weight of the LCA are composites. It would not be out of place to mention that the recent Airbus A-350 and the Boeing 787 have composites in this range of surface area and weight. This foresight has now paid rich dividends, albeit through an arduous development path.

Another daring approach was to build state-of-the-art computing systems with associated software for both Flight Control Systems (FCS) and Avionics. While the French had a quadruplex FCS, three of these channels were digital and one was analogue. With LCA, it was decided to go in for all four digital channels. This was an extremely bold decision. Together with this, it was decided to go in for Open Architecture Computer (OAC) for the avionics, facilitating better obsolescence management. Both decisions have been resoundingly successfully, making the LCA contemporary and future-proof. Since the software for all these advanced computers would be either flight or mission-critical in nature, a robust fail-free software was crucial. To ensure this, software quality was a primary consideration. The team developed something called Independent Verification and Validation (IV&V). This technology has been extremely useful in other domains as well, given the significant increase in software development in the country.

The main objectives of forming ADA were to undertake, aid, promote, guide, manage, coordinate, and execute research in aeronautical science in the country, and to design and develop various types of aircraft and rotorcraft. In short, ADA was conceived as a programme management entity created as a Special Purpose Vehicle (SPV). I guess this objective was especially important to build the technology and skill base in the country. Following this significant step, came the task of collaborating with scientific agencies, research centres, and educational institutions on specific projects and investigations in areas of technology relevant to the objects of ADA. The other major role envisaged for ADA was programme management to enable it to cooperate and collaborate with other national and/or foreign institutions and international organisations.

Following the success of some of the work carried out by ADA and its partner entities in other R&D labs, academia, and industry, some of the results would be published, and the results of research, design, development, test, and evaluation conducted would be suitably archived and disseminated.

I would now like to highlight some of the challenges encountered in the LCA development programme and its sustainability. As mentioned earlier, there had been no fighter aircraft development project in the country for more than two decades after the HF-24 (Marut) project by Hindustan Aeronautics Limited (HAL) prior to the launch of the LCA programme. This implied that the design potential in aeronautics in the country had decreased over the years, and the infrastructure at HAL and elsewhere had not been enhanced since HF-24 aircraft project to support design and development. It may be prudent to note that computers and technologies for Computer Aided Design (CAD)/Computer Aided Engineering (CAE)/Computer Aided Manufacturing (CAM) facilities were minimal or non-existent. There were no significant technology development programmes other than sponsored projects by the Aircraft Research & Development Board (AR&DB) of the Defence Research & Development Organisation (DRDO). It is therefore obvious that there was a need to bridge the divide in domain knowledge, skill sets among individuals, technology build up, infrastructure build up, test facility readiness, etc.

This hiatus in aircraft development in the country had resulted in a situation wherein aeronautics was not seen as an area of attraction for young engineers and technicians. The core team that was formed had the challenge of sourcing talent available within the country with expertise in the field of aeronautics. This core team had to be formed by drawing specialists from various aeronautical/space organisations, and some of these pioneers in this domain left their comfortable jobs and pitched headlong into this unknown and uncertain venture. Having secured some of this scarce resource, the training of this manpower was now a major task.

The knowledge base from academia and peers had to be exploited to build up the necessary skill sets in various domains that would be required for a typical ab initio fighter aircraft development. In addition, there was a need to carry out a gap analysis and identify necessary infrastructure build-up required for the programme. Additional facilities for advanced technologies needed for a typical 4th-generation fighter class of aircraft had to be created to enable indigenous design and development of these technologies. In addition, there was a need for a change in mindset regarding production technologies and capabilities required from a 'Licence Build' to building an aircraft that was indigenously designed and developed.

Once the core team was put together, initial studies for the LCA development programme were sanctioned by the Government of India in August 1983 at an estimated cost of Rs. 560 crores. The actual cost of the programme was to be finalised based on the results of the Project Definition Phase (PDP). After carrying out feasibility studies during 1983-85 and pre-definition activities during 1985-87, the project definition phase was taken up in July 1987 and completed in December 1988. This resulted in a document giving the contours of a potential 4th-generation fighter aircraft, as envisioned by the team, to be developed in the country. This comprehensive proposal for the development of the aircraft leading to Initial Operational Clearance (IOC) and Final Operational Clearance (FOC), was examined by a committee of specialists and the Indian Air Force (IAF).

After reviews and deliberation at various levels, a development strategy in two phases was worked out in 1990 that would largely be a technology demonstration in the first phase, followed by prototype vehicle development. Accordingly, a note to the Cabinet Committee on Security (CCS) was prepared and submitted to the Government of India for due consideration and approval. This note went through a series of discussions and iterations and was finally ready for consideration and approval by the CCS in early 1993. I wish to highlight the point that the *formal sanction of the LCA Programme was accorded only in 1993*, while feasibility studies and gap analysis were being done from 1983.

LCA Full Scale Engineering Development (FSED) Phase 1

Government sanction was accorded on 23 June 1993 for the Full-Scale Engineering Development (FSED) Phase 1 of the LCA programme at an estimated cost of Rs. 2,188 crores at the October 1991 price level. This included Rs. 560 crores, sanctioned earlier for initial studies of the LCA development programme in August 1983. The major milestones to be achieved during FSED Phase-1 were to build two technology demonstrators (TD) of the LCA. It was envisaged that there would be limited flight testing of these two TDs to prove core technologies planned for the aircraft. These were designated as TD1 and TD2. Along with aircraft design and development, parallel development of other technologies and their demonstration on ground/flying test rigs was another major objective. Designing and building the two TDs were in progress, along with building confidence within the team for this challenging and interesting task. While the indigenous 'Kaveri' engine had been planned as per the CCS approval, a mid-course correction was needed to fit the GE-F404-IN20 engine due to non-availability of an indigenous engine. This, of course, entailed redesigning the entire rear fuselage structure due to differences in size and mounting arrangements.

Government sanction was revised on 5 January 1998 for fabrication of two additional PVs (Proto Vehicles, PV1 & PV2) within the funds that were sanctioned for FSED Phase-1. It may be highlighted that through effective and efficient management of sanctioned funds, two PVs were built, absorbing rupee escalation and Foreign Exchange (FE) conversion rate variations. The US sanctions that prohibited imports caused a major setback to the LCA development programme, as about 40 items of equipment for the LCA were being sourced from the USA. This setback was countered through import substitution and third-country source development initiative, which was also funded out of the resources provided for FSED Phase 1. Hence, a setback was converted into an opportunity for indigenous development, albeit with a few delays.

At this point, I would like to bring out an extremely important element of flight testing and how the capable team members played a significant role in the success of the programmes. A visionary step was to create a National Flight Test Centre (NFTC) under the aegis of the ADA with test pilots and flight test engineers drawn from both the Indian Air Force (IAF) and the Indian Navy (IN). The flight test crew were active participants in the entire design and development process and worked as a team with the aircraft designers at every stage of the process. They flew in multiple types of cockpits, including various types of simulators and aircraft. The pioneer chosen to head the NFTC was Air Marshal Philip Rajkumar, who helped realise the vision by setting up the processes and state-of-the-art facilities. The step-wise approach taken by the dedicated team enabled the realisation of incident-free flight testing throughout the prototype development. As would be seen later, the processes laid down largely contributed to flawless flight testing of the Naval version of the Light Combat Aircraft (LCA Navy) as well. I am certain that this team will continue their good work in all future programmes.

A significant milestone in the LCA programme was when the first Technology Demonstrator (TD1) took to the skies for its maiden flight on 4 January 2001, piloted ably by Wg. Cdr. Rajeev Kotiyal. This was a historic moment in the annals of the country. As Dr. Kota Harinarayana famously said, '*Technologies also took off along with the aircraft*'. I was fortunate to have been in ADA as a uniformed person at that time, and it was an exhilarating moment to witness the aircraft becoming airborne and landing back safely a few minutes later. This was indeed a red-letter day in the annals of aviation in particular and the country in general. Pictures after the flight are shown on page 81.

It may be mentioned here that a young aviation reporter at that time, Mr. Anantha Krishnan, working with *The Times of India,* broke the story on 29 December 2000 about the likely flight scheduled in early January 2001. A snapshot of the newspaper report is shown. The author of this piece then went on to write a significant number of positive reports on LCA (Tejas), which also contributed immensely to spreading the right facts and figures about the national programme. Ananth's recent series 'Hamara Tejas' along with Dr. Kota Harinarayana on Tarmak Media House networks, further helped spread several unknown aspects of the LCA Tejas programme.

From here onwards, flight testing progressed at a steady pace, and the overall objectives of LCA FSED Phase-1 was achieved on 31 March 2004 with limited flight testing of 202 flights. During these flights, the aircraft achieved a maximum speed of 1.4 Mach, climbed to a height of 15 kilometres above sea level, and performed several confidence-building manoeuvres. Its handling qualities were found to be exceptionally good by test pilots of the Indian Air Force. They commented that the aircraft flew almost like a simulator, largely controlled by the control law and the digital fly-by-wire flight control system.

ONE OF WORLD'S BEST FIGHTERS AWAITS CLEARANCE

A prototype of Light Combat Aircraft set to fly any time now

LCA set to take to skies

Anantha Krishnan M.

BANGALORE: The first prototype of one of the world's most advanced multi-role fighter planes, the Light Combat Aircraft (LCA), is ready to take off any time now. High-speed taxi trials are on at the HAL airstrip.

Highly-placed sources at the Aeronautical Development Agency (ADA) and Hindustan Aeronautics Limited (HAL) associated with this sensitive project, confirmed to *The Times of India* that the Centre for Military Airworthiness and Certificate (CEMILAC) had finally given the go-ahead to LCA. "After the last-minute formalities are over, the test pilots will fly the prototype," the sources said.

It is learnt that efforts are on to make the LCA fly this year itself, to put an end to speculation. "Now that the project is heading towards take-off, we want to ensure that everything is in place. It may fly before December 31 or before January 10," the sources said.

With the visit of Defence Minister George Fernandes to the project site a few weeks ago, followed by inspections by the Chief of Air Staff and the Public Accounts Committee, it was almost certain that the much-waited moment was nearing.

Sources said the Indian Air Force (IAF) would require 200 LCAs over a period of 15 years and the induction into the Services would begin by 2004.

The LCA is irrefutably state-of-the-art now, but will it still be so four years from now? "LCA's technology is digital and it can adopt any form of modern devices. It's a flying machine available for update," the sources said.

Keeping in view that the service life of LCA is in excess of 20 years, the aircraft has been designed to achieve very low operational and maintenance cost by incorporating a high degree of reliability, good maintainability and low fuel consumption right from the initial stages.

THE FIREPOWER

- **A precision weapon-launch platform with air-to-air, air-to-ground capabilities and an armoury consisting of a wide range of weapons and stores.**
- **State-of-the-art technology cockpit and digital avionics and weapon system interface to provide point and shoot characteristics.**
- **Effective Pilot Vehicle Interface (PVI) and display cues to interpret targets with ease**
- **A wide range of sensors and data-links offer improved situation awareness and early threat detection.**
- **A high performance multi-mode radar allows LCA to launch advanced BVR missiles at distant targets with a high degree of accuracy and effectiveness.**
- **A high-performance powerful gun offering additional choice in weapon capability, especially during close air combats.**

The project entered the definition phase in 1986 and got government's nod in in 1983. Though the 1990s [illegible] slowed down the project, the scientists have managed to pull it through, thereby laying the foundation for future combat aircraft programmes.

"Considering that we started from a scratch, the time we have taken is justifiable. We have roped in the best talent in the country and given them the freedom. Despite the rough weather, they have delivered a world-class product," the sources said, complimenting the scientists.

When the LCA keeps its date with the skies, it will be a moment of glory for the ADA and 1,600-plus scientists from the DRDO, CSIR, HAL, NAL, the BEL and many more who have been toiling for the last 15 years. Once operational, it will be the nation's pride, neighbour's envy.

► **India, Russia sign Sukhoi deal, page 8**

Source: Times of India - Scoop on 29 Dec 2000.

LCA Full Scale Engineering Development (FSED) Phase 2

Following the successful maiden flight of the first technology demonstrator aircraft in January 2001, the Government of India had sufficient confidence in the LCA programme spearheaded by ADA, and hence, LCA FSED Phase 2 was sanctioned on 20 November 2001 at a cost of Rs. 3301.78 crore. The major objectives were to complete LCA development activity leading to Initial Operational Clearance (IOC) and Final Operational Clearance (FOC).

Simultaneously, it was planned to create facilities at HAL and other allied production agencies to achieve Limited Series Production (LSP) of eight LCA aircraft per annum as part of the objectives of the above sanction. HAL was also to be funded by ADA to build and deliver eight LSP standard LCA aircraft from the FSED Phase-2 sanction. These aircraft would facilitate HAL in transitioning from a prototype build process towards a full-fledged series production process. It was also envisaged that these aircraft would participate in enhancing flight test activity, especially for weapon and system-level development testing. Pictures from the maiden flight of the various prototypes are shown on page 81.

Initial Operational Clearance-1 (IOC-1) of the LCA was successfully achieved on 10 January 2011, and Initial Operational Clearance (IOC) was achieved on 20 December 2013. This paved the way for the potential formation of the first squadron of LCAs (Tejas) by the IAF of 20 aircraft. Final Operational Clearance (FOC) was achieved on 20 February 2019, leading to the formation of the second Tejas squadron with another 20 aircraft. This triggered the order of 83 improved variants of LCA Mk-1A aircraft, totalling 123 Tejas aircraft. Seven LSP aircraft were built and flight-tested. The facility to roll out eight LSP LCA has been established at HAL, and the objectives of FSED Phase 2 were achieved.

Participants in the LCA Programme

LCA is a national programme, and ADA spearheads its development effort, with HAL as the principal partner. Nearly 100 major work centres and 300 smaller work centres, CSIR laboratories, Public Sector Undertakings (PSUs), educational institutions, certification agencies, quality assurance agencies, Indian Air Force and Indian Navy establishments, Indian Space Research Organisation (ISRO), and private sector entities, among others, have actively participated in the LCA programme. With this integrated approach, the investments made in the LCA programme have contributed to infrastructure development within the country, besides developing core technologies incorporated in the LCA. Indigenous R&D efforts in the LCA programme have also established self-reliance in aeronautics other than providing substantial spin-off benefits to the defence and civilian sectors. This has certainly helped create a vibrant aerospace ecosystem in the country, instilling utmost confidence to carry out ab initio designing and development of fighter aircraft.

Manpower

As mentioned earlier, ADA started initially to meet the objectives of a single programme of the LCA, with the primary role of coordination and programme management only. However, as certain skill sets were not available in partner organisations, technology areas were taken up progressively within ADA itself in niche areas of Flight Control Systems (FCS), Avionics, Mechanical systems, Composites, Smart materials, etc. Further, multiple programmes were sanctioned subsequently, namely, the Naval version of the Light Combat Aircraft (LCA Navy), improved versions of the LCA, design studies for a 5th-generation fighter aircraft, etc.

The extent of permanent manpower sanctioned did not increase commensurate with the tasks on hand, and innovative strategies were needed to meet the requisite human capital. There was thus a need to take on additional manpower under separate categories for short-duration engagement like Project Engineers, Project Assistants, Work Package Personnel, Consultants, and Emeritus Scientists. This strategy has paid rich dividends in building up the overall skill levels required for handling multiple programmes at ADA. I wish to highlight that project engineers were inducted on a special basis in four experience categories and laterally inducted from the industry. They were provided market levels of remuneration and retained for a period of five years, extendable by another two years. In fact, this entry of highly skilled resources caused a reverse flow from the private sector to the ADA. I am particularly happy that I was able to steer through the Government approvals and provide this innovative mechanism of manpower induction.

The day of 1 July 2016 was a proud moment for the country when the first squadron of Tejas was formed with aircraft in IOC configuration. I was fortunate to have witnessed this significant event as the Director of ADA. This was followed by the second tranche of aircraft in the FOC configuration, leading to a second squadron. On 28 March 2024, another major event was the successful maiden flight of the upgraded LCA AF Mk-1A aircraft, which is the first of the 83 aircraft ordered.

Notable milestones of the overall programmes at the ADA are shown in the graphic below.

Important Milestones of LCA Programme

Broad Timelines of ADA Programme Activities			
		22-Aug-1983	**Sanction Rs 560 Cr as seed money for initiation of LCA Programme**
Registration of ADA as a Society	**16-Jun-1984**		
		Mid 1985	Start of ADA functioning
Formation of ADA Core Team	**1986**		
		1987-88	Project Defintion Phase Completion
Sanction of FSED Ph-1 for Development of 2 Technology Demonstrators (TD)	**23-Jun-1993**		
		19-Nov-1995	Roll Out of LCA TD1
Approval of two additional Prototypes	**5-Jan-1998**		
		4-Jan-2001	**Maiden Flight of first Technology Demonstrator (TD1)**
Sanction of FSED Ph-2 and Limited Series Production (LSP)	**20-Nov-2001**		
		6-Jun-2002	**Maiden Flight of second Technology Demonstrator (TD2)**
Sanction of FSED Navy for Development of 2 Naval Prototypes (NP)	**31-Mar-2003**		
		4-May-2003	Naming of LCA as 'Tejas' by the Indian Prime Minister
Shattering of Sound Barrier by LCA TD1	**1-Aug-2003**		
		25-Nov-2003	Maiden Flight of LCA PV1
Completion of FSED Ph-1 (202 Flights)	**31-Mar-2004**		
		1-Dec-2005	Maiden Flight of LCA PV2
Completion of 500 Flights	**9-Mar-2006**		
		1-Dec-2006	Maiden Flight of LCA PV3
Maiden Flight of LCA LSP1	**25-Apr-2007**		
		Jun 2007	First Sea Level Trials at Arakkonam
Air to Air R73E Missile launch Trial	**Oct 2007**		
		16-Jun-2008	Maiden Flight of LCA LSP2
Cold Weather Trials at Leh	**Dec 2008**		
		Mar 2009	1000 L. Weapons Separation Trials at Jamnagar
Maiden Flight of LCA Trainer PV5	**26-Nov-2009**		
		Nov 2009	Sanction of FSED Ph-2 Extension; FSED Ph-3 and Tech. Development
Achieving of 1350 kmph CAS	**8-Dec-2009**		
		23-Apr-2010	Maiden Flight of LCA LSP3
Maiden Flight of LCA LSP4	**2-Jun-2010**		
		19-Nov-2010	Maiden Flight of LCA LSP5
Release of CMDS	**2-Dec-2010**		
		17-Dec-2010	1200L Fuel Drop Tank Jettison Trials
Initial Operational Clearance-1 (IOC-1)	**10-Jan-2011**		
		9-Mar-2012	Maiden Flight of LCA LSP7
Maiden Flight of LCA Navy Trainer (NP1)	**27-Apr-2012**		
		31-Mar-2013	Maiden Flight of LCA LSP8
Initial Operational Clearance (IOC)	**20-Dec-2013**		
		8-Nov-2014	Maiden Flight of LCA Trainer PV6
Maiden Flight of LCA Navy Fighter (NP2)	**7-Feb-2015**		
		Jan 2016	Participation in the Bahrain International Air Show
BVR Air to Air Missile Firing	**5-Feb-2016**		
		1-Jul-2016	Formation of First Squadron (Flying Daggers) by the IAF
Final Operational Clearance (FOC)	**20-Feb-2019**		

2

Background & Summary of LCA Naval Version

The potential journey of a Naval Version of the LCA started in the 1990s when the then Programme Director of the Aeronautical Development Agency (ADA), Dr. Kota Harinarayana and his team visited INS *Hansa*, the Indian Naval Air Station at Goa, to interact with the Indian Navy (IN) team comprising, at that time, Cdr. Shekar Sinha (later Vice-Admiral), Lt Cdr. CD Balaji (later Commodore), and Lt Cdr. Vijay Kandru (later Commodore). The ADA team discussed the nuances of carrier-borne aircraft operation with the IN team, who had extensive aircraft carrier experience. This was my first exposure to a design and development environment and, I guess, the initiation of my close and future journey with the Naval version of the Light Combat Aircraft (LCA Navy). At that time, the design of the Air Force Version of the LCA was already in progress, and initial building activities were also underway, with the formal sanction being accorded in 1993, as brought out in the preceding chapter.

Based on the draft Naval Air Staff Requirements (NASR) of September 1986 issued by Naval Head Quarters (NHQ), the feasibility of developing a Naval Version with minimum structural changes of the Air Force Version of LCA was studied. LCA Navy Project Definition Phase (PDP-Navy) was initiated based on the interest shown by the IN to explore the possibility of developing a deck-based fighter aircraft within the country to meet its future aircraft carrier needs. This was a significant step forward to explore the idea of building a carrier-borne aircraft indigenously.

The ADA and HAL teams put together a study based on the LCA Air Force Version and concluded that it would be feasible to develop a carrier-borne aircraft, albeit with changes, in order to operate with the concept of Ski-jump Take-off But Arrested Recovery (STOBAR). At that time, it was envisaged that the exit Angle of Attack (AoA) would be limited to 24 degrees and the approach AoA would be 17.5 degrees in order to have a reduced approach speed to the ship. The take-off run was indicated to be about 200m with the ship's ramp exit angle of 12 degrees.

Based on the positive recommendations made during project definition for building a Naval Version and with my formal deputation to ADA in 2002, I was tasked to write a note for consideration by the Cabinet Committee on Security (CCS) of the Government of India, for the Full-Scale Engineering Development for a Naval Version of the Light Combat Aircraft (FSED LCA Navy), under the able guidance of Dr. TG Pai, Project Director (Technology Development). This document went through various iterations within the Ministry of Defence, then within the Ministry of Finance, and then in the Cabinet Secretariat over a period of about nine months. Finally, based on deliberations and reviews, CCS approval was accorded in end March 2003. The assumption at this time was that the changes to the Naval Version would be to the order of 15 to 20 per cent vis-à-vis the Air Force Version. Incidentally, the LCA AF had its maiden flight on 4 January 2001, as brought out in the preceding chapter. The team was built up over the years from a lone ranger in the LCA Navy programme office at ADA in 2002 to four members by 2005 and a lean team thereafter. The initial members of the team were Mr. TV Vinod Kumar and Mr. P Thangavel. The office was supported by young Ms. Chitra. I would like to mention here that we were always against the tide insofar as resources from various agencies within ADA and outside were concerned, since the larger focus was on the LCA AF Version.

The scope of the FSED Navy was primarily to design, develop, and build two LCA Navy prototype aircraft, namely, Naval Trainer (NP1) and Naval Fighter (NP2). To facilitate ground testing, a dedicated Naval Structural Test Specimen (STS-N) was sanctioned together with test facilities. Prior to clearing an aircraft to embark on an aircraft carrier, it needed to be tested and validated ashore. The option in front of us was to either use existing test facilities available outside the country or build our own. As will be brought out later in more detail, the only two potential facilities were with the US Navy and in Ukraine. The US Navy facility did not have a ski jump at that time and the Ukraine facility had limitations for launching of aircraft. Also, the condition of the facility itself was suspect. Accordingly, it was planned to establish a Shore Based Test Facility (SBTF) that would replicate an aircraft carrier ashore, with a ski jump for the aircraft launch (take-off) and arresting gear for aircraft recovery (landing). The scope obviously included ground and flight testing of naval prototypes and demonstrating carrier suitability on IN aircraft carriers.

The LCA Navy is the first of its kind, carrier-based fighter aircraft developed by the country. The original requirement was a single-engine light aircraft envisioned as a replacement for the Sea Harrier that was in operation with the Indian Navy. The top-level operational concept of LCA Navy was to develop it for a STOBAR aircraft carrier. INS *Viraat,* on which Sea Harriers were being operated, was a Ski-jump Take-Off and Vertical Landing (STOVL)-based type of aircraft carrier. The LCA Navy needed to be adapted for operation aboard the aircraft carrier, INS *Vikramaditya* (the erstwhile *Admiral Gorshkov*). The ship was undergoing upgrade and refitting in Russia, primarily for MiG-29K operations. The LCA Navy was also planned for operations on the future indigenous aircraft carrier, INS *Vikrant.* The requirements outlined by the Indian Navy sought development of a single-seat fighter and a two-seat trainer variant of the LCA Navy. It may be noted that carrier interface details are also critical inputs for the design of deck-based aircraft. Hence, it is vital to know the details of the carrier operating environment to facilitate meaningful aircraft design.

The design and development activities were initiated by ADA in earnest, along with HAL and other partners. As the detailed design evolved, the extent of changes continued increasing, and it started becoming essentially a new aircraft, albeit with constraints imposed by commonality. The main objective imposed on the design was to convert the land-based LCA by integrating deck interface features to make it compatible with Indian Navy carriers. Along with this requirement from the Indian Navy, the design of a trainer variant for the IAF was yet to be taken up. Hence, it was decided to design a fuselage shape that would be common to the LCA Air Force trainer as well as the LCA

Navy fighter and trainer variants. This would incorporate an additional nose droop that was required to achieve a higher over-the-nose vision angle, allowing the naval variant to approach the carrier at a higher angle of attack and hence with reduced landing speed. Inherently, commonality became a necessity, considering challenges in resources available for this programme. This was advantageous in some ways as it probably would reduce the design and development effort. However, it was problematic in other ways, as the design space became restrictive.

We had to introduce a new front fuselage (nose section), a strengthened centre fuselage to accommodate the volume and loads of a longer and stronger landing gear and the arrester hook. We had a new leading-edge control surface, and a new control law, etc. As previously mentioned, the land-based aircraft with the engine selected to suit its requirements was adapted for the Naval Version also. Incidentally, the engine was already in use in US Navy carrier-borne aircraft and, hence, was adapted for the LCA Navy without the need for additional certification. High sink rate landing and arrested landing loads associated with the STOBAR configuration necessitated higher strength landing gear, the inclusion of an arrester hook, and associated structural reinforcement. In order to reduce approach speed during the landing phase, an aerodynamic solution was introduced: Leading Edge Vortex Control (LEVCON), a flight control surface at the leading-edge apex of the wing. The dry empty mass of the aircraft was originally estimated to increase by around 600 kg, and design studies indicated that this would still permit the aircraft to remain within the hook-to-wire engagement speed limits of the carriers.

The landing gear design posed tough challenges in terms of interfacing it as a fuselage-mounted configuration within the constrained space. The requirement of a wider track to utilise the Restraining Gear System (RGS) on the carriers and bigger shock absorbers increased stowage volume, resulting in larger fairings, with the penalty being that they acted as drag contributors. Arrester hook interface in the rear fuselage of a single-engine configuration has associated challenges that require extra structural reinforcement for load transfer during arrested landing on a carrier. In the case of the LCA Navy, the rear fuselage bottom zone is completely covered by the engine bay door that has no rigidity for interfacing with the arrester hook, and hence cannot meet the large load transfer requirement. A separate platform had to be designed and appended for this purpose. This external structure increased drag, apart from the mass increase that also had to be compensated for with ballast in the nose section. The idea of mentioning these is to highlight the challenges faced throughout the design and development process, and, suffice to say, they were taken head-on and overcome successfully.

In due course, as the design effort progressed and mission performance targets were clearly defined by the user, evaluation of the attained configuration was carried out. Design optimisation effort with objectives to enhance installed thrust and mass reduction was prioritised, and a multi-disciplinary design group was formed towards defining the way ahead. Following deliberations, activities to identify weight reduction in the fuselage and landing gear were taken up. An aerodynamic solution for improving air intake pressure recovery was carried out, and as a result, a 3-door Auxiliary Air Intake Door (AAID) feature with incremental intake pressure gain was incorporated on the LCA Navy Fighter Prototype (NP2). Here, I would like to mention that the concept of a 3-door AAID was taken up as an undergraduate project by my younger son, Anuj, and his team, and they had built a concept model of the same, under the able guidance of Mr. Arindam Banerjee of the Airframe Group at ADA. This was later developed into the actual design and successfully implemented on the aircraft. I am now given to understand that there is a move to incorporate this innovative design concept in the Mk1A variant of the light combat aircraft because of its benefits for aircraft performance.

The high-strength landing gear of the LCA Navy was a totally new design with requirements for fresh sourcing of indigenous maraging steel raw material from Midhani, a Government of India material developing entity. This was followed by forging large components of landing gear that required a high-tonnage press, which was identified after considerable effort. Machining large landing gear parts of maraging steel was a challenge due to the frequent failure of cutting tools. In the wire cutting process, some of the parts were produced through identified vendors in the private sector with special purpose machines. The landing gear assembly and installation parts, totalling around 280 and 60 respectively, were then realised at various HAL Divisions. The landing gear assembly and testing were done at HAL, Nasik, which had the infrastructure to handle such large-size assemblies. The installation parts were done at the Bangalore Division of HAL.

The rotary geared LEVCON actuator integration on the stub wing and the moving flight control surface involved an innovative hinge-line device. The hinge required a long pin, and this presented unprecedented precision manufacturing challenges on a part about 1600 mm long. This challenge was overcome with innovative processes developed during machining. Prior to sourcing the LEVCON actuating system, the Central Machine Tool Institute (CMTI) at Bangalore was tasked to develop the rotary gear actuating mechanism. The challenge was to fabricate small sized gears with high precision and finish. Engineering models were fabricated, but could not meet the exacting requirements and hence had to be dropped.

In parallel with the design and development of the aircraft itself, there was a need to conceptualise and build various test facilities/rigs for proving the design prior to flight/validation. I would like to point out that building each of these test facilities was an interesting and challenging experience. It helped us gain significant insights into the overall concept of carrier-borne aircraft testing as well. Some of the major facilities were the Shore Based Test Facility (SBTF) at Goa replicating the ski-jump launch and arrested recovery, the full-scale aircraft structural test rig to load the aircraft to 1.5 times the flight loads, subsystem test rigs for landing gear, arrester hook, LEVCON, Control law, Avionics, Real-time simulator, Telemetry facility at Goa, etc.

Specific requirements for qualification of airframe and systems due to the high sink rate recovery onboard carriers and shocks due to arrestment on to the Arresting Gear System (AGS) had to be pioneered in this programme as a first-time naval aircraft development effort. Hardware-in-loop simulator, 'Iron Bird', which is LCA-Navy specific, was built. Simulation in this facility included naval aircraft-specific launch and recovery modes for certification. The design of the landing gear for LCA Navy was validated to withstand high sink rate landing loads in carrier operations on a test specimen using a landing gear drop test rig at a 7.1m/sec vertical sink velocity. The arrester hook, being a new introduction for naval aircraft, underwent testing in a dedicated test facility. All system equipment was separately qualified to withstand arrested landing shock. This phase was successfully completed with specially designed fixtures and utilisation of test facilities within the country.

Private Sector involvement

Structural design activity of LEVCON and arrester hook system activities were identified for outsourcing to a private agency as a risk mitigation strategy to meet programme schedules due to constrained human resources in ADA and HAL. The process for certification of outsourced work packages in structural design was established through ground testing and clearance for flight trials. The Arrester Hook System (AHS) design and development was outsourced to a private vendor, and a version of the AHS was fabricated and tested as a standalone system that met the requirements provided by ADA. However, due to the integration challenges and the acquisition of more details of aircraft dynamics available at a later stage, HAL designed and integrated another version of an arrester hook system, which is installed currently on the aircraft.

The aircraft was rolled out in 2010, equivalent to the launching of a ship. This was witnessed by the then Indian Defence Minister, Sri AK Antony in the presence of the then Chief of the Naval Staff (CNS), Admiral Nirmal Verma, and other dignitaries. The aircraft was then equipped, extensively ground tested, and had its maiden flight on 27 April 2012, exactly nine years after CCS approval. This is considered contemporary by any world standards, especially when we were doing it for the first time in the country.

The maiden ski-jump launch on the SBTF at Goa was in December 2014, followed by the arrested recovery (taxi-in) in August 2018. This was then followed by flight engagement at SBTF a year later. Iconic pictures of ski-jump launch and arrested recovery at the SBTF is shown in pictures at page 81. The beginning of 2020 saw a significant milestone with the aircraft successfully demonstrating arrested recovery and ski-jump launch from an aircraft carrier, INS *Vikramaditya*.

I had the opportunity of flying the aircraft that we had designed and built three days prior to my demitting office on superannuation in March 2017. The Chief Test Pilot, Cmde. Maolankar took me up for this exciting sortie. A picture of this memorable moment is on page 88.

3

THE BEGINNING: LCA AF, PROJECT DEFINITION & PRE-PROJECT PHASE OF LCA NAVY

Light Combat Aircraft (LCA) – Air Force Version

The background of design and development of the LCA Air Force Version was described briefly in an earlier chapter. Just to recall some of the salient events, the Aeronautical Development Agency (ADA) was formed in 1983 to prepare for the potential development of a 4th-generation fighter aircraft in the country. Phase-I of Full-Scale Engineering Development (FSED) of the Light Combat Aircraft (LCA) programme was sanctioned in June 1993 as a Technology Development (TD) activity by the Government of India, to design and develop an indigenous fighter aircraft to meet the requirements of the Indian Air Force (IAF), potentially to replace MiG-21s.

Design and development activities were initiated in earnest by all team members at ADA, HAL, DRDO, CSIR labs, other public and private sector enterprises, academic institutions, and others. Together with this, the build-up of technologies that were required for a 4th-generation aircraft was also taken up. In a significant number of areas, the Technology Readiness Levels (TRLs) were quite low. To test aircraft components, systems, and the aircraft itself, test facilities had to be conceptualised and built. All these activities were concurrently in progress.

Necessary tooling, jigs, and fixtures were designed and built, with participation from private sector industries to a large extent. These were installed at the LCA facility that was set up in HAL. There was also a need to develop strategies for military aircraft certification and quality assurance, to be able to validate the design and build of the aircraft. Certification ensures that the aircraft has been 'designed right', and Quality Assurance ensures that the aircraft has been 'built right'. This was followed by the actual aircraft build and ground test, followed by documentation related to certification and quality assurance.

The historic maiden flight of the LCA Technology Demonstrator (TD-1) took place on 4 January 2001, followed by successful completion of the first block of flights. Based on confidence in the development scenario, sanction was accorded by the Government of India for Phase-2 of full-scale engineering development in November 2001. The maiden flight of the second technology demonstrator, LCA TD-2, took place on 6 June 2002. By the beginning of March 2003, when the LCA Navy CCS was under consideration, the two technology demonstrators (TD1 and TD2) had completed 31 flights. HAL was also in the process of setting up infrastructure for a limited production capacity of eight aircraft per year, as part of FSED Phase-2. This was in a separate Tejas division set up at HAL. The eight Limited Series Production (LSP) as a part of FSED Phase-2 was also taken up.

Project Definition Phase (PDP) for LCA Navy

Based on draft Naval Air Staff Requirements (NASR) issued in September 1986 by Naval Head Quarters (NHQ), the feasibility of developing a Naval Version of the Light Combat Aircraft (LCA Navy), with minimum structural changes, was studied. Subsequently, NHQ issued NASR in June 1992 and a project on LCA Navy PDP was initiated in April 1995 at ADA. The first step towards commencement of PDP was to form a core team that would actively work on various aspects of a potential Naval Version of the LCA. Members were drawn from various disciplines at ADA, HAL, DRDO, CSIR, academia, and other public and private sector entities. The PDP studies were then carried out by the joint team, actively led by Dr. TG Pai, the Project Director (Technology Development) at ADA. It may be mentioned that the Indian Navy was actively supporting this activity, even to the extent of providing a small amount of funding for the studies.

As a first step, the team commenced the study of staff requirements provided by the Indian Navy and tried to understand them, both qualitatively and quantitatively. Discussions were held with Indian Navy personnel to have adequate clarity on each of the requirements. These were then compared vis-à-vis the Air Force Version of the LCA, the design and build of which was well in progress. The objective was to chart clearly the commonalities and differences as perceived and understood by the team members at that time. Further, it would also give an idea of the likely level of compliance with the requirements spelt out by the Indian Navy.

In addition to the staff requirements of the user, there would be a host of other requirements that the aircraft needed to comply with, namely, design, certification, quality assurance, reliability, testability, safety, EMI/EMC, lightning protection, maintainability, accessibility, corrosion protection, and so on. As can be understood, this stage is extremely critical in any product development cycle and especially so in the case of a deck-based fighter aircraft. Hence, it was necessary to work out a detailed compliance matrix at this stage and the team revisited it at every step to check the level of compliance. It is all the more important to assess areas of partial compliance/noncompliance and have a dialogue with the requirement-generating agency to get a sign-off on acceptability of the deviation from the stated requirements, otherwise there would be a need to request them to change these requirements. This step in the process is extremely critical to preventing 'heartburn' and avoidable arguments at a later stage.

The next stage in the process was to carry out preliminary simulation studies with the data available at that time. For example, to attain a safe fly-away speed of the LCA Navy with the allowable maximum take-off mass, from a ski-jump with a 12° ramp (as was then envisaged), a minimum deck length requirement of 200m was established through simulation studies. This was one way of looking at the parameters. The other way was, given the length of the take-off run as 200m and the ramp exit angle of 12°, then the allowable take-off mass of the aircraft was worked out. Of course, other significant factors affecting take-off mass were the wind-over-deck and the ambient temperature. Ambient conditions play a significant part in the allowable take-off mass of the aircraft.

Towards meeting the low approach speed requirement of the LCA Navy, a new aerodynamic device, namely, Leading Edge Vortex CONtrol (LEVCON) and an additional nose droop of 5° at that time (with respect to the Air Force

Version) towards providing satisfactory cockpit vision at an approach angle of attack (α) of 17.5° and glide path of 4° were found to be essential. These are some of the examples of trying to understand and check compliance vis-à-vis requirements that have been provided. As will be seen later in the detail design and development section, the geometry of the aircraft carrier was changed with the take-off ski-jump exit having a 14-degree parabolic profile. Further, the approach angle of attack was later fixed at 14.2 degrees, instead of 17.5 degrees as envisaged during Project Definition Phase (PDP). Obviously, the simulation needed to be re-done during detail design.

Gradually, the team got into as much detail as possible during the stage of Project Definition. A three-position LEVCON control surface, with 45° upwards for approach, 0° for take-off and 20° downwards for manoeuvring was developed based on LEVCON aerodynamic data from model tests in HAL and NAL wind tunnels. LEVCON loads and hinge moments obtained from Computational Fluid Dynamics (CFD) were used for finalising LEVCON layout, choice of available rotary actuators and hydraulic power requirements. From preliminary model test data, LEVCON with 45° upward deflection was found to be effective as a deceleration device with no adverse effect on lifting and pitching characteristics. Rotary geared actuators chosen for LEVCON for low-speed approach (45° up) and transonic manoeuvres (20° down) were found to be prima facie acceptable with certain changes for transonic/supersonic deceleration provided by conventional airbrakes. Thus, LEVCON in LCA Navy provides an independent pitch control (approach/ manoeuvres) and a deceleration device (air brake). Whilst this was the thought process at the time of project definition, there were significant changes made during detail design and implementation on the aircraft as part of full-scale engineering development of the LCA Navy. This will be brought out in detail subsequently.

Preliminary LCA Navy aerodynamic configuration was finalised by providing an additional 5° nose droop (compared to the Air Force Version) giving 19° over-the-nose vision and deflectable LEVCON in the wing apex region. Conventional airbrakes provided on LCA base-line configuration were deleted for the LCA Navy. However, during detail design, the nose droop of the front fuselage was reduced to 4° since the approach angle of attack was reduced. This would provide adequate over-the-nose vision for ship deck landing (recovery) of the aircraft and hence was chosen as a design parameter.

Based on test data and drag analysis, with wave drag inputs from CFD, a preliminary aerodynamic data set was prepared. The Kaveri engine performance data (thrust deck) and aircraft mass and c.g. data were other input parameters that were required. This facilitated ski-jump take-off simulation and landing approach speed analysis. Using available data, LCA Navy point-and-mission performance for a range of naval missions, (anti-shipping, strike, and CAP) was also computed. These results were then presented to the Indian Navy to indicate the extent of compliance with take-off performance, landing performance, point performance, and mission performance. Point performance would generally include the 'g' loads for which the aircraft is designed, the Sustained Turn Rate (STR), the Attained Turn Rate (ATR), turning radius, etc.

To reiterate, a ski-jump simulation study was carried out with the LCA Navy aerodynamic data set (aerodata) including LEVCON effects for a range of take-off configurations. This study included parameters such as Wind on Deck (WoD) and maximum permissible angle of attack (α) in a post-launch ballistic trajectory as parameters. The piloting technique of aircraft attitude, namely, theta (θ) capture, which was followed for Sea Harrier ramp take-off and holding attitude during launch phase, was also followed for the LCA Navy ski-jump take-off. The brake release was with maximum dry thrust and an engine response of 2 seconds was assumed to reach maximum reheat thrust in deck roll to estimate end speed in a free take-off mode. The safe fly-away speed is the aircraft launch speed for which, it does not experience any negative climb rate whatsoever in a post-launch ballistic trajectory. Typically, at the exit from the ski-jump, there would be a positive climb rate initially due to the ballistic nature of the aircraft leaving the ramp. However, the forward speed is still not sufficient for wing-borne flight; hence, the climb rate keeps dropping as the forward speed builds up. There is a balance reached at a point (inflexion) when the forward speed is sufficient to sustain wing-borne flight, and at this speed it should be ensured that there is still a positive climb rate, or at least zero climb rate as a minimum. This is the beauty and challenge for the algorithm development of the take-off control law in the flight control system.

These aspects will be clearer when we get into the details of Control Law (CLAW) development in later chapters.

The approach speed of the LCA Navy for a normal recovery mass of about 10 tons was found to be about 130 knots. The approach speed is a function of the approach angle of attack and the descending glide slope angle. This speed for an aircraft is critical from both the aircraft handling qualities perspective and the engaging speed limits of the ship's arresting gear. This parameter needs to be controlled at all times. Providing for certain allowances for recovery mass (500 kg) and engaging speed (5 knots), the arrester gear capacity is specified for recovery mass of 9,500 kg. for normal operation with an engaging speed of 120 knots and 10,000 kg. of maximum recovery mass for emergency operation with an engaging speed of 125 knots.

The airframe of the LCA Navy incorporates advanced technology in carbon-fibre composites in the primary structure including the wing, fin, rudder, elevon, a few bulkheads and skin panels of the fuselage. Major changes to the LCA Navy fuselage from the Air Force Version include nose droop to provide over-the-nose vision of 19° to ensure cockpit vision at approach attitude. Changes were also made to accommodate longer main and nose undercarriage, and the arrester hook/actuator-cum-damper installation, along with beefing up the structure to take up recovery loads, including undercarriage loads for flare-less landing with large sink rates and arrester hook loads due to large decelerations (~ -4.5 g). Most fuselage bulkheads are of aluminium alloy. The cockpit flooring is made of aluminium-lithium alloy. Laminated polycarbonate windscreen bubble and stretched acrylic bubble housed in aluminium alloy framework are used for the canopy.

Typically, a land-based aircraft approaching the runway for landing 'flares out' just prior to touchdown and then gently lands. This gives a relatively low vertical rate of descent or sink rate of the order of a limiting value of 3.0 m/s. Under normal circumstances of a shore landing, sink rates experienced are typically less than 1.0 m/s. However, when approaching a ship, the pilot needs to constantly see the lights in the optical landing system and, hence, cannot flare the aircraft. This concept is called 'Flare-less Landing/Recovery' on a ship deck.

Flare-less landing of the LCA Navy approaching at 130 knots at a glide slope of 4° with a corresponding vertical velocity component on the ship, combined with the ship's own vertical motion at the touchdown point, calls for high sink rates (~7.1 m/s) for undercarriage design. A longer and stronger undercarriage resulted in a larger main undercarriage requiring a bigger bay space in the centre fuselage. Also, with a 4° deck attitude chosen for the LCA Navy, the nose undercarriage was significantly longer with a bigger shock absorber.

Nose wheel powered steering of ±35° (later changed to ±70°) and castor wheeling were provided to meet deck manoeuvring requirements. Using the nose wheel turn radius definition of the aircraft, a typical parking scheme for 12 aircraft on the flight deck was also demonstrated. Due to limited deck space on an aircraft carrier, large angles provided for nose wheel steering facilitate the aircraft to practically turn on the spot.

A retractable arrester hook system with a yoke and two jack-cum-dampers was configured with an uplock. The hook, with a self-centring mechanism that permitted 7.5° lateral movement on either side catering to off-centre landing, was conceptualised to ensure that the hook returned to the centre position ready for hook engagement with the ship's arrester wire. The arrester hook faces large deceleration during recovery due to a short stopping distance of about 90m; hence, the arresting load is about 4.5 times the recovery mass. It may be appreciated that the structure needs to absorb and dissipate this load without any distress, on a repetitive basis.

The Kaveri engine, which the power plant under development at the Gas Turbine Research Establishment (GTRE) of DRDO, was initially chosen for the LCA Navy initially, as it was envisaged for the LCA AF Version. This engine has a 3-stage fan and a 6-stage high pressure compressor. The maximum dry thrust and maximum reheat thrust of the Kaveri engine were estimated to be about 52 KN and 80 KN, respectively. The interfaces of this power plant were taken for the preliminary design and performance estimation of the LCA Navy during the PDP. It is worth noting that engine selection at the very initial stage is a key factor and an input for aircraft design. This is because every engine would have its own mount locations, and the mass flow characteristics would be different, leading to changes in air intake design, auxiliary systems interface, fluid interfaces, etc., and unique to a particular engine. This entire evolution needed to be redone at the detail design stage later due to the non-availability of the Kaveri engine, with the interfaces of the GE-F404-IN20 engine.

The LCA Navy has seven hard points, including three below-the-wing stations on either side and one below the fuselage at the centreline. These can be used as weapon carrying stations/external fuel tanks (drop tanks). Longer undercarriage provided adequate ground clearances to install Sea-Eagle class of Anti-Shipping Missile (ASM) at the centreline station. Outboard stations are dedicated to Close Combat Missiles (CCMs). The fuselage, inboard and midboard stations are meant to carry fuel drop tanks, in addition to weapons. Rail-launched Medium Range Missiles (MRMs) are carried on the midboard stations. It is possible to carry Laser Guided Bombs (LGBs) and ASMs on inboard stations.

Based on the analysis of naval missions and functional requirements of avionics and weapon systems, the LCA Navy avionics system architecture was proposed. Cockpit Environment Facility (CEF) used for evaluation of the avionics system was upgraded for evaluation of 'ski-jump take-off', 'wave-off', 'bolter' and 'arrested recovery' of the LCA Navy. These were very preliminary studies based on inputs from the LCA Air Force programme, which itself was evolving. Obviously, during detail design, there were significant changes as will become apparent in subsequent chapters.

Based on the philosophy of aircraft carrier operations, an approach to control law development and simulation studies was suggested, highlighting efforts involved in developing and testing different control law versions using various simulation facilities. The flight control system architecture, including LEVCONs as an independent pair of pitch control surfaces and airbrakes, was discussed. Clearly, this was an area identified for significant changes from the LCA Air Force Version.

A preliminary system architecture of various aircraft systems was worked out that included the fuel system, catering to fuel jettisoning for emergency recovery, the hydraulic system incorporating arrester hook and LEVCON requirements, the electrical system, the Environmental Control System (ECS), Secondary Power System (SPS) incorporating a modified Aircraft Mounted Accessory Gear Box (AMAGB), and the Integrated Life Support System (ILSS).

Integrated logistics support for the LCA Navy, including aspects of maintenance onboard and ashore, ground support equipment, technical documentation, maintenance training and support, was discussed. An approach to reliability and maintainability study of the LCA Navy was also discussed. This included reliability apportionment and prediction, Failure Mode and Effectiveness Analysis (FMEA), estimation of Maintenance Man Hours per Flight Hour (MMHFH), evaluation of accessibility to LRUs through service panels at ground level, etc.

LCA Navy and Air Defence Ship (ADS) interface issues were discussed. They included ship motion and airflow, necessary aviation facilities onboard, ski-jump ramp for aircraft launch, three wire arresting system for recovery on flight deck, arrester gear capacity for normal and emergency recovery mass, hangar space, aircraft lift, etc. The Indian Navy's INS *Vikrant* is now what was then called the ADS.

Pre-Project Phase of LCA Navy

As part of the LCA Navy Project Definition Phase (PDP), ADA undertook a study and confirmed to the Naval Headquarters (NHQ) the feasibility of converting the LCA Air Force Version to a Navy Version capable of operating from an aircraft carrier with a ski-jump take-off and arrested recovery. The Chief of the Naval Staff and the Scientific Adviser to the Indian Defence Minister (Raksha Mantri) jointly reviewed this study. Subsequent to completion of the PDP in May 1997, a Pre-Project Phase (PPP) was initiated in April 1999 with small joint funding by NHQ and DRDO to initiate concept design activities specifically to align the basic LCA configuration for naval use, focusing on critical long lead-time areas. Some of the major initiatives were the concept design of the main and nose landing gear, the concept design of arrester hook system, the concept design of LEVCON, and aerodynamic data generation, as well as preliminary studies of LCA Navy control law, advance studies and planning for ground test facilities for launch, and recovery trials, to name just a few.

I was not present during the PDP of the LCA Navy when it was taken up earlier. However, I was extremely fortunate to be associated with the pre-project phase activities of the LCA Navy from its very inception and, of course, through the journey of detail design and development. All-out efforts were made to maximise the preliminary work that could be carried out pending formal Cabinet Committee on Security (CCS) approval for a Full-Scale Engineering Development of the Naval Version of the LCA Navy (FSED Navy). The work carried out during the pre-project phase was merged into the FSED Navy when it was sanctioned in March 2003.

This chapter summarises the Air Force Version of the Light Combat Aircraft (LCA) programme from its origin. At the stage of LCA Navy studies, the LCA AF Version had commenced flight test. This chapter then brings out the initial studies of the Naval Version of the Light Combat Aircraft (LCA Navy) through the Project Definition Phase (PDP) and the Pre-Project Phase (PPP). It thus gives an insight into the thought process of the design teams with the available information at that time. How it all changed as the detail design of LCA Navy progressed will be apparent in later chapters of this book.

4

CARRIER-BORNE FIGHTER AIRCRAFT

Need

In the early 2000s, the Indian Navy had made plans to have multiple aircraft carriers. At that time, it was envisaged that the carriers would be equipped with a Ski-Jump take-off But Arrested Recovery (STOBAR) mode for aircraft operations. This entails that an aircraft needs to get airborne in a short distance take-off run of about 200m on the ship. In ship take-off/launch, it could be either with a suitable restraint mechanism located on the ship or the aircraft could perform a free roll take-off. Compare this with land-based aircraft take-off, where the runway length required would be about 800 to 1,000m. On a ship, landing/recovery would be in just about 90m with an arrester hook engaging an arrester wire on board the ship. The wire pull-out of the ship's arresting gear would be of a constant length, as there is only a finite space in the landing path of the ship. Accordingly, the carrier-borne fighter aircraft needs to be designed for this capability of a short take-off and arrested recovery. These challenges will be discussed in more detail in subsequent sections of this book.

At the time of government sanction in March 2003 for the Full-Scale Engineering Development of the Naval Version of the Light Combat Aircraft (FSED Navy), it was envisaged to have an aircraft optimised for air defence role, being in the light category. This aircraft would co-exist with a larger aircraft in the medium weight category that would primarily perform strike missions. Hence, the country had embarked on a mission to design and develop a carrier-borne aircraft *ab initio* with this objective. At that time, it was planned to develop a deck-based aircraft as a replacement for the Sea Harrier aircraft (a light aircraft) that would be required to operate from future aircraft carriers. Further, as a long-term perspective vision of being self-reliant in the country, it was envisaged to have an indigenous carrier-borne fighter aircraft. It was expected that the LCA Navy would meet this aspiration.

Requirement

The Indian Navy provided broad top-level requirements to the Aeronautical Development Agency (ADA) that would be used during the design and development process. It was brought out that the aircraft needed to operate from an aircraft carrier having a 14° ski-jump, with a deck run of about 200m. The aircraft was to be designed to have an arrested recovery capability to stop it in about 90m using a specially designed arrester hook engaging an arrester wire on board the aircraft carrier. This would result in a sudden deceleration to the extent of 4.5g and needed to be reacted by the arrester hook and the corresponding aircraft structure.

What this means in simple terms is that if an aircraft has a landing mass of 10 tons and has a deceleration of 4.5g, then the load on the arrester hook will be about 45 tons. This enormous load acting on a single point on the arrester hook needed to be reacted in the immediate vicinity of the arrester hook shank and then diffused within the aircraft structure without distress or failure. This is a repetitive load every time the aircraft lands on a ship, and thus poses challenges for design.

The aircraft was to be designed in such a way that the landing gear and, consequently, the aircraft structure needed to withstand a high sink rate (vertical rate of descent) of around 7.1 m/s due to flare-less landing. The sink rate is nothing but the vertical component of the aircraft's approach speed. Typically, the vertical component of the approach speed, in the limiting condition, could be as much as 4.5 m/s. This, combined with the ship's heave velocity at the touchdown point of an order of a maximum of 1.5 m/s, makes the sink rate at 6.0 m/s. The value for the design of 7.1 m/s is thus taken considering scatter in landing on a ship's deck.

The aircraft structure faces a significantly larger load in both the horizontal direction due to the arrester hook and vertical load due to high sink rate landing on a ship. Both these extreme loading conditions needed to be analysed carefully during the design and subsequent testing process. This entailed an interesting design challenge to ensure load absorption and dissipation within the aircraft structure. As will be seen later, this was successfully surmounted by our highly capable design teams.

There is a critical pilot requirement to have adequate over-the-nose cockpit vision to enable the landing path and aids on the aircraft carrier to be always visible. The aircraft design needs to take care of this requirement by suitable modifications to the front fuselage of the LCA AF Version. Based on the ship's geometric characteristics of ramp profile and the ambient conditions, the allowed take-off mass is decided. For example, the allowable LCA Navy take-off mass could be 12.5 tons. However, the limit landing mass allowed from the ship's arresting gear and landing approach speed perspective could be 10 tons. There is a difference of about 2.5 tons from take-off to the allowed landing mass of the aircraft. One of the ways to reduce this is to jettison the external weapons and fuel drop tanks. However, this may not be sufficient. Deck-based aircraft typically need to incorporate a fuel jettison system that would be utilised to permit the aircraft to recover on deck in case of an emergency immediately after launch, by dumping excess fuel at a significantly high rate of discharge.

The Indian Navy projected a requirement that the aircraft should have In-flight Refuelling (IFR) capability. This would be a significant capability enhancer for operational exploitation of the aircraft during service by carrying out air-to-air refuelling. The refuelling probe could preferably be retractable as stated by the user. Considering the size of the aircraft, it was planned to have a fixed air-to-air refuelling probe installed on the aircraft. It was analysed that the impact on the aircraft control characteristics due to the external projection into the air stream could be handled by the flight control system, and hence would not impose restrictions on the aircraft.

Aircraft carriers have large lifts to take the aircraft down from the flight deck to a hangar deck below and vice-versa. Typically, there are two aircraft lifts on the ship, one towards the forward section and the other towards the aft section. The sizes of the lifts are decided by the ship's designer based on certain inputs of the types of aircraft likely to operate from the carrier. Normally, the aircraft are parked in the two sections, with a firewall in between to isolate the two parts in case of a fire. Once decided, the aircraft lift dimensions become a geometric parameter that is fixed and the aircraft weight and size needs to meet the carrier lift structure and dimensions. It may be mentioned here that there are other lifts of smaller size for weapon loads to be brought up from the ship's weapons storage areas to the flight deck.

Aircraft Carriers & Typical Carrier-Borne Aircraft

Aircraft carriers around the world are typically of various types, albeit with varying sizes and capacities in terms of aircraft and crew. These are based on the philosophy of operation and the type of aircraft that a particular country operates. Of course, the aircraft capabilities to meet both Point and Mission Performance specified by the user would have been taken note of by the country during its selection process of the aircraft. It is also important to remember that the operating philosophy and strategy need to be tailored to the type of the aircraft carrier and, consequently, there is an impact on the type of aircraft. There is a need for a close synergy between the ship's capability and the aircraft characteristics to effectively operate from it.

STOBAR Carriers

This type of aircraft carrier was originally operated only by Russia, namely, the *Admiral Kuznetsov*, operating the Sukhoi-33 aircraft. India decided to get the Russian cruiser, the *Admiral Gorshkov*, to be repurposed as a STOBAR aircraft carrier that would operate the Russian aircraft, MiG-29K. This aircraft carrier acquired by India, INS *Vikramaditya*, is currently operational in the country. The indigenous aircraft carrier, *Vikrant* (new) built at the Cochin Shipyard Ltd., is also of this type. These types of aircraft carriers typically have two take-off positions; a longer one at around 200m and a shorter one at around 125m/165m depending on a particular carrier. A picture of INS *Vikramaditya* indicating the broad features of the flight deck is shown below. We can clearly see the take-off path over the ski-jump and the angled landing/recovery path. At about 45,000 tons, this carrier would be in the medium weight category.

Ski-jump Take-off But Arrested Recovery (STOBAR)

Ski-jump Take-off and Vertical Landing (STOVL) Carriers

These types of carriers originated in the UK operating Sea Harrier aircraft, followed by exploitation in India. It may be recalled that the Royal Navy of the UK exploited the HMS *Hermes* operating the Sea Harrier aircraft during the Falkland War. This Centaur class aircraft carrier was then purchased by the Indian Navy and rechristened INS *Viraat*, which continued to operate the Sea Harrier aircraft during the period of its commission. The earlier aircraft carrier with the Indian Navy, namely, INS *Vikrant*, was converted to have a ski-jump for launch and vertical landing for operating Sea Harriers. The UK has its new aircraft carriers, the Queen Elizabeth class, in this concept to operate the Joint Strike Fighter (JSF), F35B. These carriers are bigger than INS *Vikramaditya*. Obviously, the number of aircraft and helicopters carrying capabilities are higher.

Ski-jump Take-off and Vertical Landing (STOVL)

Catapult Take-off But Arrested Recovery (CATOBAR) Carriers

These types of carriers were operated earlier by the UK and India. An earlier version of the *Vikrant*, with its Sea Hawks and Alize aircraft, was in this category where aircraft were launched off the deck by a catapult and recovery was by an arrester hook on the aircraft engaging an arrester wire on the ship. In my initial days in the Indian Navy, I had the good fortune of being the Air Engineer Officer of the Alize Squadron embarking on the *Vikrant*. The tenure of almost three years gave me tremendous exposure and experience regarding the nuances of aircraft carrier operations and maintenance. I was also able to experience, firsthand, the feel of catapult launch and recovery from the navigator's seat of the aircraft a significant number of times. I believe these experiences stood me in good stead when I was associated with conceptualising and developing a deck-based fighter aircraft in the country, namely, the LCA Navy.

The USA and France are currently operating CATOBAR carriers. China is also building CATOBAR carriers. The US Navy aircraft carriers are large carriers weighing almost 100,000 tons. They are veritable floating cities, are nuclear-powered and can stay at sea for extended deployment. A typical US Navy aircraft carrier is shown, clearly indicating the catapult take-off regions (4) and the angled arrested recovery path. From the 1950s, the launch device on the aircraft carrier has always used a steam catapult system. However, recent US Navy aircraft carriers have changed over to the new concept of the Electro-Magnetic Aircraft Launch System (EMALS). Again, since the 1950s, the arresting gear energy absorption device has been a hydro-pneumatic system and remains largely in all the carriers to date. Recent US Navy aircraft carriers have switched over to equipment called the Advanced Arresting Gear Engine (AAGE).

Catapult Launch But Arrested Recovery (CATOBAR)

Typical carrier-borne aircraft worldwide are shown below:

Type	*Aircraft*	*Comments*
Ski-jump Take-off But Arrested Recovery (STOBAR)	LCA Navy MiG-29K SU-33	Light, Indian Medium, Russian Heavy, Russian
Catapult Take-off But Arrested Recovery (CATOBAR or CV)	Rafale-Marine F-18 E/F JSF: F35C	Medium, French Medium, US Medium, US
Ski-Jump Take-off & Vertical Landing (STOVL)	Sea Harrier JSF: F35B	Light, UK (and with Indian Navy) Medium, US

Typical Aircraft All up Weight Categories

Light: < 14 tons; Medium: 14 to 24 tons; Heavy; > 24 tons

Carrier Operating Doctrine

When the Government of India was considering the approval for LCA Navy development, the Indian Navy had indicated that the carrier operating doctrine would include a mix of lightweight fighters, medium-weight fighters and helicopters. The Indian Navy's projected requirement then was 57 LCA Navy aircraft. It was envisaged that the LCA Navy would be optimised for a fleet air defence role and the selected medium category aircraft would be optimised for the strike role. Hence, different types of aircraft and helicopters would coexist on board the aircraft carrier, each performing a specific primary role. This kind of mix of aircraft and helicopters is typical onboard aircraft carriers worldwide. In fact, the Indian Navy had extensively operated on a similar philosophy with the *Vikrant*, exploiting different aircraft/helicopters, namely, Sea Hawk, Alize, Sea King, and Chetak.

Carrier Operations

It was learnt from the Indian Navy that they plan a three-carrier operating philosophy in the future with a mix of different aircraft deployed on them. Accordingly, the LCA Navy, a 12.5 ton class of aircraft, had certain operational roles as identified in the Naval Air Staff Requirements (NASR) to coexist with other aircraft and helicopters. The LCA Navy is configured for ski-jump take-off from a 14° ramp with a run up of 200m and arrested recovery with a wire pullout of 90m as per the characteristics of the *Vikramaditya*. As can be seen, the planned top-level objective of the LCA Navy was well within the carrier operating doctrine set out by the Indian Navy. This set the stage for the initiation of the Full Scale Engineering Development (FSED Navy), which would involve the design and development of a Naval Version of the Light Combat Aircraft (LCA Navy).

CCS Approval

ADA, together with its partners, undertook a study in the Project Definition Phase (PDP) and confirmed to the Indian Navy the feasibility of converting the LCA Air Force Version to a Naval Version capable of operating from an aircraft carrier with the concept of ski-jump take-off and arrested recovery. The scope of FSED-Navy included building two aircraft and a Structural Test

Specimen in Navy standard (STS-N) and flight-testing towards operational clearance/carrier compatibility demonstration. A note as per the requisite format was prepared at ADA providing information of the background, the scope of activities envisaged, the estimated cost and the anticipated timeframes for the FSED Navy.

The note for the Full Scale Engineering Development for the Naval Version of the LCA Navy (FSED-Navy) was first considered by the Cabinet Committee on Security (CCS), chaired by the Hon'ble Prime Minister of India, on 26 June 2002 and was deferred to discuss issues regarding the aircraft carrier operating philosophy of the Navy, production line capability of HAL and the development strategy to handle LCA Navy activities, in addition to the LCA Air Force Version. The CCS wanted clarity on these aspects and directed that they be incorporated in the note. The carrier operating philosophy and the estimated number of aircraft were articulated by the Indian Navy as shown above and the same was incorporated in the draft CCS note.

As for the other query by the CCS regarding production capability to handle the LCA Navy, HAL intimated that they would be setting up a production line for the LCA Air Force aircraft with an initial capacity of eight aircraft per annum in LCA FSED Phase-2. They further indicated that it could progressively be enhanced to 24 aircraft per year. Between the LCA Air Force and LCA Navy configurations, the commonality to the extent of 80 per cent in LRU and parts was envisaged at that time. Further, the front fuselage would be a common module for the LCA Air Force trainer and the LCA Navy aircraft. Thus, the assembly line created for the LCA Air Force Version would also be employed for LCA Navy production with certain changes/additions to jigs and fixtures, thus meeting the total requirements of the Navy. This clarification provided by HAL was suitably incorporated in the note to the CCS for FSED Navy.

The LCA Navy development strategy was also to be incorporated in the note to the CCS. The initiative of the Indian Navy in supporting work on certain long lead-time activities prior to launching the full-fledged development phase had afforded better clarity on the overall scope of the LCA Navy programme. Based on design studies, it was considered, at that time, feasible to have a common configuration for the LCA Air Force trainer, LCA Navy fighter and LCA Navy trainer. The extensive experience gained in developing several technologies and design tools in the LCA Air Force programme would be directly beneficial to the LCA Navy development phase and they are briefly mentioned in subsequent sections.

Advanced aerodynamic concepts were evolved using a judicious mix of wind tunnel tests and Computational Fluid Dynamics (CFD) simulations for freezing the configuration. The same strategy was planned for the LCA Navy also, with a build-up of the aerodata set, taking the LCA Air Force Version as a baseline. This would significantly reduce the time and effort of tests and evaluation. It was envisaged that suitable corrections may be needed based on simulation and delta testing. The finalised configuration is called the Numerical Master Geometry (NMG) or the outer mold line of the aircraft. This gives the external shape of the aircraft that can be used for CFD studies. Based on the feedback from simulation, NMG may need to be changed.

Strategy and processes for detail design, analysis and fabrication of the entire airframe including metallic components and primary structures made out of carbon composites were already developed for the LCA Air Force Version. Necessary fabrication and test facilities already built for the LCA Air Force Version would be utilised for the LCA Navy also. Hence, the technologies already developed for the LCA Air Force Version would be adapted right away for the LCA Navy too, wherever feasible.

System design and integration technology, particularly in avionics, flight control system, environmental control system, hydraulic system, fuel system, and secondary power system had been extensively developed for the LCA Air Force Version. It was felt that a significant extent of this could be adapted to the LCA Navy aircraft, with minor changes. Further, it was anticipated that most of the Line Replaceable Units (LRUs) already developed (90%) for the LCA Air Force would be used for the LCA Navy, albeit with additional qualification testing for arrested recovery shock loads.

Existing LRU level, system level and aircraft level rigs/facilities, ground and flight test facility, etc., already developed during the FSED of the LCA Air Force would be used for the LCA Navy. However, there was a need for new main air frame static test rig, undercarriage drop test facility, arrester hook test rig and shore-based facility for the LCA Navy ski-jump launch and arrested recovery trials. Maintenance and necessary upgradation of these rigs were catered for in the cost estimates. Additional rigs and facilities that were schedule critical for progressing both FSED Phase-2 and LCA Navy concurrently would also be established during the LCA Navy development phase, for example, the Iron Bird.

Whilst in-house knowledge and expertise would be largely utilised, as a matter of abundant caution during the first time development of a deck-based aircraft in the country, consultancy in certain critical areas like control law for ski-jump take-off and arrested recovery, undercarriage development and arrester hook design were worked out and planned to be pursued during the development phase. This would be selective and was planned to be utilised more in terms of audit and critique of the executed design. Consultancy was also planned in the area of carrier suitability demonstration aspects.

It was proposed to make use of the available weapon range and associated facilities planned for the LCA Air Force Version, largely available with the Indian Air Force, to undertake weapon trials of the LCA Navy. It was assumed that the Indian Navy would make available weapons as free issue for trials whenever they were required. Further, for common weapons, there would be a 'read across' of data and certification tests that may not be repeated for the LCA Navy.

To summarise, the operational characteristics of the LCA Navy differ from the LCA Air Force in its ski-jump take-off capability from a 14° ramp and arrested recovery within the available deck length of the aircraft carrier. LEVCON, a deflectable control surface in the wing apex region and an auxiliary deployable fore surface in the front fuselage, improves the lift coefficient during take-off and landing. Arrested recovery is achieved with a deployable arrester hook and an undercarriage capable of absorbing high energy levels associated with high sink rates of flare-less landing. A fuel dump provision is required to cater to the emergency deck recovery of the aircraft. A nose droop is provided for better cockpit vision at approach attitude.

The note to the CCS was suitably modified and submitted again in early 2003 with the above clarifications. The CCS note was first vetted by the Ministry of Defence and cleared both by the Department of Defence (R&D) and the Indian Navy. After suitable financial scrutiny at the Finance Wing of the Ministry of Defence, the CCS note was scrutinised and concurred at the Ministry of Finance of the Government of India. After several presentations, briefs and discussions on the draft CCS Note for the FSED Navy, the CCS accorded its approval at end of March 2003 for the full scale engineering development (FSED) of a carrier-borne fighter aircraft to be undertaken for the first time in the country. This heralded a significant phase towards building up the indigenous design and development capability of a deck-based fighter aircraft in the country.

In summary, this chapter brings out the need for a deck based aircraft and its design intent based on the type of aircraft carrier that it operates on. It briefly describes the different types of carriers that are operating worldwide and a brief insight into the aircraft on them. STOBAR carriers are operated by Russia, China and India. STOVL carriers are operated by the UK, earlier operated by India with the Sea Harrier aircraft. CATOBAR carriers are operated by USA and France. China is also building a CATOBAR carrier. The earlier version of *Vikrant*, with the Indian Navy was a CATOBAR carrier operating the Sea Hawk and Alize aircraft. An important aspect of the carrier operating doctrine is brought out in this chapter. This is followed by the process of getting the approval of the CCS of the Government of India for LCA Navy development.

5

COMMONALITY & DIFFERENCES WITH LCA AF AND MAJOR CHALLENGES

Commonality Assumptions

At the time of commencement of design and development of the Naval Version of the Light Combat Aircraft (LCA Navy) in April 2003, the Air Force Version of the LCA had already been designed, built, and was in the flight test phase. Effectively, the baseline was already set, and the LCA Navy would have to be developed accordingly as a derivative. This chapter attempts to bring out the aspects of estimated commonality, differences, and challenges in converting an Air Force Version to a Navy Version of the LCA.

As brought out in the preceding chapters, based on the project definition and pre-project phase activities, a commonality of the Naval Version of the LCA to an extent of 80 to 85 per cent was assumed with the LCA Air Force Version with changes due to nose droop, landing gear, and arrester hook. With limited simulation and analysis, this was the best estimate at that time. The remaining structural and system elements were presumed to be common to a large extent.

As we go along, we will see some of the assumptions made at the time of commencement of the project in some detail based on the Project Definition Phase (PDP). However, as the detail design progressed, differences started emerging that were quite challenging, as would be apparent later. I guess this was to be expected; however, there was a penalty to be paid in terms of a longer-than-anticipated development time. Notwithstanding these challenges, it is satisfying to note that the maiden flight of the first LCA Navy prototype, NP1, took place exactly nine years from the start of development. I believe this is quite a good achievement for a first attempt to develop a carrier-borne aircraft in the country.

It is worth noting that some of the other major aircraft programmes like the Boeing's Super Hornet (F-18 E/F), Lockheed Martin's Joint Strike Fighter (JSF – F35) and Dassault Aviation's Rafale aircraft largely started out with a Naval variant. The Air Force variant was derived from it, resulting in optimum solutions for each variant, wherein they could fit equipment as required for a particular variant. Unlike this, the Russian MiG-29 (Air Force variant) to MiG-29K (Naval variant), was a conversion of the Air Force variant to a Naval variant. The LCA Navy was also taking this arduous route of converting an Air Force variant to a Naval variant, resulting in certain penalties and compromises.

As a first step to understanding the extent of activities and based on the results of the project definition, a top-level planning matrix was prepared identifying major similarities and differences, as shown in the table below. This would provide a 'bird's eye view' of the commonalities and differences amongst variants. It provided a significant insight into charting out the course of the programme. The baseline chosen was the LCA Air Force fighter variant that was already developed and in flight test. The evolution process that was envisaged was to first develop the LCA Air Force trainer, followed by the LCA Navy trainer and then the LCA Navy fighter. Hence, there would be four variants of the light combat aircraft: two for the Air Force Version and two for the Naval Version. This seemed a natural process to derive the variants with incremental/significant changes in the various modules as shown.

Item	*PV5 (Trainer)*	*NP1 (Trainer)*	*NP2 (Fighter)*
Front fuselage	New to Navy Std	PV5	PV5+Mod
Centre fuselage	AF Fighter with mod. for spine merger	New	NP1+Mod for Gun
Rear fuselage	AF Fighter	PV5+AHS	NP1
Wing	AF Fighter	PV5+LEVCON	NP1
Air Intake	AF Fighter	PV5+New Splitter plate	NP1+3 Door AAID
Stub wing	AF Fighter+	New	NP1
Canopy	New to Navy Std	PV5	PV5+Rear bubble closed
Wind screen	New to Navy Std	PV5	PV5
Equipping	New	PV5+	NP1+

Key: **PV:** Prototype Vehicle (LCA AF version); **NP:** Naval Prototype; **AHS:** Arrester Hook System; **AAID:** Auxiliary Air Intake Door; **LEVCON:** Leading Edge Vortex CONtroller.

Top Level Commonality Matrix of LCA Variants

As an aside, I would like to mention here that the LCA Air Force trainer programme was steered by the LCA Navy programme office, considering the extent of similarities with the LCA Navy shaping. Hence, the first LCA Air Force trainer (PV5) development and build, leading to its maiden flight on 26 November 2009, was a result of handling the design and development by the LCA Navy programme office. It was personally exciting for me to have taken this aircraft right through from 'Paper to Flight', in fact, as the 'lead-in' to LCA Navy.

Front Fuselage

One of the critical requirements for carrier deck recovery (landing) is to be able to see the landing path of the ship and the Optical Landing System (OLS) in particular, at all times, as shown pictorially below. This necessitates the need for a good 'over-the-nose' pilot's vision from the cockpit of a typical deck-based aircraft. Hence, it was decided that the front fuselage of the LCA Navy would be drooped down by 4° as compared to the LCA Air Force Version. It was reasoned at that time that the LCA Air Force trainer would also benefit by this increased visibility, especially for pilots in the rear seat. So, it was decided to have a common structural arrangement of the front fuselage for the Air Force trainer, Navy trainer, and the Navy fighter. This was a significant step wherein the buy-in of the IAF was obtained, leading to a common structural module for three variants.

A pilot's view of an aircraft carrier during landing approach

As they say, there are no free lunches; this arrangement has a larger side projection with a penalty of reduced directional stability and needs to be handled by the Flight Control System (FCS) through suitable control augmentation. A preliminary sketch of the front fuselage is shown below clearly showing that the pilot in the rear cockpit has a good all-round view. I have been fortunate to have experienced this personally in my flights on both the LCA Air Force and LCA Navy trainers.

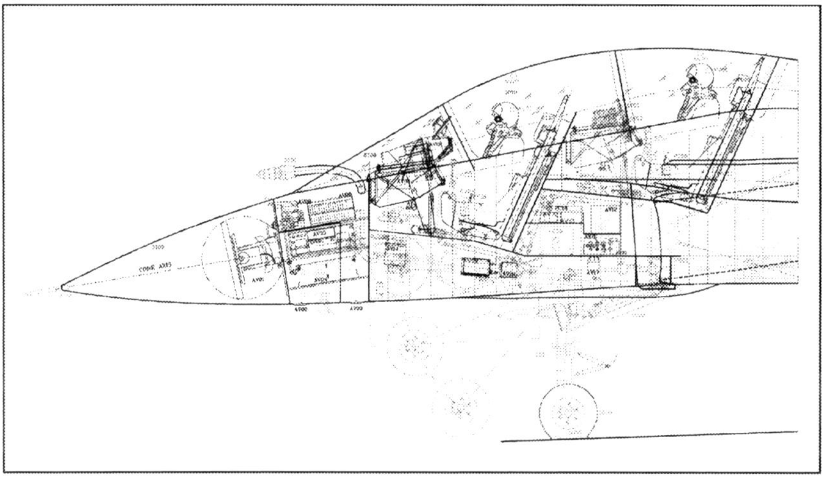

Preliminary sketch of the front fuselage

Since the trainer version would have two seats, there would necessarily be changes in avionics displays and Environmental Control Systems (ECS). In the case of LCA Navy aircraft, during deck landing and corresponding arrested recovery, there would be a tremendous downward slapping force on the nose landing gear due to a pivot action of the main wheel. In order to withstand this load, the nose landing gear needed to be longer and stronger. Hence, the attachment point is different and there is also a need for a larger volume in the nose landing gear bay. There is a single nose wheel as against a twin nose wheel in the LCA Air Force variant to facilitate better ship deck handling. Due to larger loads on the nose wheel, the wheel size is larger and therefore, there would be a 'bump' at the lower side of the fuselage surface to encompass the nose wheel.

When it comes to the LCA Navy fighter, the rear seat volume was planned to be utilised to have a fuel tank at the bottom to recover some of the lost fuel space in the two-seater. An entirely new fuel tank was to be designed and connected to the aircraft's main fuel system. The top region was planned to locate part of the avionics equipment. Some of the critical avionics system Line Replaceable Units (LRUs) were planned for installation at this location for ease of removal and replacement. This has the benefit of better equipment accessibility and improved maintainability - a huge benefit for maintainers.

Wind Shield and Canopy

With the external contour changed in the front fuselage, there was a need to have a new standard for the wind shield. The canopy would also be a new one as the shape is different due to the nose droop and needed to cater for two seats. The challenge here was to design the transparency and ensure manufacturability in such a way that there are minimal distortions. Further, the canopy needed to be designed for safe ejection, if the need arose. The ejection seat standard would also be different in comparison to the LCA Air Force fighter. It was planned that the LCA Navy fighter would have the same frame as the trainer, albeit with the rear transparency replaced by an opaque installation. Making this canopy was a significant challenge; however, it was successfully accomplished by the 'Plastic Shop' of HAL (Aircraft Division) at Bengaluru.

Centre Fuselage

There is an entirely new centre fuselage structure for the LCA Navy to react to the much larger structural loads due to carrier-based landings/recovery. Vertical loads due to a much higher vertical rate of descent or sink rates, as is usually known, of 7.1 m/s (LCA Air Force Version is designed for a sink rate of 3.0 m/s) needs to be reacted. Whilst the velocity component is more than double, it is obvious that the energy absorption is proportional to the square of the velocity and this has to be effectively absorbed. Due to this, the main landing gears are much larger and needed to be accommodated in the physical volume that was available vis-à-vis the LCA Air Force Version. This resulted in the internal layout of the centre fuselage needing complete rearrangement. A sketch of the centre fuselage module is shown below.

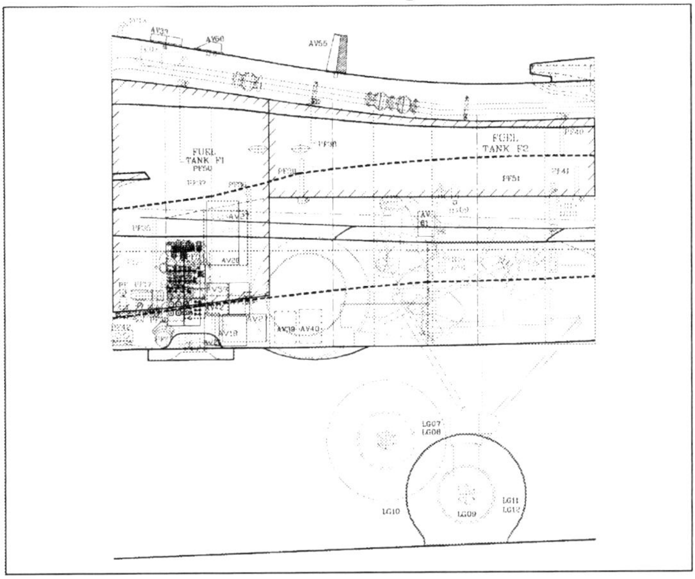

Sketch of centre fuselage

The spine region is also enhanced and would need to merge smoothly with the modified front fuselage. The fuel tank floor in the LCA Air Force Version was made of a single complex shaped composite part. However, to take the much larger vertical reactions, the fuel tank floor of the LCA Navy was planned to be made as a machined structure.

Whilst the arrestor hook installation is largely in the rear fuselage section, loads arising out of the hook engagement will be reacted in the horizontal axis (longitudinal axis) in the two bottom longerons (aircraft main longitudinal members) of the centre fuselage. Considering the landing mass of the LCA Navy to be 10 tons, with a maximum deceleration of 4.5g, the hook load is around 45 tons that is first encountered at the hook shoe. This load transfers through the hook shank to the aircraft structure via a hook system attachment. The challenge would be to design the structure in such a way that there is efficient load absorption and energy dissipation.

Due to the reduced volume available in the centre fuselage, there is a marginal reduction in the fuel volume of the LCA Navy. As was pointed out earlier, this loss has been effectively recovered by innovative management in the front fuselage of the LCA Navy fighter by introducing a new fuel tank in the region of the second cockpit of the trainer. Various LRUs also need to be relocated in the aircraft. Hence, the devil is in the detail when we move from a concept in the project definition to full-scale design during development of the aircraft. Challenges emerged as we proceeded with the detail design and each needed to be tackled. It is to the credit of the design teams that they gamely rose to the challenges and effectively surmounted them, as will be seen in the subsequent chapters.

Rear Fuselage

The rear fuselage largely houses the engine which is installed from the bottom. Due to this, there are no continuous frames in the rear fuselage structure but what are called 'horse-shoe' frames. The main mounting of the arrester hook system is located at frame station number 30, which is the last continuous frame in the aircraft. Arrester hook installation posed challenges in the single engine configuration, as arrester hook loads cannot be reacted in the rear

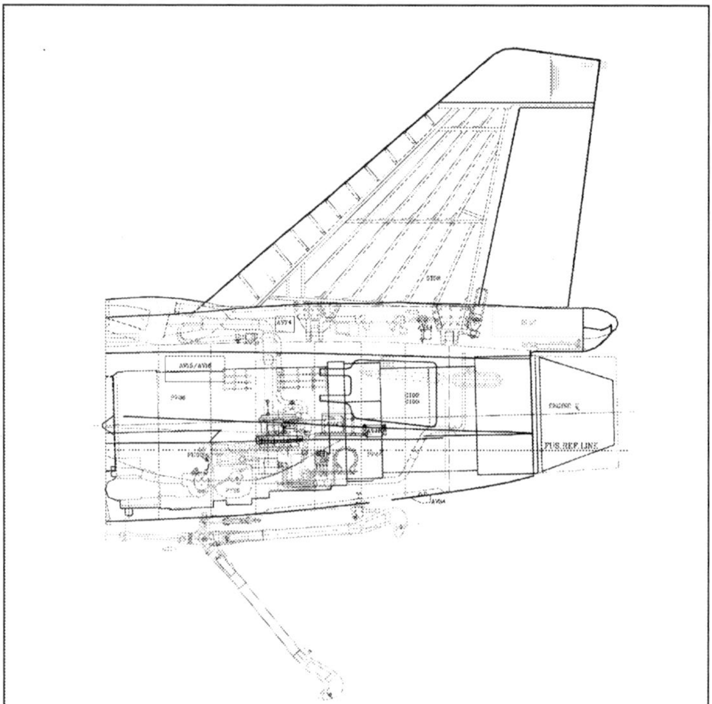

Sketch of rear fuselage

fuselage. The rear fuselage is by and large common with the Air Force version, with the engine bay door at the bottom, modified to accommodate arrestor hook system elements that included a separate platform. The other challenge was to ensure that the bottom structure and systems within the rear fuselage are not damaged if the hook shank strikes it due to hook bounce when it deflects off the deck. A sketch of the rear fuselage is shown above, indicating the arrester hook in both the extended and retracted positions. The sketch also shows the engine installation, with the access for which is from the bottom. When an engine change is envisaged, the arrester hook, along with its platform, needs to be dismounted first to facilitate access.

Wing

The wing of the LCA Air Force Version was a challenging development and was optimised based on a number of iterations. In fact, a national task force was set up amongst various agencies to conceptualise and develop the wing. This also resulted in the development of a large 'autoclave' by the National Aerospace Laboratories (NAL) to facilitate curing of large-sized composite parts. It therefore made sense to retain the wing configuration and characteristics to the extent feasible for the LCA Navy, rather than going in for a new design and development cycle.

As has been brought out earlier, the LCA Navy would have an additional secondary control surface, namely, Leading Edge Vortex CONtrol (LEVCON) at the inboard leading-edge side of the wing. Modification was necessary in the wing apex region to accommodate the LEVCON surface and the actuation mechanism to move this secondary control surface. There would be a need to have corresponding changes to the stub-wing structure, which is the interface between the wing and fuselage structure. Accordingly, there would be changes to the wing and stub-wing jigs to accommodate changes due to LEVCON. The impact of this change also affects the air-intake, primarily in the structural interface with the fuselage.

The wing structure is quite slender and, hence, innovative actuation concepts needed to be evolved keeping this aspect in mind. After a detailed market survey, it was decided to develop a rotary hinged actuating mechanism that would work efficiently in a minimal volume. The LEVCON surface can be deflected between 20 degrees down to 30 degrees up depending upon the phase of flight and would be linked to the aircraft flight control system. For carrier deck recovery, LEVCON will be deflected up by 30 degrees to enable reduction in approach speed.

Auxiliary Air Intake Doors (AAID)

These are located at the sides of air intake on both sides of the aircraft. As shown in the figure below, there is an opening with a hinged flap deflecting inwards that would be installed at this location. When the aircraft is on the ground in a static condition, the engine needs all the air it can get. The primary source of air is through the main air intake. However, it is not sufficient when the aircraft is static, as the engine has a larger potential to absorb air. There is suction in the air intake passage when the engine is running, and the free-floating flap of the AAID opens inwards to allow additional quantity of air, thereby improving the engine's static thrust.

Due to the nature of the mechanism, the actual opening area is about 30 per cent of the total capture area and, hence, the full potential of AAID was not realised. This became especially critical for the LCA Navy due to the smaller deck run (200m) available on the ship and every 'ounce' of thrust would be helpful. Hence, an innovative solution was found to have three smaller hinged doors in the same external cut-out element, thus resulting in a much larger capture area for air passage. This change was incorporated on the

Auxiliary Air Intake Door (AAID)

second LCA Navy prototype, NP2, and has given significant benefits in terms of launch performance due to a higher static thrust. When the aircraft is moving, the dynamic pressure created is sufficient and the AAID 'free-floats' to the closed position.

Systems

It is important to understand that a deck-based aircraft operates in an environment that is a 'super-set' of a typical land-based aircraft from the perspective of the structural and system capabilities. There are much larger structural loads in the vertical direction due to a higher rate of descent (sink rate) and horizontal 'g' loads due to arrested recovery. Naval aircraft operate in a marine environment; thus, structural and system items are prone to corrosion. The effects of Electro-Magnetic Interference (EMI) would be more severe as the aircraft operates close to emitters on board the ship. Hence, there was a need to design both the structural elements and systems to be safe considering these aspects. All elements taken as common from the LCA Air Force programme needed to be checked and suitably modified to meet LCA Navy requirements from the environmental clearance aspects due to loads and marine conditions.

Engine

The Kaveri engine was envisaged at the time of the project definition phase for installation on the LCA Navy. However, this had to be changed as the Kaveri engine was not ready. Accordingly, based on the decision taken by the LCA Air Force programme to install the GE-F404-IN20 engine, it was decided to use the same engine for the LCA Navy programme as well. As mentioned earlier, the engine is one of the most critical items that need to meet the operating envelope of a deck-based aircraft. Fortunately, the GE-F404 engine family is in active use on the US Navy's F-18 (Hornet) aircraft which operates in a harsher catapult launch and arrested recovery environment on board US Navy aircraft carriers. So, this fitted in well with the scheme of things since there was no need for re-certification of the engine.

The throttle assembly was sourced from the same manufacturer supplying to the F-18 aircraft of the US Navy, albeit modified for single engine operation.

The throttle assembly in the LCA Navy incorporates a back-drive mechanism to enable linking with the flight control system. This enables a feature like the auto-throttle to mitigate pilot workload during carrier deck recovery.

An issue that was not so apparent in a typical land-based take-off, but critical for the short take-off on a ship, is 'thrust droop' of the engine. When the throttle is opened, in the first few milli-seconds, the thrust actually drops by about 6 to 8 per cent, before it picks up. This is not critical in a typical runway take-off as there is adequate rolling distance available. However, in the case of the LCA Navy, the reduction in thrust occurs at the most critical phase of the short take-off over the ramp, which is clearly undesirable. From a safety aspect, the lowest momentary thrust would be assumed for computing the allowed take-off mass. This has an impact on reduction in mission performance as a result of lowering allowed take-off mass. The three door AAID installed in NP2 mitigates this effect to some extent, due to better pressure recovery. Whilst some 'work-arounds' were found for the LCA Navy Mk1 (as the first programme was later termed), the thrust droop issue has been corrected in the engine control law of GE-F414-INS6 engine for the LCA Navy Mk2.

Aircraft Mounted Accessories Gear Box (AMAGB)

CVRDE, DRDO, the developers of the AMAGB for the LCA Air Force, had to reanalyse the load cases for the LCA Navy load environment. Based on this, suitable modifications were carried out and the AMAGB was retested to the environmental specifications of a deck-based aircraft. The casing is made of magnesium alloy that is susceptible to corrosion in a marine environment. New coating technology was developed to cover the casing and environmentally tested to prove its efficacy. In fact, this coating developed for AMAGB was found useful for the LCA Air Force programme as well, as their aircraft also operate near coastal areas like Jamnagar.

Fuel System

The LCA Air Force aircraft fuel system is largely adapted to the LCA Navy platform, with some additions/changes that are essential/desirable for a deck-based aircraft. Any carrier-borne aircraft will typically have a fuel jettison/dump system. In a deck-based aircraft, there is a maximum launch mass that is dependent on the Wind-on-Deck (WoD) available on the flight deck, the ambient temperature and any other flow disturbances. This weight, of course, is below the designed maximum All up Weight (AuW) of the aircraft. Based on aircraft design and the limitations of the arresting gear on the ship, the maximum landing mass is defined, which is typically around 75 per cent of the launch mass. For the LCA Navy, the take-off mass could be around 12.5 to 13.0 tons and the maximum landing mass could be around 10.0 tons, resulting in a difference of 2.5 to 3.0 tons. When the aircraft gets airborne from the ship, if there is a need to recover immediately, then this additional mass needs to be reduced in a short time. Some of the expendables are external weapons which can be jettisoned. Another item that can be expended is fuel, wherein about 1.0 ton of it can be dumped in 90 seconds. Therefore, for emergency deck recovery, a combination of store jettison and fuel dump can bring the aircraft to a safe landing mass.

Hot Refuelling

This is a feature that is unique, as the aircraft is refuelled on the ground with its engine running and the pilot sitting in the cockpit. Adequate safety measures are in place when this procedure is in progress. This has been incorporated in the LCA Navy and, to my understanding, very few aircraft worldwide have this capability. The result is multiple flights in a 'sortie', thus enhancing the capability and flight test productivity of the aircraft. At one time, about three-hour sorties have been conducted. This is considered to be a significant performance and operational enabler. Having seen the success of this capability during flight testing of the LCA Navy, it is understood that the Indian Air Force has also evinced interest in incorporating this feature on the LCA Air Force Version.

Hydraulic System

The hydraulic system of the LCA Air Force Version is utilised with augmentation to operate the larger landing gears, arrester hook system and LEVCON. Simulation studies reveal that the existing system could handle the additional hydraulic load due to management of the loading duty cycle. The hydraulic system is a dual-redundant system catering to the requirements of redundancy and reliability. This high-pressure system operates at a pressure of 280 bar (4000 psi). There are other emergency hydraulic power sources available, primarily to cater to the flight control system in the LCA Air Force architecture, which would be carried over to the LCA Navy as well.

Environmental Control System (ECS)

The ECS of the LCA Air Force Version, with significant layout changes, is adapted for the LCA Navy Version. A new feature of 'Bleed Shutoff' has been introduced in the LCA Navy. As mentioned earlier, there is an issue of thrust droop in the GE-F404-IN20 engine at the moment of opening the throttle by about 6 per cent of static thrust. If the engine bleed going to the ECS is shut off for 30s, then static thrust recovery is better, permitting an allowable increase in aircraft take-off mass. The bleed shutoff feature was used for ski-jump launch by incorporating the same in the 'ski-jump' mode logic.

Ejection Seat

The LCA Air Force Version was installed with Martin Baker, UK ejection seat Mk-16G. It may be mentioned that Martin Baker has considerable experience with ejection seats that are carrier suitable. Due to larger loads on the LCA Navy and the cockpit dimensions being different, there was a need for modifications to the variant of the Mk-16 ejection seat to be installed in the LCA Navy. Due to the larger spine shape, the canopy breakers are longer as per installation requirements. Further, this seat needed to be analysed and tested for the larger loads due to carrier operations.

Brake Parachute

A brake parachute is deployed after the aircraft has landed on the runway to enable the aircraft to decelerate without unduly stressing the aircraft brake system. The same standard brake parachute system as in the LCA Air Force Version was planned for the LCA Navy Version also. Whilst there was a debate on the need for this system in a carrier-borne aircraft, it was decided to retain it since around 60 to 65 per cent of the time, the aircraft would operate from a land-based runway.

Flight Control System (FCS)

The FCS has various primary and secondary control surfaces like elevons, flaps, rudder, slats, and air brakes. In addition to the FCS of the LCA Air Force Version, the LCA Navy aircraft has an additional secondary control surface, namely, LEVCON. The aircraft also incorporated an auto-throttle to assist the pilot during ship deck landings. Hence, the Air Data Computer (ADC) is replaced by a LEVCON Air Data Computer (LADC) that incorporates monitoring and control functions of the additional LEVCON and an auto-throttle. The software for the LCA Navy is also different, primarily for ski-jump launch and arrested recovery capability.

Avionics and Cockpit Controls

The avionics system is largely the same, albeit with changes to the software. Head Up Display (HUD) has been modified to accommodate a larger over-the-nose vision provided in the naval version. For the rear seat in the two-seater aircraft, the HUD location is replaced with an additional Multi-Function Display (MFD) to act as a HUD repeater that receives live camera feed from forward HUD. Cockpit displays and controls cater to arrester hook and LEVCON too. There are additional lights in the landing gear and landing gear bay specifically for carrier-borne operations. The two-seater aircraft has duplicate cockpit controls and displays.

Electrical System

The electrical system used for the LCA Air Force Version was planned to be adapted for the LCA Navy with the inclusion of new systems, namely, arrester hook, LEVCON, fuel dump system, additional lights, etc. The wiring is also different for the two-seater variant (NP1), due to having a dual cockpit.

Weapons

Weapon fit requirements were planned to be the same as those of the LCA Air Force Version to begin with. The light combat aircraft has been designed with an innovative weapon management system that enables easy integration of various types of weapons. Adequate intelligence has been built into the computers located within the weapon pylons itself to take care of interface requirements. Therefore, it was felt that any new weapon/store integration was not seen to be a big challenge.

Major Challenges

At this stage, some of the major challenges involved in the LCA Navy design and development will be highlighted. They will be discussed in more detail in subsequent chapters. These challenges are depicted in the graphic below and are briefly described in this section.

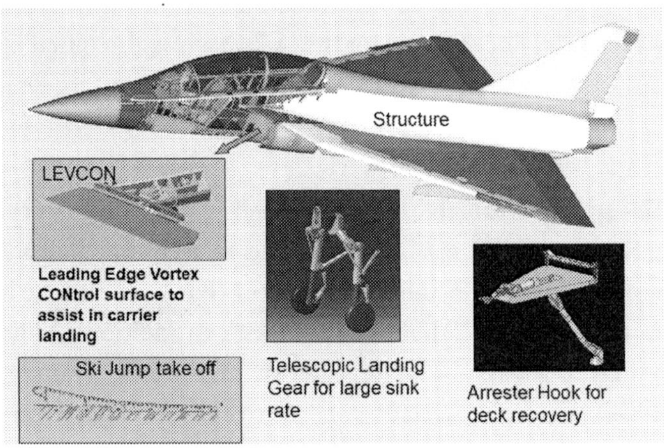

Challenges in LCA Navy development

The first challenge was the Aircraft Structure itself, due to larger structural loads encountered during carrier-borne take-off and arrested recovery. Structural design was also a challenge in packing in items in the same volume with various LRUs, larger landing gears, introduction of the arrestor hook, LEVCON, etc. The LCA Navy needed stronger and longer landing gears to take the significantly larger loads with sink rates of 7.1 m/s. Designing and building this, and also accommodating it in the small aircraft, was deemed a significant challenge.

The next system was the arrestor hook that had to be integrated to absorb the single point loading of deck recovery up to 45 tons, which posed an interesting challenge to the designers. The control law for ski-jump launch was to be designed for the aircraft to get safely airborne in just about 200m. This required a special control law mode to be developed, largely automated with minimal pilot intervention. The LEVCON posed a challenge due to the integration of a new secondary control surface, its actuation, and the control system harmonisation.

Programme Management Challenges

Formal Cabinet approval for the Full-Scale Engineering Development of the LCA Navy Programme (FSED Navy) was accorded in March 2003, a decade after the formal full-scale engineering development sanction of the LCA Air Force programme (FSED). The historical maiden flight of the first technology demonstrator of the Air Force Version of the light combat aircraft (TD1) had already taken place on 4 January 2001. Other aircraft of the LCA Air Force programme were in various stages of development, building, and flight test and, hence, the infrastructure and human resources were largely occupied with that programme.

It was a significant challenge to get some of these resources to work concurrently for the LCA Navy programme. From a very minimal team when it started in April 2003, the programme office team also had to be built up over the years. Even during the latter part of the programme, it was still modest. Many times, conflicts would occur, with each programme vying for priority, and solutions needed to be worked out. To the credit of HAL team, they did try and allocate a separate team to work on the LCA Navy programme. A pictorial representation of the four variants of the LCA is shown on page 82.

Since the LCA Navy was to be derived from the already developed land based variant, commonality was the major theme. At the time of CCS approval in March 2003, the assumption was that LCA Navy would have about 80 to 85 percent commonality with LCA. The chapter then identified major challenge areas of landing gear, arrester hook, aircraft structure, ski-jump launch, LEVCON, etc. Due to these challenges of a deck based aircraft, the extent of commonality reduced as development progressed, albeit having certain constraints due to a derived aircraft programme. These would be clearer to the reader as we move along with the forthcoming sections of this book.

6

Design & Development Cycle of LCA Navy

Process and methodology are extremely important factors for an effective and efficient product development cycle, be it a small component or a complete aircraft. Typically, every aircraft development organisation/industry develops its own methodology for its design and development process. However, a product development cycle largely follows the process that was adopted for the Light Combat Aircraft (LCA) and its variants, as shown pictorially below. There is a need for a combination of the requisite skilled human resources, software tools, simulation facilities, software coding faculties, ground test facilities, hardware-in-the-loop infrastructure, instrumentation, flight test facilities, certification, etc. This process is capable of meeting the entire spectrum from requirement capture to concept development, to simulation, to analysis, to virtual testing, to system engineering support, to detail design, to digital manufacturing, and digital assembly of the aircraft. This is followed by physical manufacturing of parts, assemblies, integration, ground and flight tests so that the intended objectives vis-à-vis requirements are met.

To achieve the above, there is a need to have software tools and the necessary skill sets to handle these tools in the product development cycle. In fact, when the LCA Air Force programme started, most of these tools were non-existent and were built up over a period of time, from basic drawing boards to 2D Computer-Aided Design (CAD), to 3D CAD, and then a concurrent engineering approach. This was another technological and skilling challenge that was traversed along with the aircraft development itself.

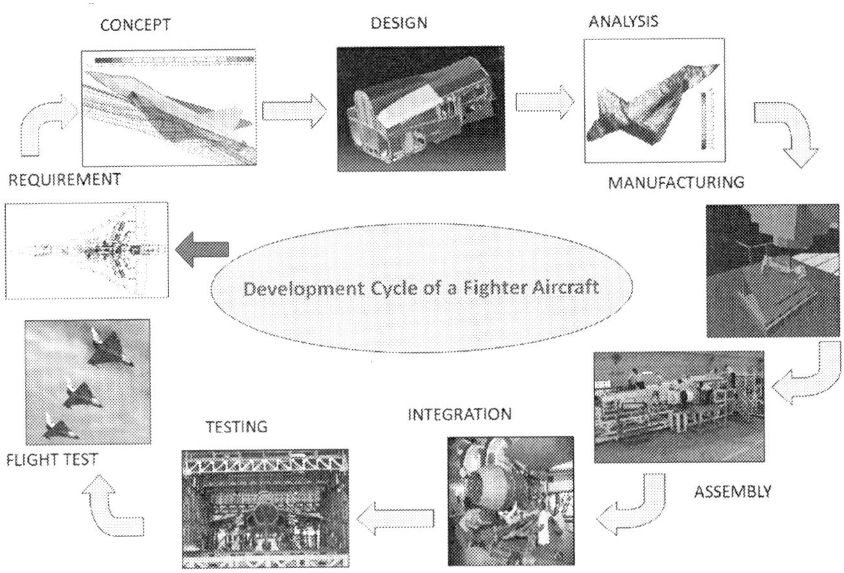

Design and Development Cycle

At this point, it will be interesting to briefly understand the evolution of the design and development tools. It all started in the 15th century when Leonardo da Vinci sketched some concepts of an aircraft. I feel sketching even today is of great relevance for an engineer as it is a universal language.

I would like to recount an interesting experience when I was dealing with the Russian design agency for some aspects of the design of the Shore Based Test Facility (SBTF) to be set up at the Indian Naval Air Station at Goa. Normally, our entire communication was through an interpreter. There was a particularly complex situation wherein the interpreter was feeling challenged, and so both the Chief Designer on the Russian side and I resorted to communication through sketching. It worked very well and was highly productive.

Coming back to the evolution of design tools, the next step was to perform engineering drawings using drawing boards with a 'drafter'. This was followed by 2-dimensional CAD, wherein drawings were created on the computer screen and printed on drawing sheets. The next evolution was 3-dimensional CAD, leading to the creation of a Digital Mock Up (DMU). Today, we have a collaborative environment, digital twin, augmented reality, and so on.

At this stage, let us start the actual development journey of the LCA Navy aircraft with Requirement Capture being a critical first step in any product development process. It is important to note that the greater the details that are noted during requirement capture, the greater will be the fidelity and understanding and will therefore result in a better design. One of the most important inputs for the LCA Navy design and development is the Naval Air Staff Requirements (NASR) promulgated by the Indian Navy (IN). This defines the functional, performance, weapon loads, operations, and maintenance requirements expected of the aircraft in the challenging environment of an aircraft carrier. Certification and Quality Assurance (QA) requirements will be another major chunk, with Certification requirements answering the question, 'Have I designed it right?', and QA requirements answering the question, 'Have I built it right?'. Manufacturability, assembly, testing, accessibility, maintainability, and product support will also dictate some of the design requirements. There is thus a need for documenting all requirements and tracking their extent of compliance during the design and development process. A typical requirement tree is depicted below.

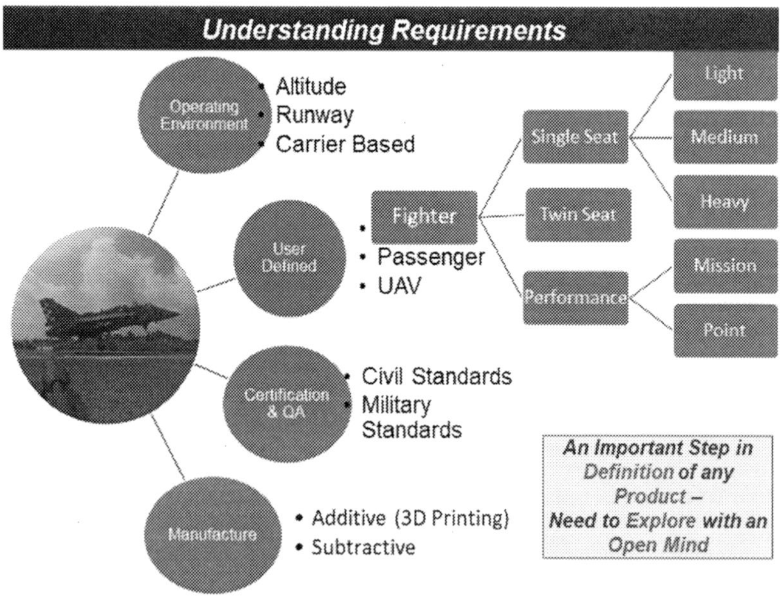

Typical Requirement Tree

The typical Design Stage Process Flow is shown below. It shows Systems Requirement Review (SRR), which is a means of tracking compliance of all the requirements that have been captured. This is the stage wherein a detailed compliance matrix of various requirements is generated with clearly identified partial/non-compliance areas, if any. Stakeholders need to scrutinise the compliance matrix and sign off the document as having accepted it, especially in areas of non-compliance. In the case of non-compliance, the user would need to either modify the requirements or provide a concession for that specific requirement. All these need to be carefully collated and documented for later reference and acceptance by all the stakeholders.

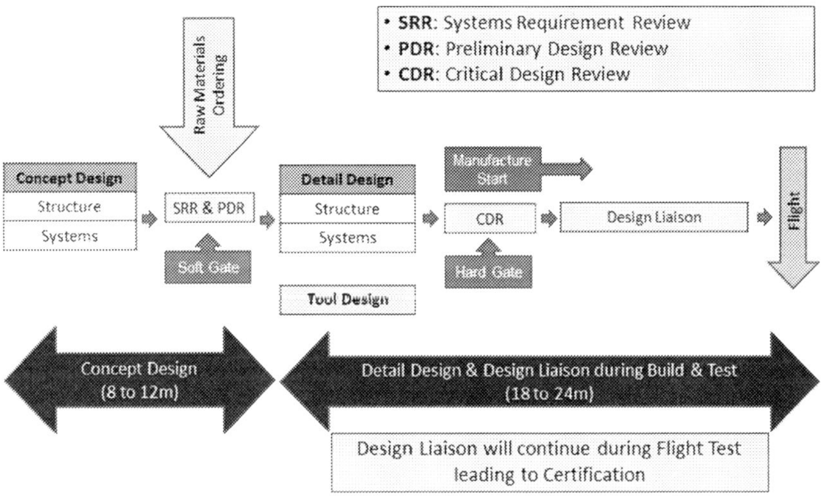

Design Stage Process Flow

Successful completion of the SRR lays the foundation for checking aspects of concept design, leading to a potential finalisation of the configuration. A Preliminary Design Review (PDR) will then be conducted at the culmination of concept design. The PDR can be considered a 'Soft Gate', as it is still in the realm of paper or in a digital mode and iterations are still possible without significantly impacting time and cost, albeit investing additional effort. Compliance to requirements is again checked at this stage. Further, at the completion stage of the PDR, there is sufficient confidence for ordering raw material as this has a long lead time for supply, typically of the order of 36 months.

Once there is a sign-off on the PDR, the next major step is the detail design process, at the end of which there will be a Critical Design Review (CDR). This stage is considered as a 'Hard Gate', as the next stage will be manufacturing and assembly of the aircraft. Any change suggested after this stage will be extremely costly in terms of time and cost. Even at the CDR stage, the requirements are once again checked for the extent of compliance, and stakeholders need to confirm acceptability. Post CDR, designers will perform the role of 'Design Liaison' when the manufacture, assembly, and test phase is in progress. The design liaison team acts as a bridge between the production and design teams to clarify doubts during manufacture, assembly, and testing. In parallel with aircraft detail design, tooling, fixtures, and jigs are also designed and built to be available when the CDR is complete. Whilst this is the ideal process, it had not been followed entirely in the LCA Navy development, and some of the aspects have come with 'Hind-Sight Wisdom'. However, it is an important lesson learnt and has been applied to a large extent on the next variant, namely, the LCA Navy Mk2.

Concept Design

Concept Design was earlier carried out to some extent in the form of preliminary sketches during the Project Definition Phase (PDP). However, it needed to be revisited vis-à-vis formal requirements provided by the user and other requirements that were discussed and finalised during the SRR. Any new inputs that became available needed to be addressed in the concept design stage. With the Kaveri engine not being available, the preliminary design of the rear fuselage assembly had to be redone with the interfaces of the GE-F404-IN20 engine; this was one of the examples of a major change.

Concept design is the phase wherein alternative solutions are explored and a number of iterations are carried out. The advantages and disadvantages of each of the solutions are studied in detail, keeping requirements in mind at every step. In the concept design phase, preliminary 3-view drawings were first generated, as shown below. The general shape and size of the proposed aircraft start to become visible. Some of the key elements of the aircraft are defined, namely, the arrester hook, the larger landing gear, the distinctive front fuselage nose droop, the LEVCON, the In-Flight Refuelling (IFR) probe, etc.

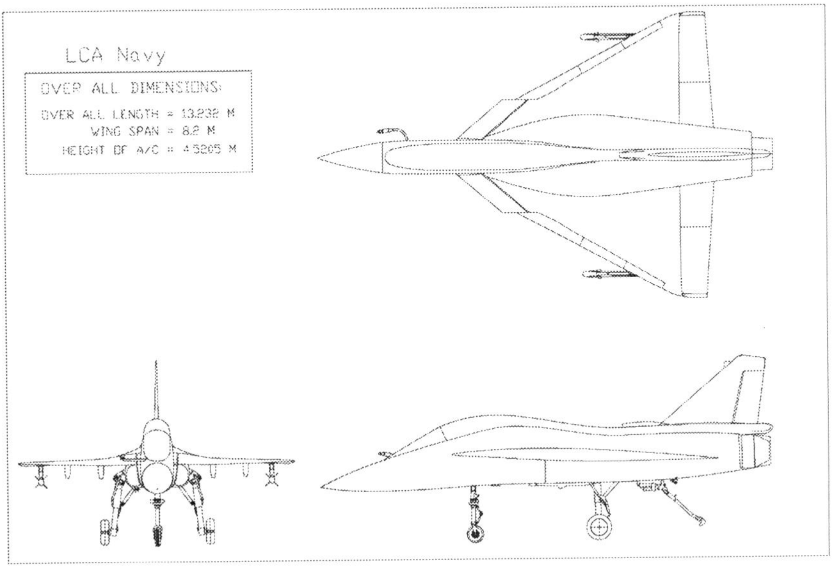

Preliminary 3-View Drawing of LCA Navy

With some of the major internal elements added to the aircraft and based on the 3-view drawings, the 3-dimensional external shape begins to emerge. This results in the preliminary outer geometry of the aircraft, called Numerical Master Geometry (NMG). This is also termed as the 'Outer Mold Line'. NMG is a key element in the design process of the aircraft and typically becomes proprietary to an aircraft design house. The preliminary NMG will be the medium used to check whether the aerodynamic requirements are met or if any suitable streamlining needs to be done to minimise unnecessary drag. This NMG forms the basis for initial Computational Fluid Dynamics (CFD) simulation to obtain the aerodynamic characteristics, termed 'aerodata set' or simply 'aerodata'. The resulting structure is also used for preliminary stress analysis.

Preliminary inboards (internal layout) with all equipment and systems are prepared to verify that all items are installed within the defined outer shape. This may result in iterations on NMG based on ability to accommodate all items and systems. At this stage, preliminary mass and inertia data, item-wise, are prepared and tabulated. This is called the mass properties of the aircraft and will also define its Centre of Gravity (C.G). The C.G margin based on the aircraft's control characteristics is also defined, and the location of each equipment/items installed needs to be tabulated, which also includes information on its relative position vis-à-vis C.G. The inboards and mass properties will be updated as the design progresses to address specific challenges that may be encountered. There could be situations when some of the equipment/LRUs may not fit in the space allocated, necessitating modifications to NMG or creating local 'bumps'. A typical inboard picture of the first LCA Navy prototype (NP1) is shown below.

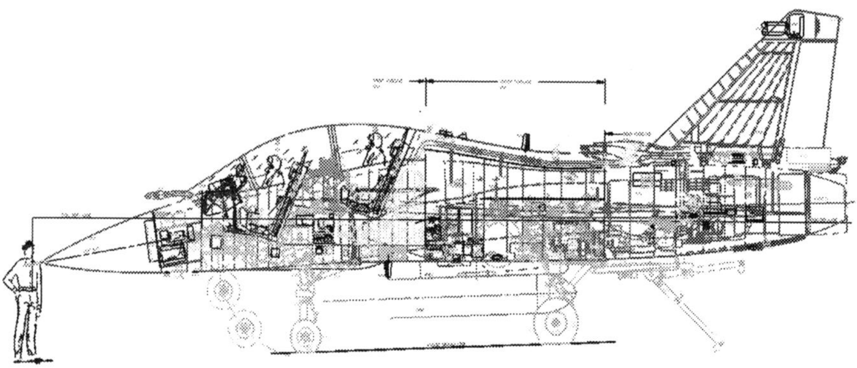

Preliminary Inboards of the LCA Navy (NP1)

Wind Tunnel Model Test

As a result of CFD studies and the iterated NMG, low-speed and high-speed wind tunnel models were designed, fabricated, and tested to obtain refined aerodata sets. This will facilitate correlation of the aerodata obtained by CFD, and if necessary, the simulation model is corrected. The aerodata set thus obtained will be one of the inputs for the Control Law (CLAW) team to generate algorithms. A picture of a 1:20 scale high-speed wind tunnel model under test at NAL wind tunnel is shown below:

1:20 Scale LCA Navy Wind Tunnel Model at NAL Tunnel

Design and Ergonomics

CAD tools are used to create parts of the aircraft in three dimensions (3D). From these parts, assemblies are created and visualised. Let us take an aircraft cockpit as an example for a 3D assembly and the design iterations thereof. In earlier days, a physical mock-up of the cockpit was fabricated and assembled. There was a need to check the position of various elements of the cockpit, from the seat to the control stick, to switches, to displays. To check that these were in the right positions, a number of pilots of different sizes would be made to sit in the cockpit and confirm the reach of both hands and feet, and also comfort. This entailed a significant effort and time. Any change that was required as feedback from checks entailed a change in the physical mock-up until satisfactory results were achieved. This is extremely laborious and time consuming. Digital tools are now available that mitigate this effort to a large extent. We can have mannequins in the 3D space that can be used for ergonomic studies, both internal and external. This has become quite a game-changer in the design and development process of an aircraft.

Simulation

Once a concept design has been made, the next step is to simulate/analyse it to check if it is satisfactory from various aspects of strength, durability, and life. These are primarily structural simulations using techniques of Finite Element Methods (FEM). Every structural component and assembly needs to be first checked for its strength in static and then carryout a dynamic analysis. The items are then checked for fatigue capability defining life. For instance, if the design life of a structure is defined as 3000 hours, then the structure needs to withstand at least four times this when analysed. Design has to meet both the requirements of strength and fatigue. Every simulation needs to be validated by ground and flight tests. Once validation is established, then for the bulk of design studies, decisions can largely be taken based on simulation.

Correlation

Correlation is an important aspect of a design and development process, wherein the design simulations are validated with tests of different types. Typical bomb drop trajectory prediction was done using CFD. These were then validated by actual flight tests, and pictures of the drop were taken from another aircraft. It can be seen from the pictures below that there is an excellent correlation between simulation and flight tests. In fact, these simulations were first correlated with wind-tunnel testing as an interim step. This shows that simulation tools available today have come of age. Hence, there is an increasing reliance on simulation, thereby reducing physical testing and thus resulting in significant savings in cost and time.

Prediction Flight Test

Correlation between CFD and Flight Test of 1000lb bomb

Simulation Capabilities

There are a number of simulation capabilities available today, namely, finite element analysis, thermal analysis, dynamic analysis, fatigue analysis, bird strike analysis (explicit), non-linear analysis, heat transfer simulation, and studies for computational electromagnetics, etc. Using these simulation technologies, it will be possible to carry out structural optimisation and hence facilitate lighter structures.

Electrical Harness Design & Installation

There are a significant number and types of electrical cables and connectors that need to be installed in an aircraft. They could be system cables, data cables, power cables, etc. There is a need to scientifically route these cables in an aircraft in the most optimum manner. It has to be ensured that they do not clash with any other structural or system elements. This will enable subsequent physical installation while supporting maintainability and testability.

Harness design tools enable generating details of cables, looms, and connectors and provide digital data. From 3D routing as installed on the aircraft, a concept called flattening is done, which is virtually laying out the cable assemblies in 2D, enabling exact lengths to be available. Further, this facilitates generating a Bill of Material (BoM) used for fabrication of cable looms for subsequent installation on the aircraft. With the electrical harness design process, we can generate a database of all the cable harnesses in the aircraft that would facilitate subsequent checks efficiently. Continuity and insulation (Megger) checks are carried out using an automatic harness check rig to ensure that the system integrity is sound. This facility was first built as part of the LCA Navy programme and has saved significant time and effort. This has become a standard checkout system for production of LCA (Tejas) also.

Piping and Tubing

An aircraft has many mechanical systems, namely, fuel, hydraulics, environmental control, lubrication, braking, flight control systems, etc. All these systems need piping and tubing, together with connectors, to be installed in a logical sequence in an aircraft. There is a need to correctly allocate space within the structure, without clashing with other elements, equipment, cables, etc. This is possible in a digital environment, where a clear 3D installation is possible, facilitating a virtual walk through.

From the previous sections, it is apparent that the structural design defines the overall internal 'real-estate' of the aircraft. This permits installation of the engine, LRUs (equipment), electrical harnesses, piping and tubing, etc. The DMU is thus evolving, at every stage checking that there are no clashes and interference, and that accessibility for maintenance is adequate. During this process, there is a possibility that some of the items may not fit within the defined NMG, resulting in further iterations of the shape of the aircraft. However, it may be noted that whenever there is an NMG change, the aerodynamic characteristics need to be rechecked and aerodata set updated.

Having the DMU of the cockpit and other areas of an aircraft, various items/elements can be positioned in the digital space. With ergonomic capability, animated mannequins of differing sizes, from 3 to 97 percentile of the population, can be placed in the cockpit and analysed for reach and comfort. Iterations are easily achieved and the cockpit can be finalised without the need of a physical prototype, as previously brought out. The DMU of the LCA Navy is shown on page 82. As can be seen in the graphic, the aircraft structure is available, with the installation of all equipment, engine, systems, pipelines, cables, etc. Engineers can virtually walk through and see the internal details and check various system installations, electrical harnesses, piping, tubing, etc. Accordingly, an installation scheme can also be generated and this will be an extremely useful tool for shop floor professionals when building the aircraft. This is considered a game-changer in design and development.

Aircraft Build Process Flow

We had earlier seen the aircraft design process and we also navigated through some of these aspects in previous sections. Similarly, there is an aircraft build workflow as depicted below. You would recall that the raw material ordering would have been done at the stage of completion of the PDR. When the CDR has been completed and the 'go-ahead' is given for part manufacture, raw material for the same will be available. There are roughly 12,000 parts to be manufactured, divided between structural parts and system parts. Fabrication and readiness of each of these parts needs to be tracked individually using a dashboard to ensure timely availability for the assembly process. At this stage, necessary tooling, jigs, and fixtures are also manufactured and assembled in preparation for aircraft part availability to proceed with the next steps of building up the sub-assemblies as shown.

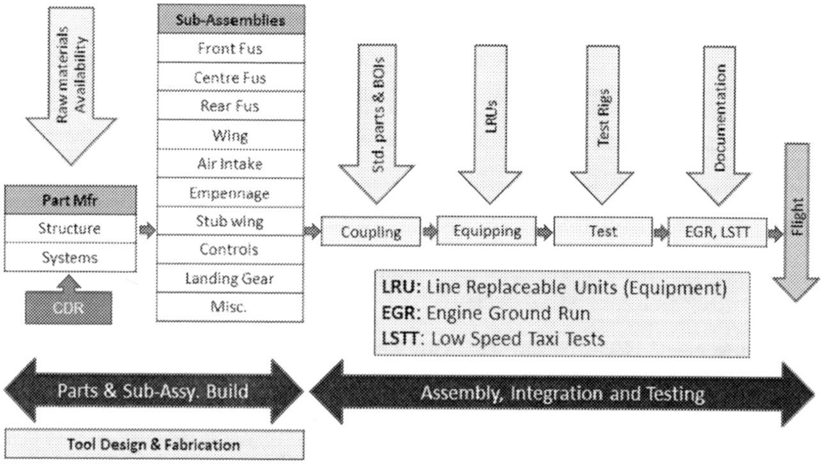

Typical Aircraft Build Process Flow

When the part manufacture is initiated, it must be ensured that requisite standard parts and Bought out Items (BoI) are also ordered. These would include fasteners, cables, electrical connectors, pipelines, fluid connectors, equipment trays, etc. These would be required in the subsequent stages of coupling and equipping as shown by place markers in the aircraft build process flow diagram. Thus, there are a number of interconnected activities that have to be tracked to prevent delays from seeping in during the build. This is a challenge in Programme Management, and the LCA Navy programme office had created tracking dashboards for both the design process and the build process.

I recall that Dr. VK Aatre, the then Scientific Advisor to the Defence Minister, insisted on a detailed PERT chart to be prepared, printed out on a large sheet, and kept in my office for ready programme tracking. During every review, he would ask me about the chart and how the activities were progressing vis-à-vis the tracking chart.

To facilitate configuration, variant, and change management, there are

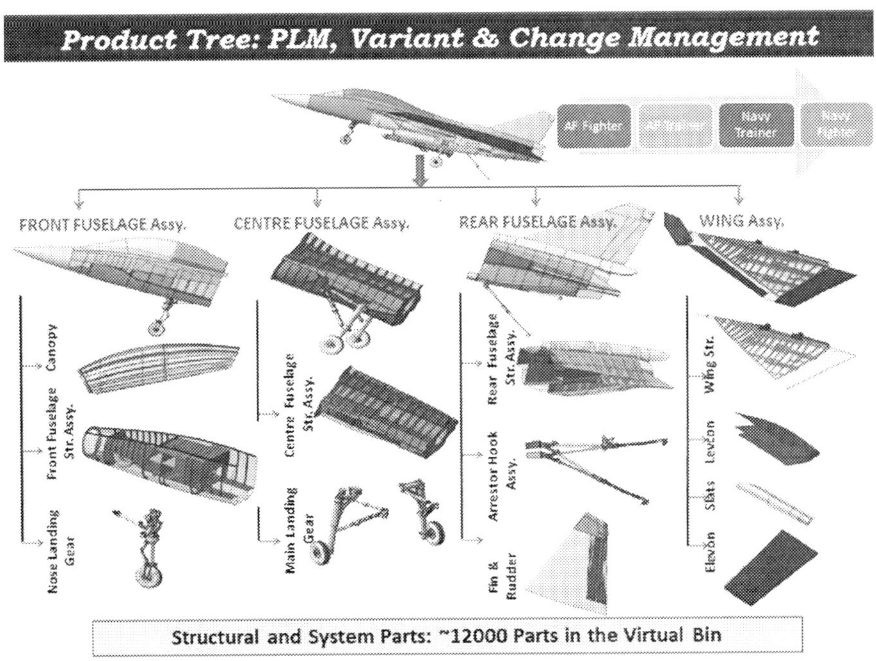

Product Tree Structure of the LCA Navy

digital tools available that can track parts as they are designed and also check for reuse from other variants. This process is called Product Lifecycle Management (PLM). It was previously mentioned that some of the parts and assemblies of the LCA Navy were common with the LCA Air Force. PLM enabled identification of these common parts in the digital environment and the tree structure was built up. This capability lends itself efficiently to variant management. The product tree at a macro-level is shown above.

We can visualise both a top-down and a bottom-up approach. At the highest level, the product is the aircraft itself. From this, we go down to major assemblies like the front fuselage, centre fuselage, rear fuselage, and wing. Each of these major assemblies has sub-assemblies as shown. Sub-assemblies are made up of parts. Hence, at the lowest level, we have a number of parts available to us in a basket to pick from. If there are other variants, then those additional parts are also designed and put in the basket. Based on the required variant, parts are picked up to build sub-assemblies and thereafter the aircraft is built up. As can be seen, there are four variants shown, namely, LCA AF fighter, LCA AF trainer, LCA Navy trainer, and LCA Navy fighter.

Manufacturing

Manufacturing is a costly process, especially with exotic materials used in the aerospace industry. In order to 'get it right' the first time, extensive simulation of the manufacturing process can be done in the digital environment. Tooling, jigs, and fixtures can also be finalised first in the digital environment. Manufacturing process planning can be optimised to minimise time and materials, thus saving costs. At the end of this process, the result would be to obtain the machine codes (NC codes) suitable for interfacing with the Computer Numerical Control (CNC) machines. The benefits of the digital environment are therefore enormous and valuable. In addition to aircraft part manufacture being digitally simulated, tooling design is also underway.

Once the manufacturing process has been established using digital manufacturing tools, the actual part manufacturing is initiated. This involves various types of parts to be manufactured and inspected, namely, metallic parts, sheet metal parts, and composite parts. Each of these types of materials will have their own raw material requirements and processes. If we have a metallic part to be manufactured, then the raw material needs to pass the requisite quality check and this billet is tagged for traceability. Depending on the final part configuration, an interim process of rough machining may be carried out in a conventional machine, followed by CNC machining. The part is then finish processed and suitably inspected to check whether it meets the design and drawing requirements. Similar processes are available for sheet metal parts or composites. Of course, additive manufacturing has evolved to the extent that it is being used in various portions of the aircraft.

For each of the sub-assemblies of the aircraft, there will be separate jigs that need to be available. Some of the jigs had to be specifically designed and built for the LCA Navy, such as the front fuselage jig, centre fuselage jig, LEVCON jig, stub wing jig, etc. Some of the other jigs that were common with the LCA Air Force variant were replicated with necessary changes incorporated to suit specific LCA Navy interface needs. These jigs and fixtures were carefully checked by quality assurance agencies and cleared to facilitate assemblies. The fidelity and close tolerances that are required to be maintained in the jigs will greatly assist in ease of coupling various assemblies and make the modules interchangeable. This is especially critical during the production stage.

Once the jigs are available and the parts are manufactured, the sub-assembly build stage starts. As the sub-assemblies are built, they move on to the stage of coupling, where the aircraft starts coming together as shown below, with the front and rear fuselage assemblies being placed in the coupling jig.

Front and Rear Fuselage in Coupling Jig

The centre fuselage is then brought in and inserted into the coupling jig between the front and rear fuselage sub-assemblies as shown below. This is a critical operation where the interfaces between the front and centre fuselages, as well as between centre and rear fuselage assemblies, need to be matched. It was indeed a sight to behold as the aircraft started to take shape in front of our eyes. This stage was reached after a lot of sweat and toil among all the stakeholders.

Centre Fuselage being placed between the Front and Rear Fuselage

We have seen that from individual parts that were digitally developed, physical manufacture was done, followed by sub-assemblies being built. The next step was to build the major assemblies as shown above, and they were brought together to assemble a full aircraft, digitally. The designers can render it and visualise both the externals and internals. They can animate some of the elements, for example, landing gear extension and retraction. This capability helps carry out the entire process of virtually building an aircraft and assessing it in all its facets, which is a significant benefit.

A pictorial representation of a virtual assembly in progress vis-à-vis physical assembly is shown below. This is precisely what today is termed as 'Digital Twin'. In the picture, the entire fuselage assembly is in the coupling jig and one can correlate it with the virtual assembly. The interface fastening is completed and certain pre-equipping activities are also carried out. This is also the stage where other interfaces are prepared. One of the critical activities is the wing mount reaming and preparation to install the wing, once it is out of the coupling jig. Other interfaces include the vertical fin, landing gear, arrester hook, etc.

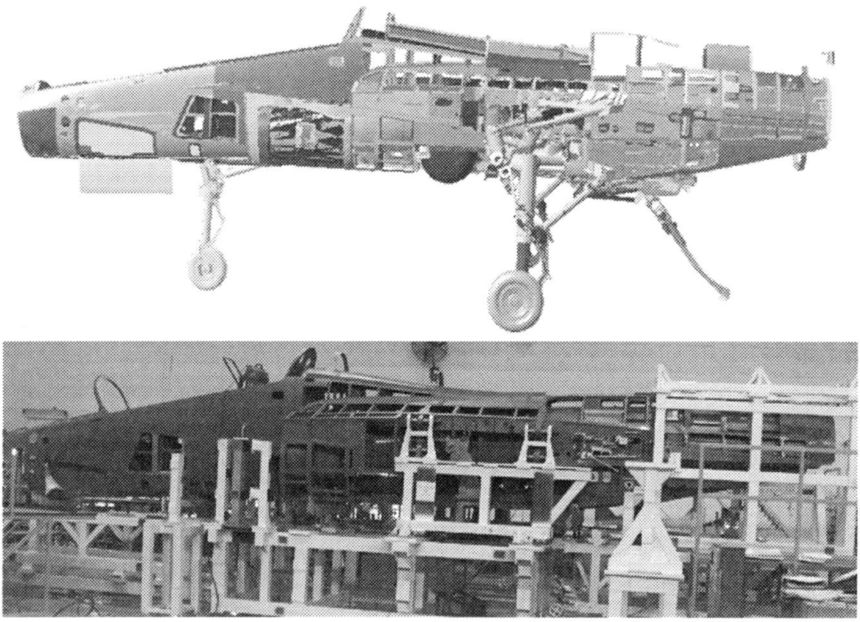

Coupling of Front, Centre and Rear Fuselage of LCA Navy

Coupling of major assemblies is an important milestone in the build of the aircraft, as its shape emerges surely and steadily. At this stage, the stub-wing and air intake have also been integrated into the coupling jig. Another important element that is integrated is the canopy and windshield frame. The main body of the aircraft structure has now been completed.

Equipping and Integration

Equipping and Integration are the next critical steps in the process of building the aircraft. Brackets and trays to install LRUs (equipment) shall be fitted at the predetermined locations. At this stage, cable harnesses of all the systems would have been prepared based on the design and digitally located in the DMU. In some cases, especially in the prototype stage, there is a process called 'One-side connectorisation'. In this case, connectors at one end are installed in the shop floor in the cable harness assembly. This process is used when the exact length is uncertain due to some circumstances, especially in the prototype stage. The other end connector is installed after the cable harness is routed on the aircraft. If the installation is found satisfactory and exact lengths are known, then this process can be dispensed with in production. Similarly, piping and tubing for various systems are prepared and installed in the aircraft. Some pictures of this stage are shown below.

Equipping – Pre Coupling

Engine Integration

Aircraft on Equipping Jig

Equipping and Integration Stages

Pre-equipping activities can be carried out at the sub-assembly stage, as shown in the rear fuselage build, to save time during the final equipping. At this stage, the engine is also installed and integrated with the aircraft systems. Other major assemblies and LRUs, namely, wing, vertical fin, canopy, landing gear, etc., are installed. The physical aircraft starts to take shape from the earlier virtual aircraft that we had as a DMU.

As mentioned above, the aircraft is starting to look complete, and being the first ever attempt in the country to develop a deck-based fighter aircraft, it was decided to have a formal 'Roll-Out' ceremony of the first LCA Navy prototype (NP1). A roll-out is akin to the launching of a ship, where the aircraft is exposed to the outside world from its earlier secluded environment in the build and assembly hangar. The act of 'Roll out' marks a significant milestone in the development process of an aircraft, where it is structurally complete, with equipment installed, and plumbing and wiring completed. The aircraft is on its wheels and can be moved by assisted power, which is a precursor to the phase of ground-based system integration testing leading to the engine ground run, taxi tests, and flight.

There was palpable excitement leading up to the roll out. I can vividly remember a distinct scene when the then Chairman HAL, Mr. Ashok Nayak, was himself present in the aircraft hangar supervising preparatory activities.

The day of the NP1 roll out on 6 July 2010 was possible through the active involvement of HAL as the principal partner of ADA and support by DRDO, CSIR labs, IAF, IN, CEMILAC, DGAQA, NFTC, public and private sector industries, educational institutions, and a host of other agencies. "*I wish to salute all of those who have contributed as a composite LCA Navy Team in realising this important milestone and look forward to the same spirit to take the aircraft towards its maiden flight at the earliest.*" I had made this statement to the dignitaries and audience present during the roll out event.

The chief guest at the roll out function was the then Indian Defence Minister, Shri AK Antony. The other dignitaries on stage included the Chief of the Naval Staff, Secretary Defence (R&D), Secretary Defence (Production), Chairman of HAL, Director of ADA, and others, including the author. Other eminent dignitaries were the former Chief of the Naval Staff, Adm. OS Dawson, former Programme Director of ADA, Dr. Kota Harinarayana, and a host of other eminent personalities as well as the personnel who had put their heart and soul into realising the wonderful machine. The Indian Navy band added to the fanfare of the occasion. A snapshot showing various facets of the roll out is on page 83.

The next important step was to carry out systems integration checks of all the aircraft systems. Some of these will be elaborated in later sections; however, one of the tests is pictorially represented below, depicting the automatic harness check out to verify continuity of cable connections and insulation integrity. This is commonly called Continuity and Meggar checks. It should be noted that in the LCA Air Force programme, the process of continuity checks and insulation integrity was carried out manually and could typically take months, as one can imagine checking about 40km of cabling in an aircraft. However, the testing process had evolved in the LCA Navy, wherein this could be automated due to having digital data. The process was completed in weeks. Also, during the checks, any faults would be indicated in the results. This enabled easy pinpointing of defects and thus facilitated quick and easy defect rectification. Subsequently, this process has been automated and standardised across the LCA fleet. The development of the automatic harness checking process and equipment has been a major enabler for the integrated testing of the aircraft. This has been one of the significant benefits of digital platform usage.

Systems Integration Tests and Automatic Cable Harness Checks

'Iron Bird' is a 'hardware-in-the-loop simulator', sometimes also called 'HILS', used to test the system integrity of the entire Flight Control System (FCS). A new Iron Bird was set up in HAL for the LCA Navy programme. In the Iron Bird, the aircraft FCS, hydraulics, and associated system elements are installed in a near identical fashion to that of the aircraft. A cockpit replica is installed to enable the pilot to 'fly' different sortie profiles and completely exercise the FCS. The software in the Digital Flight Control Computer (DFCC) is validated through what is called 'Fault-Free' tests. Failures can be intentionally introduced to check system behaviour, which obviously cannot be done in actual flight.

A number of other ground tests were carried out on the aircraft; a snapshot of some of the test facilities is shown below. Every aspect of individual systems needed to be tested and validated against simulations and predictions that were accomplished during various design stages. For LCA Navy testing, some of the ground test facilities already available from the LCA Air Force programme were utilised to the extent feasible. Some new ones were set up specifically where required. These will be highlighted in a subsequent section on test rigs. However, it should be noted that extensive ground testing was conceptualised and executed to build confidence and also validate simulation activities that were carried out in certain cases.

Ground Test Facilities

Once the ground tests were satisfactory and the results were verified by the Certification and Quality Assurance (QA) agencies, the aircraft was cleared to undertake yet another significant milestone in the process of developing a carrier-borne fighter aircraft, namely, Engine Ground Run (EGR). For the first time, the pilot got into the cockpit to energise the beauty that had been so carefully crafted and built. He undertook extensive pre-start checks of the aircraft, externally and internally, prior to asking for external power supply to

Unlike the LCA Air Force variant, the LCA Navy has a large steering angle of ±70 degrees, especially critical for ship deck operations with an extremely limited deck space. This design feature is intended to facilitate the aircraft to have a very tight turning circle. This feature was first successfully proved and the aircraft clearly demonstrated that it could practically turn on the spot. In the next step, the aircraft was taken to the runway for the LSTT, up to about 100 to 120 kmph. It was indeed a sight to behold, seeing the beauty racing along the runway.

The next major step was HSTT, where the aircraft was taken up to unstick speed. The aircraft needed to obtain flight clearance, as at the speeds of HSTT, there are chances/circumstances that may force the pilot to get airborne. It has apparently happened in some development programmes earlier in other countries. After due completion of a mountain of paper work, clearance was obtained from both Certification (CEMILAC) and QA (DGAQA) agencies, the first LCA Navy Prototype (NP1) successfully completed HSTT. A picture of the second LCA Navy aircraft, NP2 having completed HSTT, is shown below.

NP2 completing Taxi-Tests

Successful completion of HSTT of NP1 paved the way for its *maiden flight*. All systems were checked again in the ground test rig, a planned sortie was flown by the test pilot in the Real-Time Simulator (RTS), the test plans were worked out, the aircraft was again checked thoroughly, documents were re-checked, and then the clearance was given for the maiden flight.

It was a page for the history books on 27 April 2012 that the NP1 took to the air, ably piloted by Cmde Jaideep Maolankar, with Gp. Capt. M Prabhu in the rear seat. It was a glorious day and moment for the Team LCA Navy in general and for me in particular. The bird was in the air.

I was able to monitor the progress from the telemetry station of the National Flight Test Centre (NFTC). As is a common practice for the maiden flight of a new type of aircraft, the landing gear remained in the extended position throughout the flight.

The aircraft landed after flawlessly completing the objectives set forth for its maiden flight. It was a dream come true due to the hard work and toil put in by the LCA Navy Team over nine years. It should be mentioned here that the landing gear was retracted during the maiden flight of the second LCA Navy prototype, NP2. A picture of NP1 taken from another aircraft (Chase) during its maiden flight is shown on page 83. 'Paper to Flight' of the LCA Navy programme that started in April 2003 culminated in the flight of the beautiful machine exactly nine years later in April 2012.

In conclusion, a very important aspect of product development is the design and development process that was followed as clearly brought out in this chapter. The process used can be applied in general to any product development. The chapter traces the design and development journey starting with requirement capture, building a concept model, simulation, refinement of the design, detail design, build, ground and flight tests. The important aspect of correlation of the simulation model with test is clearly brought out. This helps in refining the simulation model, thus having the potential to reduce actual testing effort in the future. A brief mention of the programme management challenges involved in such a multi-agency venture has been made. Management involved coordination with about 100 major and about 300 minor work centres.

be connected. He then carried out system-level checks to validate the system's health. The aircraft also has 'Built-in-Test' (BIT) capability that would supplement information on system health. Once he was completely satisfied, he initiated engine start.

A number of EGRs were carried out, including engaging the afterburner to ensure that the aircraft is fully serviceable. Between EGRs, the data of each system was analysed and checked to ensure there were no failures prior to clearing for the next one. A picture of one of the aircraft EGR in progress is shown below.

I would like to recount that during one of the EGRs, it started raining quite heavily. However, it was decided to continue with the engine run, with the aircraft and all of us outside getting fully drenched. However, to the credit of the build team, there was no distress and water ingress into the aircraft, and the test was completed as per plan. This, de facto, also proved the waterproof integrity of the aircraft.

NP1 Engine Ground Run (EGR)

Once the series of EGRs were satisfactorily completed, it was time for the aircraft to move under its own power, called 'Taxi Tests'. There were three steps in which this was done, with the first being nose-wheel steering tests, followed by Low Speed Taxi Tests (LSTT) and then finally, the High-Speed Taxi Test (HSTT).

Snap Shots of the Roll Out Function of NP1

Maiden Flight of NP1 on 27 Apr 2012

Highlights at Shore Based Test Facility (SBTF), Goa

LCA Navy Night Ski-Jump Launch in SBTF

Pictures of CAS Flight in PV6 in May 2016

LCA Navy Prototype (NP1) at Def Expo in Goa

Formation of 45 Squadron of IAF with Tejas on 01 Jul 2016

Tejas Trainer PV6 at Leh for Hot-High Alt Trials in Aug 2016

Tejas participation in the Republic Day Event – 2017

Aero India 2017 & LCA Display

Flight of Director ADA (Author) in PV6 on 29 Dec 2016

Director ADA (Author) Flight in NP1 on 28 Mar 2017

7

Shore Based Test Facility (SBTF)

In this section, let us first look at the 'Need' and 'Genesis' for setting up a Shore Based Test Facility (SBTF). Operation of aircraft from an aircraft carrier is an extremely demanding task and even more demanding is the flight testing of prototype aircraft in this challenging environment. As a prelude to actual operations from an aircraft carrier, the aircraft needs to be flown at facilities ashore that simulate an aircraft carrier environment, namely, ski-jump launch and arrested recovery (landing on the ship), in the Indian context, having a STOBAR capability carrier. Further, it is prudent to conduct extensive ski-jump take-off and arrested recovery tests at a shore base to evaluate structural integrity, engine performance, and aircraft handling qualities. Enough confidence is generated by a series of shore-based tasks and data for the aircraft is gathered, which would be useful for actual ship-borne application.

When the LCA Navy programme was conceptualised in the early 2000s, a shore-based ramp, or ski jump for take-off and arresting gear system to facilitate landing or recovery was not available in India. Hence, for the purpose of testing, they would have to be either built at a selected location within the country or utilise existing facilities elsewhere in the world. Facilities that already existed at that time were at Saki, Ukraine, and in Naval Air Stations, Lakehurst and Patuxent River, USA. However, the facility in Saki has a ramp, but there is no restraining gear to assist in the take-off process to hold the aircraft back till it is ready to roll. Also, since the breakup of the Soviet Union, the facility was not much in use, and maintenance and upkeep of the equipment were suspect. US Navy facilities had the requisite landing facilities, but they did not have a ramp or ski-jump. They exploit the catapult take-off; hence, it became obvious that we had to build our own SBTF. As a result, SBTF conceptualisation and build were included as part of the Full-Scale Engineering Development of the Naval Version of the Light Combat Aircraft (FSED-Navy) sanction by the Government of India. It may be of interest to note that the Russians built an SBTF after our facility was built, and it is understood that the Chinese have also set up an SBTF of their own, subsequently.

Let me give a little history of Naval aviation vis-à-vis shore-based testing. Eugene Ely did the first ship take-off from a specially built 57-ft wooden platform from the USS *Birmingham* in a Model-D Curtiss bi-plane on 14 November 1910. On 18 January 1911, Eugene Ely carried out the first ship landing on a wooden platform, 120 ft x 30 ft, built on the USS *Pennsylvania.* However, before he did them, typical markings were done at a shore base for practice prior to actual take-off and landing on ships. Thus, the need for a shore facility to carry out aircraft tests prior to operation from a ship date back to the early 1900s.

A look at three representative carrier-based aircraft programmes would highlight the need for shore testing prior to actual tests and operations on an aircraft carrier. Some of these aspects will be briefly discussed in order to get an idea of why an SBTF is required and what can be achieved during prototype development, prior to actual embarkation on a ship.

The Rafale Marine (Rafale M) aircraft has been designed to operate from French Navy aircraft carriers with catapult launch and arrested recovery. Since there are no shore-based test facilities available in Europe and the UK for developmental testing, the French arranged to utilise US Navy facilities available at Patuxent River (Pax River), Maryland and Lakehurst, New Jersey. There were four land-based campaigns conducted at the US Navy facilities from July 1992 till December 1995 with one prototype aircraft (M01). As the shore test campaigns were in progress, the French Navy was also progressing with the carrier-based trials on the FNS *Foch,* from April 1993 till September 1995, again in four tranches. During the latter part of the ship campaign, the second prototype (M02) had joined for the trials.

Shore-based test campaigns were designed to check the validity of technical decisions made for carrier-based versions, especially with regard to landing gear and its compatibility for carrier-borne operations. The purpose of full-scale tests in the US Navy facilities was to validate and confirm that take-off was satisfactory from a simulated aircraft carrier environment, structural checks following heavy stress, and checking the ability of Rafale M to operate from carriers with runways much shorter than those on an airbase.

During the first phase of shore-based testing, thirty-nine catapult launch tests were performed. Each of these had been previously simulated, and it was found that the flight control system operated as predicted. A total of sixty-eight rolling arresting tests (or taxi-in arrestment) were performed. The overall deceleration envelope was tested with both on-centre and off-centre modes of operation. Fourteen Field Carrier Landing Practice (FCLP) landings were also performed to measure loads on the main gear at touchdown. The campaign ended with six fly-in arrestment. During a strong fly-in arrestment, a faulty operation of the hook damper actuator was recorded, which needed modification.

Prior to the second campaign, modification resulting from tests in the first campaign was incorporated and qualified on ground-based rigs in France. A total of forty-two each launch and fly-in arrestment tests were performed during the second campaign. In the third phase, forty-nine reeled engagements and forty fly-in engagements were performed. The results of these launch and arresting tests at US Navy test facilities proved satisfactory, paving the way for the first carrier operations from the French aircraft carrier, FNS *Foch.*

T-45A GOSHAWK is a US Navy two-seater, single-engine trainer aircraft. Significant modifications had to be made to adapt the British Aerospace Hawk design to the extreme environment of a US Navy aircraft carrier. It is interesting to note that this was a single-engine aircraft operating from an aircraft carrier, similar to the envisaged LCA Navy. T-45A design specifications require the capability for arrested landings with touchdown sink rates of up to 24 feet/sec (7.3 m/s) and approach speed of 125 knots (232 kmph). The aircraft needed to be tested at shore facilities prior to its embarkation on the aircraft carrier.

Carrier suitability demonstration followed by a basic flight test programme was initiated in March 1991 with ninety-nine taxi-in arrestments at the US Navy facility in Lakehurst. A structured build-up in gross weight, engagement speed, and arresting gear setting was performed until limit arresting hook loads were attained. Engagements were accomplished up to 124 knots ground speed and up to 20 feet off the runway centre line. Jet blast deflector (JBD) tests were also carried out to check the impact on the aircraft. After this, 122 arrested landings were performed during this period to acquire landing and arresting gear loads at various aircraft weights and landing attitudes.

Arrestments were first carried out at nominal approach attitude and then at nose down (<3.5 deg pitch angle), nose high (>9.5 deg pitch angle) and rolled/yawed (5 deg yaw and roll angles) attitudes. Both the On-centre and Off-centre engagements (up to 15 feet) were accomplished. Landing sink rates up to 21 feet/sec (6.4 m/s) were demonstrated. The first carrier landing was carried out in December 1991. Procedures for crosswind landings were then established. After initial trials, envelope expansion, weapon load analysis, etc., were undertaken.

Moving over to the Sukhoi – SU33 Programme (Naval Version), on 28 August 1982, the first take-off on an SU27 prototype (Air Force Version) that was suitably modified was carried out using a T-1 experimental ramp at the NITKA ground testing complex at Saki, Ukraine. For this test, the take-off distance was 230m at a speed of 232 kmph and aircraft weight of 18,200 kg. In the summer of 1983, the first landing test stage began using the Svetlana-2 ground arresting gear at the NITKA complex. The trials led to the conclusion that the ramp was suitable for combat aircraft take-off while, for landings, a modified arresting gear was required. The Nevskoye Ship Design Bureau (NDB), St. Petersburg, Russia, developed the ramp design. The new T-2 ramp had a cubic curve profile with a length of 53.5m, a height of 5.6m, a vanishing point width of 17.5m, and a vanishing point angle of 14 degrees.

In 1985, design approval was given and the SU27 was taken up for upgradation with reinforced undercarriage, arrester hook, increased flaperon area, wing folding, etc. Two prototypes were tested at the NITKA complex at Saki in Ukraine. One of the aircraft was fitted with a canard for checking the aerodynamic characteristics of the aircraft. Tests were carried out in September 1986 on the T-2 ramp. Testing continued through 1988, with around three hundred test flights. The maiden flight of SU33 (the Naval Version of the land based SU27), took place in August 1989 and then preparations for actual deck landing in November 1989 followed.

It is evident from the preceding three programmes of Rafale-M (France),

T45A Goshawk (USA) and SU33 (Russia) that shore testing in an adequately simulated test facility has been considered essential prior to actual ship landing and take-offs.

Let us now look at some of the aspects of the philosophy of structural tests. Landing an aircraft on an aircraft carrier imposes severe loads on the landing gear and airframe. A flare just prior to touchdown should not be done, as the pilot will lose sight of the landing system on the ship. Immediately after landing, decelerating loads of arrestment are encountered. Glide slope or line-up corrections in the last second due to turbulence caused by carrier structure can cause high aircraft touchdown sink speeds or rolled/yawed attitudes. Shore-based arrested landing tests are conducted to evaluate structural integrity when landing in different conditions that may be encountered aboard the carrier.

The first condition to be checked is the maximum arresting gear engaging speed that produces limit arresting hook loads and longitudinal deceleration. The next tests are the rolled and yawed attitudes at touchdown to simulate a last-minute line-up correction. With a target roll and yaw angle of 5°, tests are to be performed with roll and yaw, both in the same as well as opposite direction.

Occasionally, an arresting hook point will engage the arresting gear deck pendant prior to landing gear touchdown. This could happen with an in-close pitch-up attitude change or wave off. This type of engagement is called a 'free flight' engagement and is intentionally performed during a shore-based test programme as it corresponds to a high loading case, so that critical load cases are tested and the integrity of the aircraft is ensured.

All landings do not occur in the centre of a landing area. Off-centre arrestments, ranging from 3 to 6 meters on either side of the centre line, depending on the size of the carrier, are performed to investigate the high lateral loads and landing moments exerted on the arresting hook and airframe structure, and to evaluate lateral tracking during run out. Generally, the most critical testing is high sink rate arrested landing. Landings are made at increasingly higher touchdown sink speeds until limit sink speed is achieved. The limit sink speed to be checked for is 7.1 m/s. Normal carrier touchdown sink speeds are around 4.5 m/s. Sink speed during shore-based testing is increased by slowly increasing the angle of the optical glide slope until as close to the target sink rate as possible is reached. In addition, this sink speed is tested in three aircraft pitch attitudes, namely, normal landing attitude, nose down (three-point landing or nose gear first) and tail down at a pitch attitude of about 3° higher than the normal landing attitude.

We now discuss the planning and preparatory activities that were required for carrier suitability tests for the LCA Navy. It is apparent from the above three representative aircraft programmes that extensive shore-based testing of carrier-borne aircraft is required prior to embarking the ship. If facilities needed to be set up in India, it was expected to be a long lead activity. Hence, advance planning and execution towards that was needed to be developed concurrently with aircraft development. For the purpose of carrier suitability testing of the LCA Navy, it was decided to build a shore-based ramp and arrested landing facility in India, preferably at a naval air station. This would provide flexibility for testing the aircraft within the country at any convenient time slot. The added advantage was that the facility would be available to the Navy subsequently for *ab initio* and continuation training of pilots prior to embarkation on the carrier.

Once the decision was made to set up an SBTF in India, the next obvious question was 'where to set it up?'. A joint team of the Indian Navy (IN) and the Aeronautical Development Agency (ADA) personnel studied the pros and cons of setting up at various major naval air stations, namely, INS *Hansa* at Goa, INS *Rajali* at Arrakonam, INS *Garuda* at Kochi, and INS *Dega* at Visakhapatnam. Considering various aspects, it was decided to set up the SBTF at the naval air station at Goa. Of course, historically, carrier-based aircraft operated from this naval air station right from Sea Hawks and Alizes from the early 1960s to Sea Harriers from 1983 and presently the MiG-29Ks.

The next step was to decide on the potential locations of the take-off area, landing area, telemetry facilities, and other services within the naval air station at Goa. Dabolim Airport in Goa has a runway located largely in an east-west orientation and a parallel taxi-track to the south of the main runway. It was planned to set up the take-off area, with a ski-jump, at the west end of the parallel taxi track. At this location, there is a cliff at the end of the track leading to the open sea. When the aircraft leaves the ramp, there would be a safety height of about 42m and then it flies over the sea, almost replicating the carrier itself. It was decided to locate the landing area between the main runway and the parallel taxi track with an overall length of about 1.2 km. The telemetry building was planned to be located within the line of sight of the arresting area and in the same line laterally as the main Air Traffic Control (ATC). The general layout sketch made at that time is shown below.

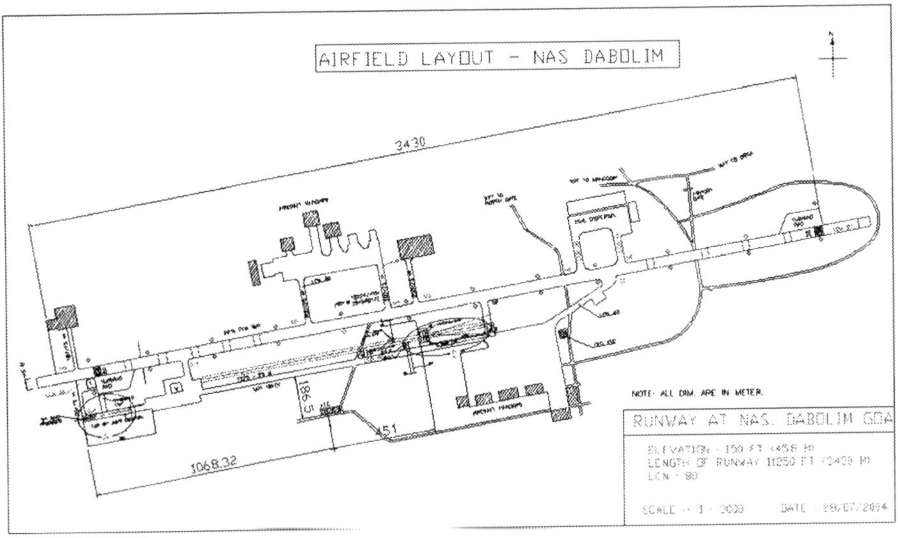

SBTF planned location at INS Hansa, Goa

In order to assess the soil structure and condition at the naval air station, ADA engaged with the Geological Survey of India (GSI) to undertake a study of the proposed areas of the take-off and landing zones. The team from GSI carried out a detailed site survey to characterise the soil condition in Goa at the potential areas for setting up the SBTF, including both the take-off and landing zones. This would facilitate suitable civil structural design that was necessitated. They submitted a detailed report in May 2003, an abstract of which is enunciated in subsequent paragraphs.

Geotechnical investigations were carried out in two phases to evaluate the foundation conditions for construction of the proposed SBTF structures at the naval air station, Goa. Geophysical surveys followed by subsurface drilling, were carried out at the proposed sites, where it was found that there was a multilayer subsurface media. The bedrock, comprising meta basalt, is capped by a 20 to 36m thick residual laterite and compacted laterite fill material. The groundwater table is encountered in this area at depths varying from 9 to 13.5m. The bedrock below the laterite is weathered up to a thickness of nearly

1.5 to 3m (saprolites). A thick layer of lithomargic clay marks the zone between the saprolites and the laterites.

The subsurface media was tested both on site and in the laboratory. Their physical and engineering properties were determined for effective use while designing the proposed project structures. The studies indicated that both the proposed ski-jump concrete/masonry structure and underground area at the arrester gear site were to be constructed over consolidated and seasoned hard/dense lateritic fill material. The anchor pillars at the arrester gear zone were proposed to be taken down to a depth of 10m from the existing ground level in hard and very dense duricrust. The existence of any cavities below the foundation level of all the anchor pillars was to be confirmed, and such cavities, if any, were to be filled by concrete or grout packing before laying their foundation. A seismic coefficient of 0.05 g was suggested for incorporation while designing the proposed structures. I must acknowledge the significant contribution of the GSI for their extremely professional study that was so critical for the design of the facility.

Based on the studies of the GSI, a number of bore-holes were sunk to check the characteristics at the exact foundation locations during the detailed design. Extensive soil testing was undertaken by another private agency that was a professional in the field. This agency was identified by the civil engineering arm of the Defence Research & Development Organisation (DRDO), namely, CCE (R&D). These formed the basis for understanding the local conditions that would help in civil engineering design. I believe these extensive preparatory steps taken for soil analysis and topographical generation stood us in good stead when actually executing the SBTF project at Goa.

One of the most critical elements for the landing area is the arresting gear. Preliminary studies and extensive market surveys were carried out on the various types of arresting gears possible and available in the worldwide market. Typically, the most widely used type of arresting gear for ship-borne applications is the hydro-pneumatic arresting gear developed in the 1950s in the UK. A schematic of a typical hydro-pneumatic arresting gear is indicated below. The idea of showing this picture is to highlight that what is seen on the flight deck are the wires and pulleys (like they say 'tip of the iceberg'), but what is below deck is a complex and large hydraulic jack with other equipment.

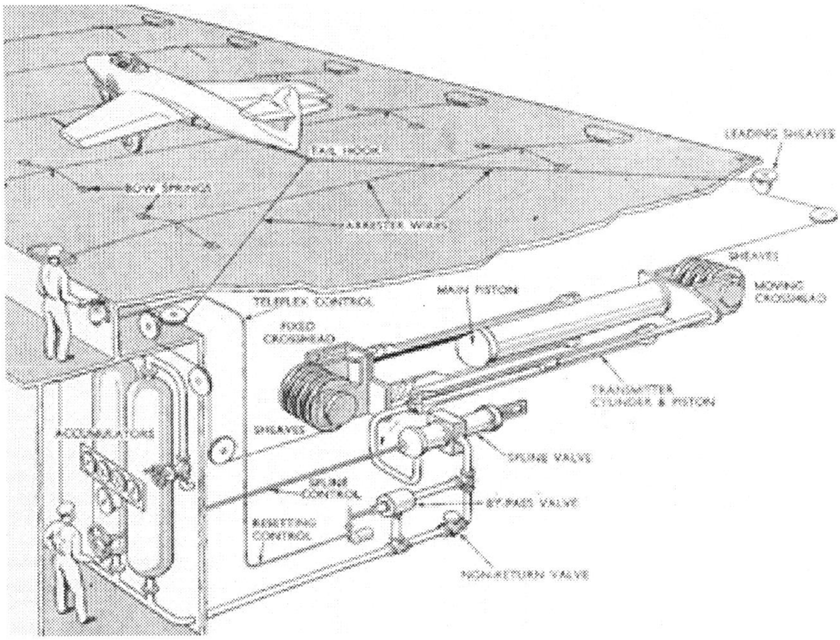

Typical Hydro-Pneumatic Arresting Gear

This was the type of recovery equipment used on UK, US, French, Russian, and Indian carriers. The essential features are to arrest multiple types of aircraft having varying landing mass and stop at the same distance, coining the phrase 'Constant Run-Out Arresting Gear'. The shock encountered at the moment of engagement and then during the period of run-out of around 90m must be regulated. Otherwise, there will be extremely high loads on the arrester hook of the aircraft and consequently on the aircraft structure. This is achieved by varying the valve opening of the Constant Run-Out Valve (CROV). Heavier aircraft will have a smaller opening while for lighter aircraft, the restriction is reduced to allow the full 90m of wire pull out. Also, the deceleration needs to be restricted to around 4.5g. I wish to point out at this stage that the Indian Navy had experience with this type of arresting gear system from the 1960s till the late 1980s on the INS *Vikrant*. I was also part of the INS *Vikrant* (earlier avatar) journey with the Alize aircraft from 1983 till 1985 as the Air Engineer Officer of the Squadron. It was indeed one of the many exciting phases of my life in the Indian Navy. Admiral Arun Prakash (then Cdr.) was the Squadron Commander of the Sea Harrier Squadron, embarking on the

Vikrant and it was indeed an honour to have interacted with him then and, of course, subsequently.

As was apparent during the time frames of 2003-2004, information regarding some of the agencies that originally had arresting gear or were currently having arresting gears was identified. Mac Taggart Scott, from Scotland, which made arresting gear from the 1950s and supplied it to the UK carriers, was one such potential source. Discussions were held with them regarding supply; however, they had closed down that side of their activities since UK moved on to STOVL carriers (ski-jump take-off and vertical landing) with the Sea Harriers and now with the F35B variant of the Joint Strike Fighter (JSF). Hence, this was obviously not a viable route because they mentioned that it would not be feasible to restart the build of arresting gears.

ESCO Systems (Zodiac), USA, which make emergency shore-based arresting gear for emergency recovery of land-based aircraft, were the next potential source. The wire run-out is typically of the order of 150 to 200m depending on the aircraft's landing mass and speed and, hence, is not constant as is required for a carrier application. Discussions were held with them regarding the feasibility of adaptation for the SBTF planned at Goa; they were not found to be possible.

The US Navy built arresting gears, for their own aircraft carriers and also for the French aircraft carriers, was the next source explored. Whilst discussions were initiated at that time (2003), it did not appear feasible for supply from their side as they were moving to a new philosophy of arresting gear and would stop production of the hydro-pneumatic devices. Hence, it became apparent that this route was also not possible.

Proletarsky Zavod, St. Petersburg, Russia, had supplied the arresting gear for the shore facility at Saki in Ukraine, installation on the Russian aircraft carrier Adm. *Kuznetsov* and the installation on the modified Adm. *Gorshkov* for the Indian Navy (*Vikramaditya*). Considering the above factors and to maintain commonality with the aircraft carrier, it was decided to proceed with the Russian-built arresting gear option. Incidentally, the *Vikrant* also has arresting gear from Proletarsky Zavod, ensuring commonality.

A joint team comprising members from the ADA and Nevskoye Design Bureau (NDB) from Russia, who were the designers of the arresting gear,

Indian Navy (IN), R&DE(E) Pune (DRDO), Goa Shipyard Ltd. (GSL) and CCE (R&D), was formed to frame the technical specifications for setting up the SBTF at Goa. While the primary objective of the SBTF was Carrier Compatibility Tests (CCT), it was decided initially to make the facility compatible with operating the MiG-29K aircraft also. This would meet both ADA's test requirements as well as the training requirements of the Indian Navy, leading to a win-win situation.

Broad technical specifications are tabulated and appended in the last section of this book at page 235 for reference. While detailed specifications were drawn up, the effort here will be to provide top-level highlights.

The features of the SBTF to be set up at the Naval Air Station in Goa needed to be defined for a Ski Jump Take-off But Arrested Recovery (STOBAR) concept of operations. The ski-jump or ramp would have a 14° parabolic profile replicating the aircraft carrier as designed by the NDB. There would be hydraulic chocks (or restraining gear) at the take-off point to hold back the aircraft till it was ready for launch. There would be a take-off control post for providing controls and communication. There would be a two-wire arresting gear with a 90m wire pull-out capable of handling the aircraft with different landing weights. Whilst the ship is installed with a three-wire system, a one-wire system may suffice for shore application. However, for redundancy in operation, it was decided to have a two-wire system. There would be a landing and arresting gear control post, light signalling system, optical landing system, landing monitoring TV system, and other auxiliary services, namely, compressed air, power, firefighting, cooling system, photogrammetry, etc.

As stated earlier, the ski-jump would be located at the western end of the parallel taxi-track, beyond which would be the open sea. The height above sea level at this point was about 42m and would be prone to wind shear when it blows from the sea due to a cliff effect. This aspect needed to be assessed to determine the exact position of the ramp along the parallel taxi track. A contract was awarded to the Russian Aircraft Corporation, MiG (RAC-MiG), in 2004-2005 to develop a scale model of the take-off region, including the cliff region, and to carry out wind tunnel testing. Based on the results, the ramp exit location was decided that would have minimal effect on the wind shear at the ramp exit.

Salient features of the ski-jump were that it would be a welded metallic structure mounted upon concrete supports arranged in a foundation pit enclosed by cast ferro-concrete retaining walls. The ski-jump plating would be a continuation of the runway and include means for water drainage. There would be provision for installation of hydraulic chocks/restraining gear. Some of the broad geometric characteristics of the parabolic profile ski-jump were: a length of 67m, a breadth of 16m, an overall height of 6m, and a breaking off angle of 14°.

The Take-off Control Post was for providing visual control of the aircraft positioning and was a suitable low sheltered structure located near the start point. It provided control for operation of the restraining gear/hydraulic chocks, having suitable light signalling and communication facilities with the aircraft and other designated areas. The lateral distance from the post to the taxi-track centre line had to be more than 42m.

At the arresting gear site, the approach and exit paths were located between the main runway and the parallel taxi track. The arresting gear compartment was a 3D welded metallic structure mounted on supports in a special concrete foundation pit, enclosed by cast ferro–concrete retaining walls. The underground space needed to be air-conditioned and suitably ventilated. A mechanism had to be available to drain or pump out water collected in the pit automatically to prevent flooding. The broad geometrical details of the ferro-concrete pit were: a length of 40m, a breadth of 45m, and a height of usable space is 3.6m. The upper surface of the arresting gear compartment would have steel plate flush with the runway surface and would be designed for LCN40 capability to facilitate aircraft movement, with the landing area being similar to that of a ship.

The approach part of the aircraft taxi path till the arresting gear compartment had a length of about 400m and the follow-through length after the arresting gear compartment was about 800m. In continuation of the follow through area, there was an additional 400m hard standing, hence the total distance beyond the arresting gear was about 1200m. This facilitated the 'taxi-in' tests to be carried out, wherein there was adequate run up distance to build up the speed of the aircraft, as well as sufficient length to stop the aircraft after the arresting gear compartment. There was a gradient up to the arresting gear region and a down slope beyond it. This gradient needed to be factored in for simulation.

The Arresting Gear System (AGS) was located largely underground and part of it was over ground. One of the major items was the two-wire arresting gear with wire pull-out capability of 90m and auxiliary facilities, wherein the arresting engine was located below. The arrester wire system was located over the deck with inter wire spacing being 12m. There were several other systems, namely, the hydraulic system, compressed air system (mobile, located outside), electrical power supply (~300 kw), lighting (main & emergency), air conditioning, firefighting, cooling water system, landing monitoring TV system and control post, communication system, office space, watch keeper's post, etc.

The Landing Control Post (LCP) had a structure above the ground co-located with the arresting gear site to provide means of viewing aircraft on the approach path located on the port side (left side). There were various kinds of equipment and monitors for control of aircraft located in the LCP. There was a watch-keeper's post within the AGS, with facilities for internal and external communication. Weight setting of the arresting gear based on the landing mass of the aircraft could be remotely done from the LCP. The controller had wind speed and wind direction information, enabling him to suitably advise operations. A monitor of the TV landing system provided visual inputs for the aircraft position vis-à-vis the landing path.

In the earlier days, when the Indian Navy operated the INS *Vikrant* with Sea Hawk and Alize aircraft, the Optical Landing System (OLS) was a mirror-assisted landing system, where the light from a source would be reflected onto a concave mirror, and the reflected light would be used for glide-slope sighting by the pilot for landing. This light was called the 'Meat Ball'.

The US Navy currently operates the Improved Fresnel Lens Optical Landing System (IFLOLS). The resolution provided by this system is significantly higher. The Russian version of the OLS (LUNA-3) is a light-based system and provides visual information to the pilot about aircraft location relative to the glide path of descent while landing. There is an adjustment possible to vary as per glide slope requirements of different aircraft. When the pilot's eye sees the 'meat ball', the hook point needs to catch the wire. The location of the hook point vis-à-vis the pilot's eye is called 'eye hook' distance and is based on the size of the aircraft. There is also a provision to adjust it to cater to different 'eye hook' distances of the aircraft.

The Russian OLS has an assembly of indicator lights located vertically, with a set of five lights, and with an overall height of 2.5m. The centre light will be steady green, the one above will be steady amber, the one below will be steady red, the topmost will be flashing amber and the bottom-most will be flashing red. It may be noted that the datum lights are located horizontally, with the distance between the taxi track centre line and the near point of the horizontal bar of datum lights will be ~ 10.5 to 13.5m.

The OLS also has a set of wave-off lights installed, which will be activated by the ground Landing Safety Officer (LSO) in case of any obstruction in the landing area. If the pilot sees the flashing wave-off lights, then he should not attempt to land. If the pilot is on the correct glide path and is making a steady approach for landing, then he sees the steady green light (meat ball) that will be in line with the fixed datum lights on the OLS. This is the ideal situation and, in this condition, the arrester hook will most likely snag the centre wire on the ship, which has a three-wire system. If the aircraft has a slightly higher glide slope angle, the pilot will see a steady amber light and is likely to catch the third wire (forward). On the other hand, if the aircraft has a slightly lower glide path angle, the pilot will see a steady red light and is likely to catch the first wire (aft). If the pilot sees a flashing amber or red light, then he should not attempt a landing as he will be beyond the range of successful arrestments.

The Landing Monitoring TV System is an aid to the LSO for visualising the location of the aircraft approaching to land on the ship's deck. It provides information to him about the aircraft's location relative to the touchdown point while landing. There are typically four cameras installed that are embedded in the structure of the arresting gear area, with two cameras on the centre line and two cameras on either side. These cameras have shielded covers on top with an overall height of 40mm and are well rounded so that they are not an impediment to aircraft operations. The video information is transferred to the landing controller in the landing control post, and there is a provision for recording video pictures.

A detailed work plan for the build of SBTF was prepared to ensure effective execution of the project. The table below indicates the major partners identified for development and the build of the SBTF. ADA, being the prime entity, entered into a contract with Rosoboronexport (Russian Government agency) in March 2009 for various Russian-origin activities/supplies. Project sanction was accorded to the Goa Shipyard Ltd. (GSL), a defence public sector undertaking (PSU), to handle the steel structural work, equipment installation, operation, and maintenance of all specialised equipment and its connected auxiliary systems. Project sanction was also accorded to Chief Construction Engineers (R&D), the civil engineering arm of the DRDO (CCE R&D), for all the civil works activities, and with R&D Establishment (Engineers), Pune, a DRDO lab, to provide supervisory cover for the activities of CCE (R&D).

Agency	*Activities*
ADA / NFTC	Overall Programme Coordination, Telemetry, Video Monitoring and Instrumentation
Indian Navy	Location and On site support
Goa Shipyard Ltd (GSL)	Steel Structural work, Equipment installation, Commissioning, Operation & Maintenance
R&DE(E) & CCE(R&D) West	Civil Engineering, Power, Water and Data Acquisition

Rosoboronexport (Overall Contract)	• Detail Design (NDB)
	• Specialised Equipment Supply
	  * Arresting Gear (Proletarsky Zavod)
	  * Restraining Gear (RAC MiG)
	  * Optical Landing System (Electropribor)
	  * Landing Monitoring TV System (TV Inst)
	  * Light Signaling System (Aerosvet)
	• Installation and Testing Support (All)

Responsibility Matrix for setting up SBTF

The overall programme management to set up the facility and handling of telemetry rested with the ADA, with an ambitious target to set up the entire facility in about four years. It was a challenging task for ADA, located in Bangalore, to coordinate the activities of SBTF in Goa, and to interact with multiple Russian agencies, Indian agencies and, of course, manage the major task of LCA Navy development itself. I would say with pride that the SBTF was set up on time, with the take-off area completed in March 2013 and was fully operational from October 2013. The landing area was operational from January 2014. To enable close coordination, a detailed work-share matrix was prepared along with project tracking charts as shown at the table appended in the last section of the book for reference at page 236.

We will now briefly discuss the work execution of the three major zones, namely, the take-off area, landing area and the telemetry-cum-workshop facility. The take-off area comprised the ski-jump/ramp, the restraining gear and the take-off control post. As stated earlier, the exit coordinates of the ski-jump were located at the west end of the parallel taxi track based on the wind tunnel test results provided by RAC MiG. All other dimensions were relatively fixed based on the position of the ski-jump. Design drawings for civil works, steel structures, drainage arrangements, and equipment installation were prepared and used for construction of the take-off area; the brief evolution of which is shown pictorially below. The facility was fully operational from October 2013.

Take-off Area of SBTF at Goa

The first picture shows bore holes being drilled for collecting soil samples to decide the type of foundation design. This was followed by soil excavation to the requisite size to accommodate both the ski-jump area and the restraining gear system. Then the civil works of necessary concrete housing and supports were done by CCE (R&D). In the meantime, GSL was pre-fabricating the steel modules at the shipyard itself and transporting them for on-site installation, assembly, and integration. Then the entire profile measurement of the ski-jump was carried out and compared with the theoretical profile given by the design house. Since care was taken during every stage of integration, the actual profile achieved was remarkably close to the theoretical profile. The actual installed picture with LCA Navy on the ramp, both at the Restraining Gear System (RGS) and at the exit of the ski-jump shows the result of the intense coordination and successful execution.

In the landing area, an arresting gear compartment was created, replicating the ship with all the internal compartments to house the individual arresting gears, system compartments, control compartments, etc. There was a need to excavate a large-sized pit measuring about 35m x 30m x 10m to house the steel structure similar to that on the ship. The Landing Control Post (LCP) is also part of this structure. Installation of arrester wires on the top, Optical Landing System (OLS), Cameras for landing monitoring system, necessary cabling, plumbing, etc., were also completed. The other major activity was to prepare the approach path to the arresting gear of 400m and the follow-through path of 800m, with a portion of these with steel plate cladding. A brief pictorial

Landing Area of SBTF at Goa

evolution of the landing area is shown above. The facility has been fully operational since January 2014.

As in the case of the take-off area, a number of bore holes were drilled to obtain the local soil samples to enable foundation design. There was significant excavation required to accommodate the entire arresting gear compartment underneath. The civil engineering team provided ferro-concrete housing for the entire excavated portion and also installed requisite supports for the steel structures within this concrete box structure. The GSL had prepared some of the modules in the shipyard itself and brought them on-site for installation and integration, which involved extensive welding activities. It was a challenge to continue with the various installations as Dabolim, Goa, is a busy airport with both military and civil aircraft operations, and the landing area is sandwiched between the main runway and the parallel taxi track.

Another challenge was the heavy monsoons in this coastal city, which brought heavy rains for at least four to five months. Undeterred, the teams erected tents and continued working, even during the rains. There was outstanding teamwork and enthusiasm to complete the construction of this challenging facility on time and with high quality. The last set of pictures above shows the final result of the landing area, with the aircraft operating. One can see the optical landing system, a view of the computer screen of the TV monitoring system showing the approaching aircraft, and a picture depicting the arrested recovery of the LCA Navy, with the arresting cable pulled out.

A state-of-the art telemetry facility, with the National Flight Test Centre (NFTC) located in Bangalore as a reference, has been built. Photogrammetry and SBTF instrumentation are additional features incorporated into the telemetry setup at Goa. Workshops and office/conference facilities are also available within this building. The facility boasts state-of-the-art flight test infrastructure and has provided exceptional flight test support, not only to the LCA Navy, but also to the Air Force Version of the LCA during various trials.

We will now briefly discuss aspects of SBTF testing and certification, starting with defining the overall philosophy. The primary objective was to ensure that the equipment and facility could undergo testing and demonstrate their capability to meet the requirements set out in the technical specifications. This would involve system-level tests on the take-off and landing areas, as well as holistic tests of the entire SBTF. At the outset, it was planned that the facility specification would cater to both the LCA Navy and MiG 29K aircraft, each with its own weight class and other characteristics. At each step, quality checks were carried out to ensure that there would be no or minimal deviation from the stated specifications. This resulted in minimal rework, thereby resulting in significant cost and time savings.

The overall design concept and drawings of the facility were provided by Nevskoye Design Bureau (NDB), Russia. They were designers of the *Vikramaditya,* and it was considered prudent to engage with them to provide details that would replicate the carrier. Further, the NDB was also involved in setting up of the shore test facility at Saki in Ukraine. It may also be relevant to mention that the NDB was the design consultants of the aviation complex for the indigenous aircraft carrier, INS *Vikrant.*

The SBTF was built according to design documents provided and under supervision and clearance of the NDB, especially the specialised Russian-origin equipment. Profile and level measurements of the ski-jump were carried out using a laser tracker to confirm data of 'as-built' vis-à-vis 'as designed'. In addition to internal quality inspection of Goa Shipyard, independent inspection by inspectors of Indian Registry of Shipping (IRS) was undertaken to ensure quality standards were maintained. Detailed test plan documents for take-off and landing area, prepared by ADA, were vetted by the NDB to ensure that the SBTF was built as envisaged. It was decided that the final facility clearance would be taken up by a joint team consisting of both Indian and Russian personnel.

Factory Acceptance Tests (FAT) of all the major equipment like arresting gear, restraining gear, optical landing system, TV monitoring system, light signalling system, telemetry equipment, photogrammetry items, etc., were carried out at the vendor sites. This is an extremely important milestone to ensure that all systems function according to their stated specifications at the manufacturing facility. Upon satisfactory completion of tests and certification, the equipment was shipped to Goa for installation at the SBTF.

I will take the FAT of the Arresting Gear System (AGS), manufactured by

M/s Proletarsky Zavod, Russia, as an example. This test was carried out in January 2010 at their facility in St. Petersburg, Russia, where they used a locomotive engine to pull out the entire wire, simulating a static wire pull out as shown in a picture below. This also enabled us to verify the cable mechanism's functionality, since the entire system was installed at the test site in the factory. A static wire pull out is necessary even when the arresting gear system is installed either on a ship or at the SBTF. Typically, a heavy duty tractor is used for this purpose, wherein the entire 90m of pull out is done, confirming that there are no kinks or potential failures in the arresting wire. It was a rare experience to bear the harsh Russian winter during the test that was largely outdoors.

Static Wire Pullout of AGS using a Locomotive Engine

Once built, the take-off area needed to be certified. As previously stated, the take-off area comprised the ski-jump/ramp built according to the provided profile, the Restraining Gear System (RGS) also called the hydraulic chocks, Light Signalling System (LSS), and the Take-off Control Post (ToCP). The first step was to accord structural clearance for the ski-jump based on the quality inspection report. Towards this, as mentioned earlier, profile checks of the ski-jump were carried out to ensure compliance with the specified tolerances compared to the theoretical profile. In parallel, functional checks of restraining gear and associated accessories in take-off area without an aircraft were carried out as a no-load test. Once this was satisfactory, taxi-in of an aircraft onto the chocks and loading was checked with full engine thrust. A MiG-29K was used for this purpose due to its higher loading. This would also check clearances of the RGS in relation to the aircraft, confirming that there was no obstruction.

With the aircraft restrained by the chocks under full engine dry thrust, the flaps of the restraining gear were lowered and the aircraft started moving forward. The throttle was pulled back the moment the aircraft's main wheels crossed the chocks, bringing it to a stop. These tests were conducted for both normal and maximum take-off mass. Based on successful testing using the MiG 29K aircraft on 14 March 2013, the facility was ready for operation. At this stage, the team proposed that it would be desirable to demonstrate the take-off over the ski-jump.

As built, the landing area needed to be certified prior to its use for aircraft testing. The landing area had the two arresting gear equipment, the optical landing system, TV monitoring system, landing control post, light signalling system, other connected auxiliary systems, the landing surface itself, etc. The first step was the structural clearance of the arresting gear structure based on the quality inspection report provided by inspectors from the Indian Registry of Shipping (IRS). Surface and topographical checks of the entire landing path 'as-built' were correctly captured and plotted, which would be required by the aircraft simulation team. Functional checks of the arresting gear system with static wire pull-out using a tractor were carried out to ensure that there was no interference and the cable had no kinks. Alignment checks of the optical landing and TV monitoring systems using helicopters and fixed wing fighter aircraft carrying out simulated carrier landing approaches and wave-off were then undertaken. All these individual system-level tests ensured that they were functioning in a satisfactory manner. To prove the entire landing area as a holistic system, it was planned to carry out 'taxi-in' tests of the aircraft at increasing energy levels and correlate with theoretical characteristic curves. The joint facility clearance team indicated that it would be desirable to check the facility, including flight engagement, using a known aircraft, namely, the MiG-29K.

Since the LCA Navy would have to undergo *ab initio* testing, it was considered prudent to prove the facility with a known certified aircraft. The newly minted MiG-29K aircraft of the Indian Navy had arrived in Goa in 2013 just when the SBTF was in readiness. However, there was a peculiar circumstance in that the SBTF was built under the aegis of ADA and the MiG-29K belonged to the Indian Navy, with Indian Navy pilots yet to undergo training on the MiG-29K for carrier operations. The only option was for ADA to enter into a contract with RAC-MiG for their test pilots to fly the Indian Navy MiG-29K to prove the SBTF.

It was an extremely happy circumstance that all the entities came together and ADA was able to finalise the contract with RAC-MiG within two months of the process conceptualisation. Trials were planned and held in the last quarter of 2013 and early 2014.

Test pilots and engineers from the Russian Aircraft Corporation – MiG, Moscow, Russia (RAC-MiG), along with Russian teams from the Nevskoye Design Bureau (NDB) and the various OEMs of specialised equipment, arrived in Goa for a joint discussion. These Russian teams, along with the Indian entities, formulated detailed test plans for demonstrating the capabilities of the SBTF. The RAC-MiG team went through all the installation and test reports to satisfy themselves on the state of readiness. They made a few minor observations, which were immediately attended to by GSL and CCE (R&D) teams on-site. The facility was then declared ready to undergo ski-jump launches and arrested recoveries.

The team decided that a two-seater MiG-29KUB aircraft would be used for the tests. It was planned to have four take-offs, with three flights by day and one flight by night to assess the suitability of the take-off area. For assessing the landing area, a dynamic test (taxi-in) using the MiG-29KUB was first planned. Aircraft mass would be at 16,000 kg and there would be three runs each at 120, 160 and 200 kmph for wires Nos. 1 and 2. Once satisfactory and correlated with theoretical profiles, a flight test for landing area readiness using the MiG-29KUB was planned with seven flights by day, including checking OLS, TV system, and light system, and three flights by night. A picture of a MiG-29K carrying out a successful ski-jump take-off and arrested recovery at the landing region is shown below. It was a proud moment to see the SBTF coming to life with successful validation flights.

MiG-29K executing a ski-jump launch and Arrested Recovery

With this, the SBTF was formally cleared, albeit with some observations to be attended to, based on the trials. These were completed in good time and the facility was utilised by RAC-MiG to train Indian Navy pilots for carrier operations to enable them to embark on *Vikramaditya* in early 2014. This, of course, was followed closely by extensive LCA Navy testing prior to its historic operations from INS *Vikramaditya* in January 2020.

A significant aspect of any aircraft development is the testing, both on ground and in the air. A newly developed deck based aircraft would not be allowed to go on to an aircraft carrier unless it is tested at a shore facility. The chapter on SBTF brings out the exciting journey of conceptualising and building a facility that would replicate an aircraft carrier on a shore base to the extent feasible. This facility has been of immense value for the testing of LCA Navy. With a farsighted vision to build the SBTF capable of handling heavier aircraft also, it has become an asset with the Indian Navy for training their pilots on other deck based aircraft. A snapshot of take-off and landing area is shown in page 84.

8

ARRESTER HOOK SYSTEM (AHS)

Landing on an aircraft carrier is an extremely challenging task, as the available length is limited, typically to the order of 90m, as against about 3 km available on a land-based runway. The landing on a ship is termed as recovery on the deck of the aircraft carrier. An arrester hook is a device installed on a deck-based aircraft that facilitates this short recovery by 'hook snagging' one of the arrester wires aboard the ship to rapidly decelerate and stop the aircraft within the limited space available. As a result, there are tremendous structural loads that needs to be reacted to and diffused within the aircraft structure.

The LCA-Navy is designed to take-off from an aircraft carrier, having a 14° parabolic profile ramp with a deck run of about 200m. The landing of the aircraft will be achieved by using an arrester hook installed on the aircraft bottom rear section, engaging a ship's deck pendant (steel wire rope). The arrester hook is deployable during carrier-borne or shore-based operations (emergency) and should be capable of stopping the aircraft within the short

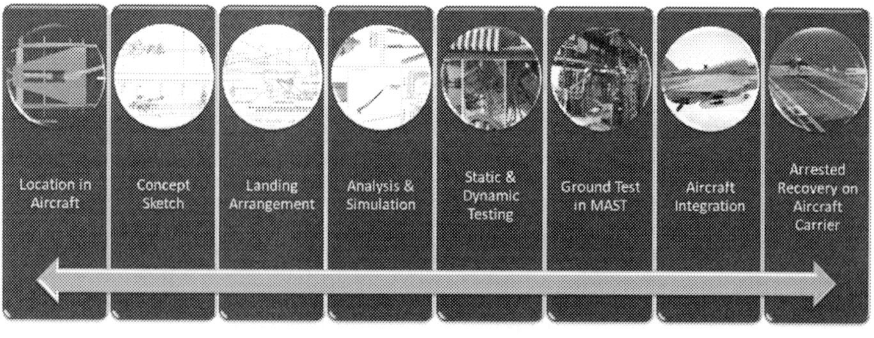

Overall Development Journey of the AHS

distance of around 90m available on the angled deck of the ship. Loads of 4 to 4.5 times the landing mass (up to 4.5g) is expected on the arrester hook, which needs to be reacted to at the airframe attachment point and then diffused along the bottom longeron. The development journey milestones of the Arrester Hook System (AHS) are summarised in the above graphic.

During the pre-project phase, covering the years 2000 to 2003, advance actions were taken to explore the challenges of developing the arrester hook system, which would be a new inclusion in the overall LCA Navy development. From my personal experience operating carrier-borne aircraft, especially with Alize aircraft on board the INS *Vikrant* (older), its system documents and configuration were studied. The Alize arrester hook has a 'V' shaped configuration, pivoting about mountings in the bottom longerons (akin to the chassis of a land vehicle). A picture of the Alize aircraft with the 'V' arrester hook is shown below.

Alize Aircraft and the 'V' Arrester Hook

Considering the LCA Navy bottom longeron spacing of ~900 mm as against a narrower longeron spacing in the Alize, using that configuration was not considered because the hook shank would be quite unwieldy. US Military Spec. MiL-A-18717C, which is the specification for 'aircraft arrester hook installation' was also referred to. It was decided to proceed with the development of an engineering model as described in succeeding paragraphs. A broad configuration for the LCA Navy was sketched out as shown below, indicating a straight shank type of arrester hook.

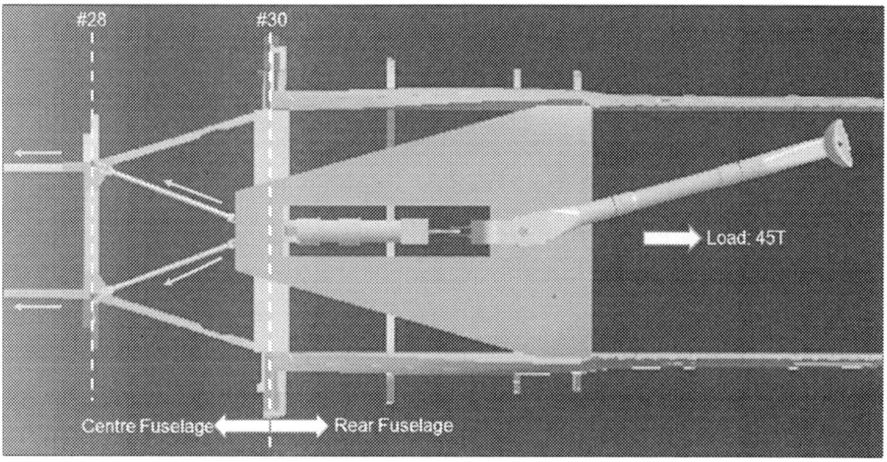

Layout of Arrester Hook with Load Path

We will now look at some of the design considerations that go into the development of a typical arrester hook system. Based on extensive literature survey and studies, design considerations were developed that would form the guiding set of documents, references, specifications, testing methodology, etc. This has been an extremely important step in understanding the arrester hook system and how it would interface with the aircraft. I believe it would be prudent to go through them, as it will give the reader an idea of the interplay with other systems and structures. Points in succeeding paragraphs elucidate some of the key attributes and requirements to consider while developing the arrester hook system.

The arresting (or arrester) hook is so located that the aircraft is maintained at an attitude which ensures clearance of all non-contact parts of the aircraft and stores over 150mm obstructions when the aircraft is subjected to the forces applied during an arrested landing. The general arrangement drawing and details on a typical carrier flight deck are shown below. When determining the location of the arresting hook, it is crucial to consider its effect on nose wheel loads, store clearances, and main wheel-to-deck contact. As can be envisioned, when the hook engages with the wire, it causes a pivoting action about the aircraft's main landing gear, exerting a slap down force on the nose landing gear.

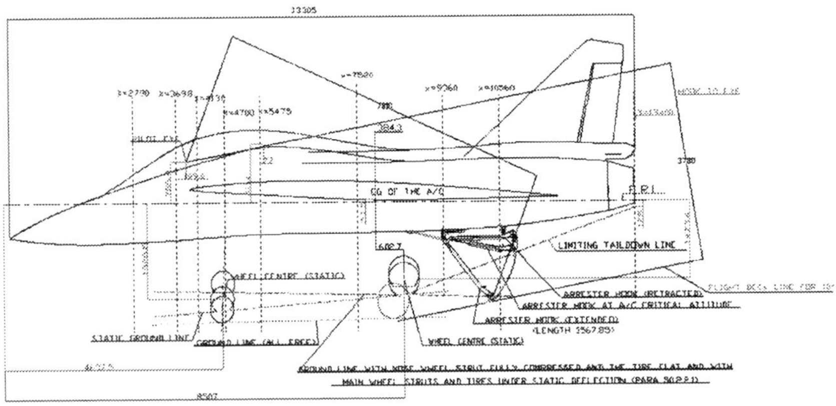

ARRESTED LANDING ARRANGEMENT DRAWING - LCA NAVY
AS PER MIL-A-18717C

General Arrangement Drawing of Arrested Landing

The arresting hook should be located or supporting structures provided on the aircraft, where necessary, to prevent the deck pendant from damaging the aircraft. During hook engagement, there is a sudden jerk on the arrester wire that translates into a wave motion. This requirement should be carefully studied with adequate simulation to identify the potential of wire flailing that may cause structural damage, necessitating suitable preventive measures.

The arresting hook should be designed and located relative to the landing gear to ensure engagement of the deck pendant by the hook after displacement by the nose wheel and main wheel of the aircraft passing over it. The arrester hook point should be sufficiently located aft of the main wheel to allow time for the wire to rise after being pressed down by the wheel, facilitating positive hook engagement.

The arresting hook must be free to move laterally, not less than 20° on each side of the centre position, to align with applied arresting forces in an 'off-centre' or 'skid' landing, unless the hook is designed as a laterally rigid structure to withstand specified designed side loads.

The 'V' hook configuration of the Alize aircraft, for instance, was designed as a laterally rigid structure. A centring device must be provided to keep the hook centred against aerodynamic and lateral loads. In addition, when the hook is laterally displaced upon contact with the deck or a deck protrusion, the centring device must return the hook to an 'arrestment ready' position, minimising side loads on the aircraft structure by providing a pivoting motion.

The aircraft must be protected from upward swing of the arresting hook shank assembly during arrestment and retraction. If the swing is not controlled, the hook may strike the aircraft structure, potentially causing damage. The arrester hook retraction mechanism must include adequate damping to meet this requirement.

A shock absorber must be provided within the retraction jack to control hook bounce. The shock absorber also acts as a damper to hold the hook down on to the deck after the bounce, at about 100lb. (45kg) force. Consequently, the internal features will be complex and pose a challenge to model and simulate. Therefore, the retraction jack must combine the functions of extension-retraction, damping, shock absorption, and self-centring.

Military specifications of MIL-A-8860 series is used as a guideline for strength of installation of arrester hook system, acting as the guiding set of documents to ensure structural integrity of the arrester hook system itself, and also receiving structures on the aircraft. Structural load transfer and diffusion path within the aircraft structure will be a critical requirement.

Any aircraft coming in for a carrier landing may engage a deck pendant in free flight or two-point attitude. Generally, at the instant that the arresting hook engages a deck pendant, the aircraft can be assumed to be in contact with the deck, with its main landing gear struts and tyres under static deflection. For analysis purpose, the main landing gear struts and tyres are assumed to remain under static deflection during the entire arrested run.

To estimate the hook length required, the hook point-ground line relationship recommended in MiL-A-18717C is used. This specification states: "*with the hook trailing aft, nose wheel strut fully compressed, nose wheel tyre flat, main wheel tyres under normal static load and main gear struts in normal static position, the hook point should touch or extend below the resulting ground line.*" The arrester hook length needs to be optimised to cater for positive hook engagement while minimising the weight of the hook assembly. This is ensured by referencing the general arrangement drawing of the arrested landing shown earlier.

The arrester hook must trail sufficiently aft to prevent the aircraft sitting on the hook in a normal 'full-stall' carrier landing. In general, hook bounce is reduced when the hook trail angle is increased, since the initial rotational acceleration resulting from kinematic bounce is less when the hook is subjected to initial impact at a decreased angle with the deck. An increase in the hook trail angle, together with a corresponding increase in the hook length, will improve the engaging attitude of the hook head for normal engaging positions of the aircraft. However, an increase in the hook trail angle has the penalty that a longer hook is required, which will add to the weight and installation complexities.

Hook deck angle is related to the hook trail angle and is the angle between the hook axis and flight deck line. The limiting value of the hook deck angle should be 65 degrees, as hold-down force increases rapidly at greater angles.

The hook shank needs to cater for adequate torsional stiffness, keeping weight at a minimum. The configuration is also governed by installation constraints on the aircraft. This is the primary load transfer member of the arrester hook system. The design of the arresting hook point (hook shoe) is critical as it governs the right engagement with the arrester wire on the ship and must do so safely without failure. The design should preclude the chance of engaging multiple deck pendants. Generally, shortening the hook face and increasing the hook face angle will improve the hook's ability to shed a second deck pendant. However, some compromise in hook point design will be required, as factors that improve the hook's ability to shed a second wire decrease its ability to pick up a deck pendant after aircraft wheels have depressed the pendant.

Toe radius is important in determining the hook point's ability to pick up a deck pendant. A small toe radius facilitates pick-up, especially from a depressed condition; however, an unduly small toe radius can damage the deck pendant. A minimum toe radius of 16mm shall be used. Transverse curvature of the hook face and cable groove have a large enough radius to minimise bending stresses in the deck pendant when it wraps around the hook point. The throat radius of the hook point should be large enough to accept deck pendants up to $1^1/_2$-inch nominal ($1^5/_8$-inch max) diameter.

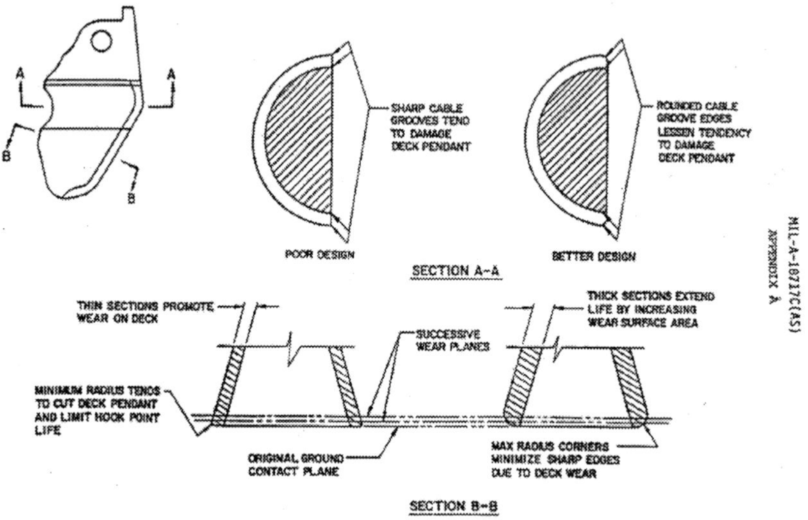

Hook Shoe/Hook Point Design Features (MiL-A-18717C)

Wear faced by the arrester hook is severe. During off-centre arrestments, the deck pendant tends to slide through the hook throat with rubbing velocities of the order of 12 m/s. The hook point throat must be made of materials that prevent welding of the deck pendant to the cable groove under conditions of heat and pressure that exist during off-centre engagements. Portions of the back of the hook point and the toe radius are subjected to severe abrasion during arresting. The hook point should incorporate a back-face wear plate that will be replaced when it has reached the maximum limit. The hook point design shall ensure that the back-face plate, and not the hook point itself, bears the entire back-face wear. Suitable cues to estimate wear shall be provided if a wear plate is not used.

The arrester hook point weight influences the hold-down force required to resist hook bounce. Hook point and shank weight must be kept to a minimum. Consideration should be given to transverse contours of the toe and back of the hook point to ensure that the point can properly engage the deck pendant with the aircraft in a rolled or yawed condition, or when the hook is displaced from its centred position.

The optimum face angle is a compromise between positive deck pendant engagement and retention, as well as shedding characteristics. A sharp face angle will promote the pickup of a low pendant and retention during the early part of the run-out, while a shallower face angle will facilitate pendant shedding at the end of the run-out.

Hook shoe attachment to the shank should be by a single bolt arrangement to enable quick replacement on the ship's flight deck with minimal tooling. Typically, at short intervals, the integrity of the hook shoe needs to be checked by Non-Destructive Test (NDT) methods. There will be a need to keep a tested shoe available for quick replacement on the flight deck itself in the shortest possible time with minimal tooling. I distinctly remember that with one torque spanner, we could open the retaining nut and replace the Alize aircraft hook shoe on the flight deck in less than five minutes.

Provision must be made for pilot operations of lowering or raising the arresting hook by a control mechanism. Control must be from the aircraft hydraulic system operating at 280 bars (4000 psi) hydraulic fluid pressure through an electro-hydraulic selector valve. The arresting hook control must be located in the cockpit, guided by MIL-STD-203G. The control must have a unique design to be readily distinguishable from adjacent cockpit controls, both by day and night, so that the pilot need not divert his attention to locate and check the control.

In fact, on the US Navy's F-18 Super Hornet, the hook operating switch is shaped like the arrester hook itself to be intuitive to operate. An actuator must be provided to raise and lower the arresting hook. The arresting hook must be designed to raise the hook to the stowed position within four seconds and to be fully extended to the 'arrestment-ready' position within two seconds after the cockpit control has been actuated.

The arresting hook control must be designed to allow the pilot to lower the hook, with the arresting hook itself remaining down in the event of a failure of the power system or control system. Typically, the actuator design is such that the retraction is hydraulic against pneumatic pressure, and extension is by release of the built-up pressure. This acts as a fail-safe design, wherein in the event of hydraulic system failure, the hook will extend with gravity assist. The arresting hook control must be interconnected with the angle of attack approach lights as specified in MIL-L-6730 (Spec. has been cancelled, but content can be used as a guideline).

The arresting hook installation or structure must be designed to absorb the shock loads caused by sudden extension of the arresting hook when the aircraft passes over the forward round down of the carrier angled deck after missing a deck pendant engagement. The hook must be assumed to extend from the 'full-up' position. The shock absorber must include a hold-down feature to minimise the bounce of the arresting hook when it strikes the deck protrusion during a carrier landing. The hold-down feature must return the arresting hook rapidly to the deck following initial hook bounce. The first bounce must not be more than 20 feet long and four inches high. The wire lifters or bow springs lift the wire to a height of about six inches. At the midpoint between two springs, there is a sag and the height above the deck is about four inches. Hence, the requirement of four inches has been indicated to ensure the hook snags the wire, even when there is a sag. 'Hold-down' force associated with the 'hold-down' moment must not be less than 100lb measured at the hook point, perpendicular to the hook shank.

The shock absorber must be designed so that the arresting hook can be released and lowered at all flight speeds of up to 2.5 times the power approach speed at maximum arrested landing weight. The arresting hook must also be capable of remaining in the full-down position at all flight speeds up to two times the power approach speed at maximum arrested landing weight. The shock absorber and its supporting structure must be designed for limit loads equal to the loads imposed on it when the design ultimate vertical bending moment is applied to the arresting hook. This requirement will ensure the structural integrity of the shock absorber during the acceptance tests when the shock absorber loads are varied to determine optimum orifice size.

From the hydraulic system perspective, a typical arrester hook system would consist of an arresting hook operating jack, an electro-hydraulic solenoid-operated control valve, and other features. The hydraulic system of the aircraft at 280 bars would be utilised to actuate the arrester hook system. Redundancy would be ensured by the alternative hydraulic system providing the requisite fluid in case of failure of the main system. Hook extension must be pneumatic using nitrogen stored under pressure in the jack itself. Just prior to this, the uplock must be released by aircraft hydraulic pressure. Retraction of the hook must also be by aircraft hydraulic pressure. It is also brought out that in the hook extended position, the jack will be retracted, and vice-versa for hook-retracted position.

AHS: Back to LCA Navy

Using the above design requirements, preliminary layout and design considerations for the LCA Navy were envisaged. Some of the major parameters and features are brought out in subsequent sections to see how the generic requirements were translated to the specific needs of the LCA Navy aircraft design and development. This will also bring out the criticality of considering not only the system level of the arrester hook system, but also the aircraft-level, holistically.

Generally, aircraft carriers incorporate a constant run-out type of arresting gear, as mentioned earlier. This means there is a fixed run-out distance regardless of the weight or engaging speed of the aircraft. At the Shore Based Test Facility (SBTF), on INS *Vikramaditya* and INS *Vikrant*, now operating with the Indian Navy, this value is 90m. The arresting gear system of the ship includes a '"Constant Run-Out Valve (CROV)' adjusted to accommodate different aircraft landing masses. For example, the Svetlana-2N arresting gear in the SBTF is capable of arresting aircraft from 7 to 20 tons. The lighter the aircraft, the more the valve opens, reducing throttling to enable full 90m run-out. The schematic of a typical arresting gear arrangement was shown earlier. The adjustment of the CROV for different aircraft masses can be performed from the local position on the arresting gear or remotely from the Landing Control Post (LCP) on the flight deck.

The hook assembly is planned for installation at frame station 30 (longitudinally aft along the centreline axis at X=9360mm), being the last continuous frame of the centre fuselage of the aircraft. The engine is located aft of this station, necessitating bottom access and precluding mounting the arrester hook in this area. There will be a single attachment at the bottom of station no. 30 on the aircraft to which the hook could be attached. A jack attachment will be located at station no. 31 (X=9785mm) onto the tie-beam assembly. Any changes in this concept must be frozen during review after the preliminary design phase. The arresting load at hook attachment at station no. 30 needs to be dissipated to the shear wall at frame station no. 28

(X=8655mm) through tension struts. Load transfer will occur through a pivot joint at station no. 30 that prevents lateral loading on the aircraft structure.

A full-scale test facility needed to be set up, which would simulate the loads faced by the arresting hook. Further, dynamic testing to simulate hook bounce and assess the efficacy of damping needed to be established. Tests and certification were required to be undertaken as per standard norms laid down for airborne stores. Extensive test facilities and infrastructure needed to be set up as will be apparent later.

At the completion of the design phase, an engineering model was planned to be fabricated using industrial-grade components to prove the design concept. This unit was intended to simulate the aircraft's standard system in form, fit, and function. Based on the feedback and experience gained in the engineering model, the design had to be refined. This was envisioned as the phase-I of arrester hook system development to understand subsystem behaviour. For the first phase, activities would be restricted to design, development, fabrication, and limited qualification testing of the engineering model. This will help in gaining appreciation for the complexities involved and help develop the final version. The engineering model development was undertaken by a private entity, namely, Turbotech.

Having the general layout, it was essential to carry out preliminary stress analysis and component sizing in accordance with established standards and practices based on data provided. Likely changes in parameters and configuration needed to be accommodated. Also, in parallel, materials and manufacturing process selection were done. Preliminary weight estimation was carried out to check conformity with weight budget and to check on aircraft Centre of Gravity (C.G). This factor will have a significant effect, as the arrester hook is at a considerable distance aft from the aircraft c.g. This then led to the study of system kinematics and dynamics, including hook bounce and damping characteristics. Mechanical, electrical, and hydraulic interface data were to be defined at this stage for aircraft-related activities. Input on the extent of nose gear load due to hook bounce needed to be provided to check the effects of the same on the nose landing gear.

Preparation of Qualification Test (QT) plan including Acceptance Test Procedure (ATP), for both the arrester hook system and test rigs, by ADA, HAL, Centre for Military Airworthiness and Certification (CEMILAC), and

Directorate General Aeronautical Quality Assurance (DGAQA), was the next important step in the process. These tests would include component-level, sub-system-level, system-level, and aircraft-level tests. There would be static strength tests, dynamic tests, functional tests, environmental tests, etc. This was all the more critical due to first-time development of the arrester hook system in the country.

Concept drawings of test rigs based on preliminary design, capable of performing static, functional, and hook dynamics testing were another major step. Extensive ground testing was needed to validate simulation and to understand the behaviour and functionality of the system. The test rig design itself needed to be analysed to ensure it would suffice for the tasks at hand. The concept stage CAD sketches of the arrester hook system layout that were developed are shown below.

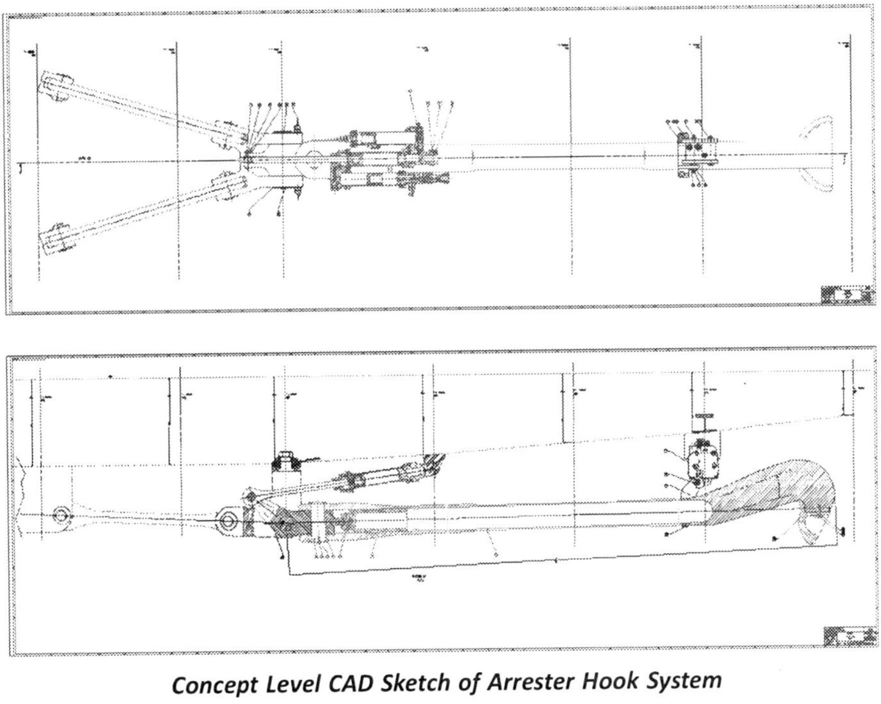

Concept Level CAD Sketch of Arrester Hook System

The strength and life analyses of all critical components, including fatigue and failure mode analysis, needed to be checked for both allowable strength and expected life. Once these were checked, the critical of the two cases would be used for component sizing. With this stage completed, assembly, sub-assembly, and component manufacturing drawings needed to be prepared for checks, verification, and approval during design review. During stress analysis, each element was analysed separately to check for regions of high stress and efforts were made to mitigate them. Assembly-level static and dynamic analysis and simulation were carried out. Life estimation was also carried out by imposing repetitive cycles of loading as per typical operational loading.

With the above steps taken, the stage was set for the preparation of the Bill of Material (BoM) that would serve as the input for material ordering for the fabrication, assembly, and testing of engineering units of the arrester hook system. Refinement of weight estimates was also carried out in parallel. Simultaneously, preparation of assembly and disassembly procedures was undertaken. Preparation of installation drawings and procedures for the entire arrester hook system, inclusive of mechanical, hydraulic, and electrical interfaces to aircraft, was carried out.

The final design of the test rigs was completed to undertake testing activities for validation of the geometry, kinematics, and structural tests including strength tests. Plans were made for endurance testing, which is critical, especially for hydraulic elements. The design of the hook dynamics test rig to facilitate development tests, including drop tests to simulate hook bounce, damping and traverse, extension/retraction, damper tuning, and wear testing, was then taken up. A pictorial depiction of both the static and dynamic test rig to facilitate the standalone testing of the arrester hook system is shown below.

Static & Dynamic Test Rigs of Arrester Hook System

The test philosophy and Route to certification strategy document were prepared that would validate the arrester hook system. As already mentioned, the design, development, fabrication, and testing of engineering units to understand the behaviour of the system in a standalone mode was the first step in this journey. The initial designs were then optimised based on test data. In parallel, fabrication and qualification testing of test rigs and facilities, both static and dynamic, were undertaken. Limited environmental qualification testing, which typically constitutes 25 per cent of endurance testing, was done.

The next step involved integration and functional testing on 'Iron Bird', which is the hardware in loop flight control system. This was followed by the static strength test using a Main Airframe Static Test (MAST) rig and correlation of load diffusion path within the aircraft structure using a Structural Test Specimen (STS), which is actually a full-fledged aircraft structure. This step would instill confidence at the overall aircraft level to facilitate integration and testing on the prototype aircraft itself. In addition to functional operations of hook extension and retraction, 'Taxi-in' engagement in the SBTF would be carried out to validate the results of simulation, standalone static testing, and STS testing on MAST. The final test would be the arrested recovery on the SBTF followed by arrested recovery on the aircraft carrier.

The above stages concluded with a Preliminary Design Review (PDR) of the entire arrester hook system development. This provided a clearer picture of the nuances involved in the design and development activities, the interplay that the arrester hook system would have on other aircraft systems, and the manufacturing and testing challenges that may be encountered. This was an important milestone as it showed the development team the mirror on where the design stood vis-à-vis requirements.

By the end of 2004 or early 2005, the engineering units of the AHS were complete, and the PDR of this configuration was also completed. However, as a matter of abundant caution, it was decided to get an independent opinion from another aircraft house that had already developed arrester hook systems, to view it from a holistic aircraft integrated installation scheme. The possibilities were the US, French, and Russian organisations doing similar work. Since it was envisaged that the Indian Navy would be getting the MiG-29K aircraft along with the aircraft carrier, it was decided to approach RAC-MiG, the designers of MiG-29K, to carry out an audit of the LCA Navy engineering model of the arrester hook system.

RAC-MiG reviewed the design and results of simulation of the engineering unit of the arrester hook and made a few observations. They suggested shifting the arrester hook attachment aft from station no. 30 to station no. 32 for better aircraft stability. However, this would not be feasible in the LCA Navy as the last continuous frame in the aircraft was the junction between the centre and rear fuselages, namely, station no. 30. The frames in the rear fuselage were all horse-shoe type, enabling installation of the engine from the bottom. Further, this would reduce the length of the arrester hook itself that would pose challenges for sustained recovery. Hence, this was not considered.

The next suggestion was to lower the hook attachment point by 100 mm to provide better clearance for hook bounce at the time of engagement. This was favourably considered. RAC-MiG suggested that the actuating jack be positioned forward of the hinge point to take compressive load at the point of hook engagement. This would entail jack redesign and had constraints of space. Hence, this was not considered. While inputs were obtained from the audit of the design by RAC-MiG, some of their suggestions could not be taken up or were not feasible to be incorporated. However, it was beneficial to interact with another aircraft house that had already developed an arrester hook.

Based on the feedback of various tests carried out on the engineering models of the arrester hook system, feedback from RAC-MiG, and integrated aircraft level simulation, certain changes were planned in the design and a revised concept was formulated. This was termed Phase-2 of the arrester hook system development. The engineering unit stage was exploratory, as the system was being conceptualised and developed for the first time. However, having completed one full cycle of development at the system level during the engineering unit development, there was better clarity for adopting a revised design. The experience during engineering development was extremely exciting, with many challenges being overcome. Earlier in my career in the Indian Navy, I had looked at the arrester hook from the operations and maintenance angles; however, here I was considering it from a system design and development perspective.

Changes were made as more details were explored and knowledge gained, resulting in further iterations, especially when considering the combined effect of the landing gear and arrester hook at the aircraft-level. I suppose that keeping an open mind during development is critical and helps in achieving a good design. An interface platform between the arrester hook and the aircraft needed to be developed as well. A CAD model was prepared to facilitate integration checks, as shown below. It also includes a picture of the actual aircraft installation of the revised configuration in the inset.

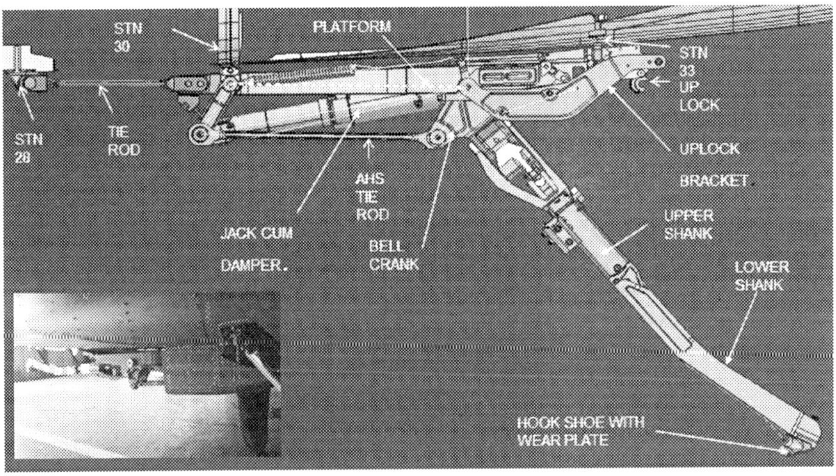

Revised Arrester Hook System

As mentioned earlier, considering a typical LCA Navy landing mass of 10 tons at a peak deceleration of 4.5g during arrested recovery on an aircraft carrier over a length of 90m, the load on a single point of the arrester hook is around 45 tons. This load is transmitted to the hook shoe and then along the hook shank to the two tie-members connecting station-30 to station-28. At station-28, the tie-members are attached to the aircraft's bottom longeron, where the load dissipates into the longeron and gets diffused as it moves forward within the centre fuselage itself. This entire process was simulated using analysis software and needed validation. For this purpose, the arrester hook, tie-members, and bottom longerons were extensively instrumented.

At this stage, the design was finalised according to the revised configuration, and comprehensive reviews were conducted with the participation of certification and quality assurance agencies. Once a go-ahead was given, parts were manufactured, assembled, and simulations carried out. The next step in the validation process was to perform integrated testing on a structural test specimen, which represents the full aircraft structure. The arrester hook system was integrated on the STS and loaded in a newly-developed Main Airframe Static Test (MAST) rig as shown below.

Arrester Hook Testing in MAST

As part of Phase-1 ground testing, the arrester hook was loaded in steps up to the limit load of 45 tons, and the results were compared with simulation at each stage of loading. Due to the care and caution taken by the design teams, the results correlated well with simulation and provided significant confidence for actual aircraft-level clearance up to two-thirds of loading done in the MAST. This clearance facilitated the commencement of 'taxi-in' tests at the SBTF. Phase-2 of STS testing was primarily related to flight load cases.

In Phase-3 of STS testing, the arrester hook was loaded to 1.5 times the limit load (~68 tons), namely, ultimate load, and the integrity of both arrester hook and structure were found to be satisfactory. This provided 100 per cent loading clearance for progressing to aircraft-level testing, first at the SBTF and then on to the aircraft carrier itself.

Successful load testing in phase-1 to limit load on the structural test specimen allowed the arrester hook to be integrated onto the aircraft and initially cleared for functional and carriage trials. A picture of the arrester hook installed in the LCA Navy is shown below, taken at the 2017 Aero India International Air Show in Bengaluru, India. With the arrester hook in place, the aircraft exemplifies a deck-based aircraft distinct from a land-based aircraft.

Arrester Hook integrated in LCA Navy

The next step was to carry out functional checks on the ground, with the arrester hook extension and retraction successfully proven, including the requisite timings of both actions. This control was activated from the switch located in the cockpit. The jack-damper had to be tuned to achieve the specified timings of extension and retraction. Once this stage was successfully achieved, it paved the way for carriage flight trials to assess the aerodynamic and structural behaviour of the aircraft across various flight regimes. This would correlate the aerodynamic characteristics observed in flight with CFD and wind tunnel test data.

With ground rig testing and validation, as well as successful carriage flight trials, completed, the next important step was to verify the integrity and correlation when the arrester hook actually engages the arrester wire at the SBTF to assess dynamics. This stage begins with a 'Taxi-In' engagement, where the aircraft taxies towards the arrester wire and the hook is lowered just short of the wire, allowing the aircraft's arrester hook to snag the SBTF's arrester wire. A detailed test matrix for taxi-in engagement, specifying parameters such as taxi distance to achieve a particular engaging speed, was worked out. These aspects will be discussed in more detail in subsequent chapters.

'Taxi-in' starts at lower speeds, resulting in lower loads and energies to observe structural load transfer within the aircraft. The engaging speed is progressively increased until reaching the limit engaging speed of 140 knots. Results in this phase have been very encouraging and have validated predictions, instilling tremendous confidence in the process, albeit progressing step by step. The first taxi-in engagement took place on 2 August 2018 at a speed of 50 knots. A picture of the LCA Navy engaging the arrester wire at the SBTF is shown below. Although I had retired from ADA by this time, I was invited to witness these activities and provide my inputs on the test result. I wish to acknowledge the support of ADA management for having given me this opportunity.

Taxi-In Arrestment at SBTF

The maiden flight engagement of the LCA Navy at SBTF was carried out on 13 September 2019. This marked another historical milestone and bolstered confidence in the country's progress in this complex process of testing and validation. A picture taken moments before flight engagement at SBTF, with the extended arrester hook clearly visible, is shown below.

LCA Navy approaching SBTF for Flight Engagement

The successful arrestment of the LCA Navy on INS *Vikramaditya* on 11 January 2020 was the culmination of the effort and dedication of the LCA Navy team in particular and the country in general. It was indeed a proud moment; my only regret was not being there to witness it myself. However, my joy knew no bounds upon hearing the news and seeing the pictures. A photograph of the aircraft landing on the ship, with the hook engaging the arrester wire, is shown below.

LCA Navy landing on INS *Vikramaditya* on 11 January 2020

While aircraft is the overall product, there are aggregates within it that are also products. Arrester hook system is one such aggregate that is one of the critical elements of a deck-based aircraft. This chapter traces the development journey right from concept to integration on the aircraft. It brings out the value of a stepwise progression with validation of simulation at each step of the development journey. It starts with the right location and being able to integrate the arrester hook on the aircraft within the defined boundaries. This is the beauty of design that you always need to work within constraints and find optimal solutions.

9

Landing Gear (LG)

The LCA Navy is designed for landing or recovery on board an aircraft carrier with a limited runway distance of 90m. This would entail a higher rate of descent (sink rate) necessarily due to the need for a concept of flare-less landing to maintain constant visibility of the optical landing system on the ship at all times, as opposed to a gentle flared approach and landing on a shore runway. Hence, the vertical component of the typical approach speed of 130 knots (67 m/s) would be about 4.5 m/s at a glide slope angle of 4 degrees. The ship itself would be pitching and the local vertical velocity could be as high as 1.5 m/s. Hence, the coupled sink rate could be around 6 m/s. With scatter margins due to the vagaries of landing on a ship, the sink rate taken for LG design is 7.1 m/s. In comparison, the LCA AF landing gear is designed for a sink rate of 3.0 m/s. A typical picture of the main and nose landing gears of the LCA AF version is shown below.

LCA AF Version – Main and Nose Landing Gear

The Main Landing Gear (MLG) design of the LCA Navy was originally envisaged as a scaled-up unit of the LCA Air Force Version, taking a higher sink rate into consideration. The retraction mechanism for this design was similar to that of the kinematics of the LCA Air Force, which is an articulated type of MLG. Modifications to dimensions for various linkages like the leg, shock absorber, and direction bar, etc., were made to suit the LCA Navy requirements for absorbing the significantly higher energies. The shock absorber stroke required for LCA Navy was also higher at ~500 mm to absorb the larger sink rate compared to the LCA Air Force Version MLG with a 146 mm stroke. The concept CAD models of the landing gears were prepared in the early days of the LCA Navy Programme based on a scaled up version of the LCA AF landing gears.

At about this time, interactions with the Russian teams had commenced for the Shore Based Test Facility (SBTF) to be set up at the Naval Air Station at Goa. Considering the operation of the MiG-29K aircraft and the Restraining Gear System (RGS) on the aircraft carrier, there were a few major observations

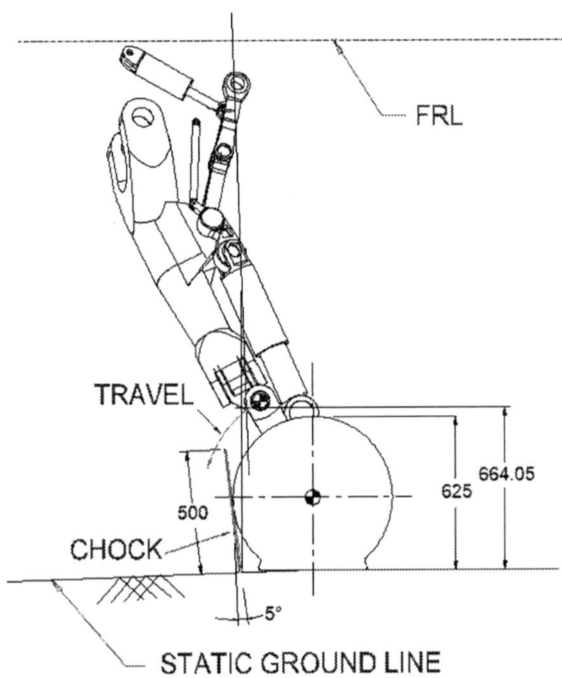

Interference of Articulated LG element with Flap of RGS

regarding the simplistic scaled-up design of landing gears envisaged for the LCA Navy. It is relevant to mention here that the restraining gear holds the aircraft's main wheels against full thrust, until the pilot is ready for launch from the ski-jump. There certainly would be interference between landing gear components and the ship's hydraulic chocks or restraining gear mechanism that acts as a hold-back unit. This would result in the main wheels not touching the hydraulic chocks, while part of the linkage itself may touch it, as shown in the sketch above. This is clearly unacceptable, as the requirement for hold-back is for the main wheel to be against the restraining gear flap.

In the original MLG concept, there may be a possibility of the aircraft having a higher toppling tendency during deck landing due to a lower stability angle of 24 degrees, compared to the Russian philosophy that uses a minimum of 30 degrees. Further, the wheel track of an articulated arrangement was 2630 mm, which was lesser than the 3120 mm for the MiG-29K. This would have imposed limitations on the aircraft carrier for operation with both the MiG-29K and the LCA Navy due to the RGS. Thus, this constraint necessitated the design of the LCA Navy landing gear arrangement to have a wheel track of around 3100mm. The arrangement with the arrestor hook position at the junction between the centre and rear fuselages was analysed in a dynamic situation post aircraft arrestment. The nose landing gear load was also found to be higher than originally planned for in this integrated simulation.

A re-evaluation of the concept design was undertaken to work out a solution to the challenges that were present in the original landing gear concept for operating on the aircraft carrier. A telescopic type of shock strut concept in the main landing gear was opted for as a solution that would satisfy the revised requirements for the LCA Navy as shown in the sketch below. This concept would provide nearly direct vertical shock absorption during high sink rate landing and enable the load to be transferred to the centre fuselage structure. However, a revised concept of landing gear needed to be accommodated within the existing centre fuselage volume as well as provide increased wheel track. Hence, there was a need to provide an extension leg, which would have an acute angle, resulting in an inefficient load transfer path. Given the constraints of commonality, this is a solution that emerged, albeit with some weight penalty. This is another example of design choices to be made within the constraints according to requirements.

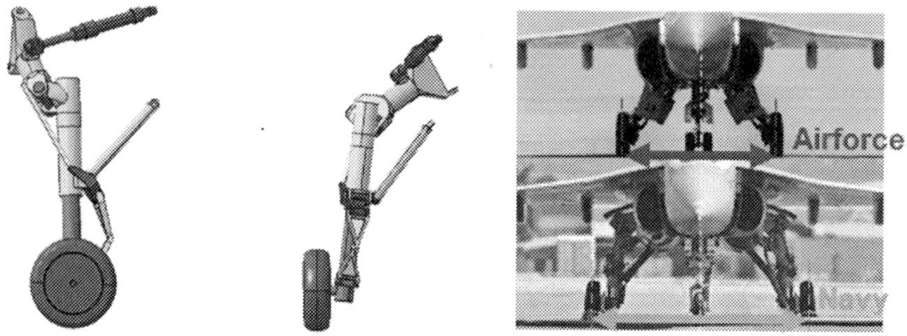

Revised Concept of LCA Navy MLG with larger wheel track as compared to LCA AF MLG

The table below provides a comparison between articulated arrangement (old configuration) and telescopic arrangement (new configuration):

Data Type	*Earlier Design*	*New Design*
Type of landing gear	Articulated landing gear	Telescopic landing gear
Wheel Track	2630 mm	3130 mm
Wheelbase	4011 mm	4089 mm
Retraction mode	Aft and inboard	Forward and inboard
Vertical Wheel Travel	500 mm	500 mm
Wheel Offset	175 mm	265 mm
Landing gear bay	Smaller	Larger
Leg material	Al alloy forging	Maraging steel forging

Comparison of two Concepts of Main Landing Gear

Broad layout sketches were then made, superimposing MiG-29K wheel size and track to check compatibility with the RGS or hydraulic chocks at the take-off point on the aircraft carrier/SBTF. Front and side views of these sketches are shown below. These sketches show that the design was converging, with the aircraft carrier interface requirements being met. An overall equipment layout drawing with the landing gears and arrester hook was then prepared with these inputs, demonstrating that the new configuration could be incorporated in the aircraft and would meet functional requirements of deck-based operations of the LCA Navy.

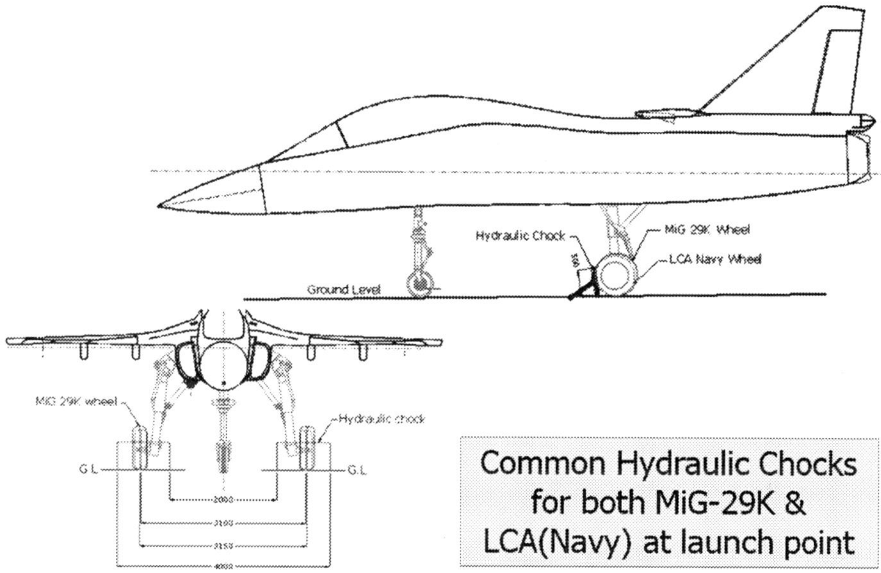

Sketch showing relative size and position on RGS

Once the revised concept was formulated, the next logical step was the detail design and development of the LG. Based on acceptance of the preliminary design, various teams embarked on the detail design and realisation of parts of the LG system. Due to high strength requirements, maraging steel (M250/MDN 250) was extensively used in the design process. This material was developed by MIDHANI, a defence public sector undertaking in Hyderabad. It was also a programme challenge to identify agencies in the country to undertake parts manufacture and assembly. Various private sector agencies were roped in to support the initiative at the parts level. HAL Nasik came forward to carry out some of the parts manufacturing and assembly of both the main and nose landing gears. Wheels and brakes were developed by HAL Lucknow. Some of the challenging forgings, like the main strut, were developed at HAL (Foundry and Forge). A CAD depiction of the main and nose landing gear elements and assemblies is shown below.

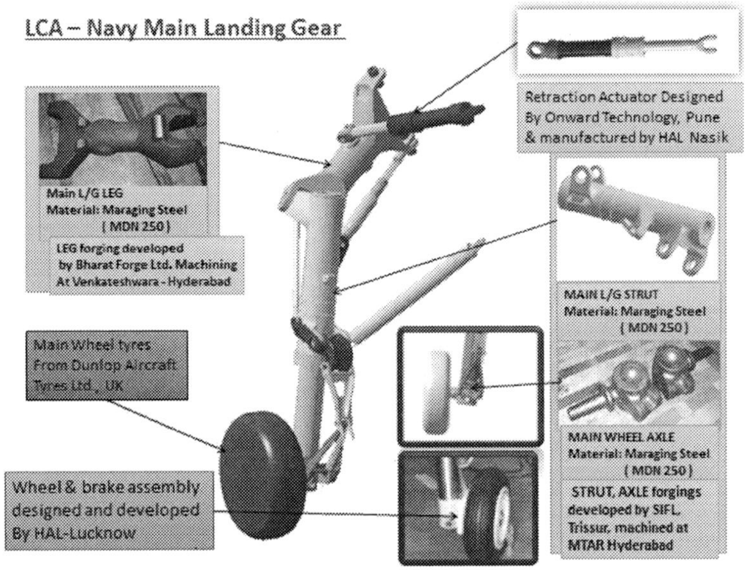

Main Landing Gear (MLG) of LCA Navy

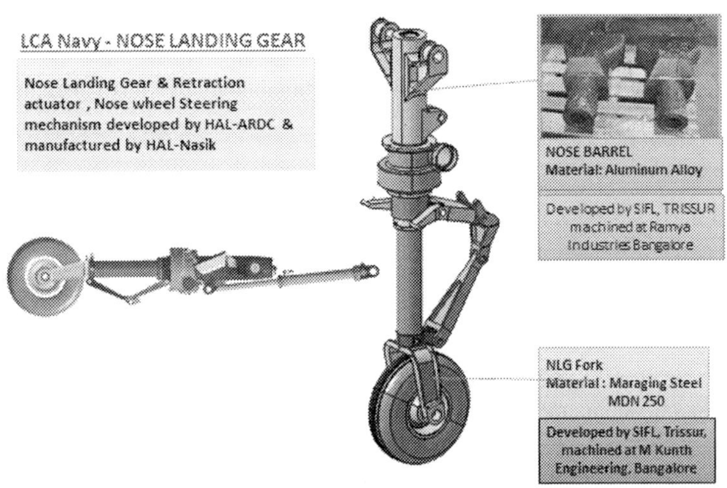

Nose Landing Gear (MLG) of LCA Navy

Once all the parts were designed and virtual assembly carried out, the next step was to define the door configuration, as shown below.

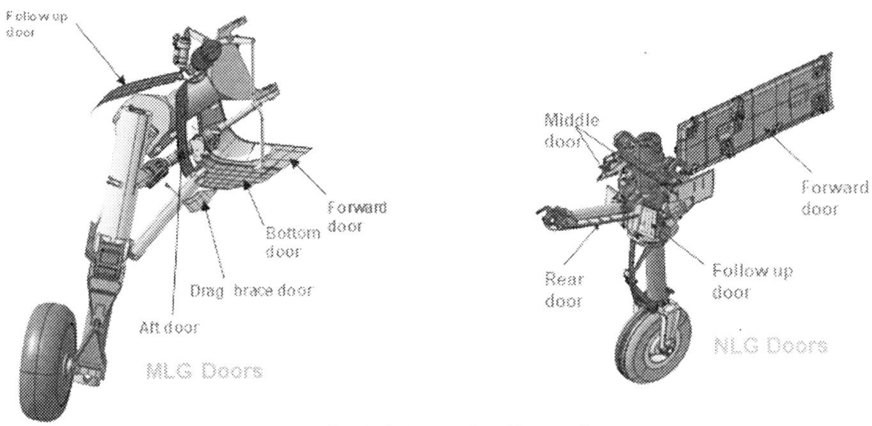

MLG & NLG Door Configuration

Initial versions of the landing gears were built with industrial-grade materials to have the requisite form, fit, assembly, and function so that the design and kinematics could be validated. Assembled landing gears were then installed on the aircraft for fitment and kinematic checks to validate simulated installation that was earlier done in a digital environment. This also ensured that there were no interference issues with the surrounding structures. A view of the LCA Navy MLG installation is shown below. Stand-alone LG testing was progressed in parallel.

MLG Installation on LCA Navy

A pictorial view of the nose landing gear is shown below. The nose landing gear needed to be designed with adequate shock absorption and strength to handle the significant vertical loads during arrester hook engagement. The nose landing gear also needed to be designed for a significantly higher steering angle to facilitate easier ground manoeuvring on board an aircraft carrier. It would also include a light box that would indicate the attitude of the aircraft to the Landing Safety Officer (LSO) located on the flight deck of the ship. There is a green light in the centre, an amber light above and a red light below. This box gets inputs from the angle of attack sensor of the aircraft. If the aircraft is on the correct glide slope, the LSO will see a green light. If the attitude of the aircraft is higher, then he will see an amber light and similarly, if he sees a red light, then the attitude of the aircraft is lower than it should be. Hence, it is an additional visual aid to guide the LSO, who could take decisions on allowing the aircraft to land on the deck of the ship or not. The landing gears also needed to be designed for a sudden expansion of the shock strut when the aircraft gets airborne from the ramp as well as during a missed wire approach, a 'bolter'.

NLG Installation on LCA Navy

The next major step was testing of landing gears to enable certification. These tests include component-level tests, assembly validation, functional tests, endurance tests, environmental tests, load tests, etc. The wheels and brakes also undergo testing in a brake dynamometer to check efficacy, in addition to other tests. Another interesting aspect is the tyre crush test, wherein the tyre is forced down on a piece of steel wire rope with the diameter of the ship's arresting gear pendant, simulating the crushing load faced by the tyre. This test is critical for a deck-based aircraft because the aircraft wheel routinely tramples the arrester wires on a ship's deck, thus we need to make sure there is minimal damage to the tyres. The integrated test of landing gear is carried out in a facility called a drop-test rig. This rig simulates the condition of the aircraft's mass component on each landing gear and the sink rate up to 7.1 m/s. Landing gear test specimens are extensively instrumented to validate the simulation and analysis results previously carried out. Picture of the brake dynamometer and CAD model of landing gear drop test rig are shown below.

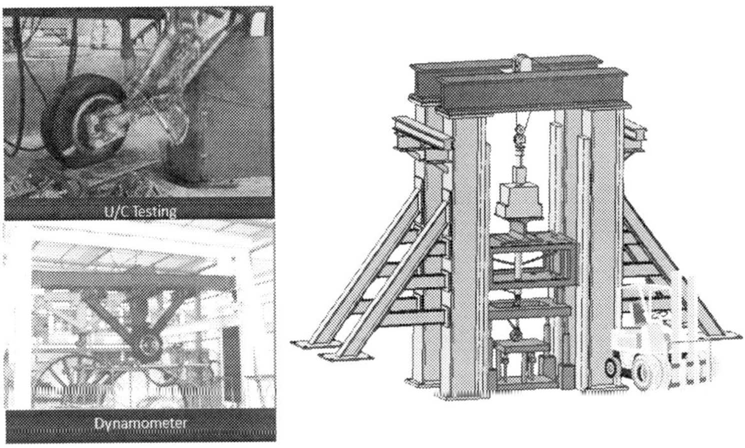

Brake Dynamometer & LG Drop Test Rig

During endurance tests of the landing gears, some component failures were observed. These were attributed to non-adherence to strict manufacturing processes as initially specified in the design. However, discussions between manufacturing and design teams revealed that there was a need for a few design changes to improve repeatable manufacturability, for example, in the nose wheel steering collar. These changes were implemented, and new parts were then re-assembled. Repeat endurance tests were carried out, and they were successful. This shows the critical interplay between design and manufacture. It also demonstrates that failure must be viewed as a challenge to do better and learn from, rather than be cowed down.

Qualified landing gears were installed on the aircraft, and system integration checks were carried out. The initial tests included timing checks of both retraction and extension of the landing gears. There was a need to ensure that the sequencing of the doors was also achieved, confirming that there were no interferences with the aircraft structure. While this was well simulated in the kinematic model in a virtual environment, there were some apprehensions due to possible deviations in actual build. This stage was successfully completed, albeit with some minor changes required as a result of the tests. However, these changes were not significant and were implemented quickly. A picture of the LCA Navy with the landing gear elements clearly visible, taken at the shore-based test facility in Goa, is shown below.

Landing Gears of LCA Navy

The next step was to observe the behaviour of the landing gears when the aircraft was moved. For this, the aircraft was first towed around using a tractor, followed by slow taxiing to check for any signs of distress. Typical dynamic behaviour of the landing gears was observed. Instrumentation available on the landing gear elements and the corresponding structural interface regions of the aircraft would also provide inputs to the design teams. Subsequently, a Nose Wheel Steering (NWS) test was conducted to check the efficacy of the aircraft in performing a spot turn. It was impressive to see the aircraft practically turn on the spot, which would facilitate manoeuvring on the ship's deck. In the picture below, one can see the nose wheel fully turned to the left to perform a spot turn on board the aircraft carrier, INS *Vikramaditya*.

Nose Wheel Steering Test

The instrumented landing gear itself was put through its paces during low- and high-speed taxi tests, followed by flight tests. At every step, instrumentation results were compared with analysis and simulation results that had already been available. Once correlated and accepted by the design and certification teams, the subsequent step in the test process was retraction and extension of the landing gears in flight. The aircraft was equipped with video cameras as part of the instrumentation package capable of observing the movement and behaviour of the landing gear during retraction and extension while in flight. This provided visualisation of the sequence of lowering and raising the landing gears, including landing gear door sequencing. This capability enabled the design team to gain a clear picture of landing gear behaviour and aided in fine-tuning the process. Thus, instrumentation at both the system- and aircraft-level was a significant tool in the development journey.

The next major challenge was to check behaviour and functioning of the landing gear during the ski-jump launch process. There was a need to check for interference with flaps of the restraining gear, loading on the ramp itself, and snubber loading after the aircraft leaves the ramp due to sudden extension. The first check involved towing the aircraft to bring it up against the extended restraining gear flap at the take-off point of the SBTF. This check ensured that there were no obstructions at the aircraft-level with the restraining gear. The aircraft was then started up and brought to full thrust to check again for interference, ensuring that the aircraft was held back against the restraining gear flaps. A picture of the aircraft against the restraining gear at the SBTF in Goa is shown below.

Main Wheel of LCA Navy (NP1) against RGS at SBTF, Goa

After successfully confirming that there was no interference, the landing gear was to be tested during the ski-jump launch, initially over the ramp. Since the ramp profile is parabolic, it was expected that the load build-up would be gradual. This was indeed the case, and hence validated the expectations from simulation. As the aircraft left the ramp, there was a sudden unloading of landing gears which would impose a load on the end of the shock absorber. The efficacy of the damping of the shock absorber during unloading was checked to ensure that the snubber loads would be within limits. It may be mentioned here that the INS *Viraat,* which earlier served in the Indian Navy, had a circular ramp profile that imposed sudden loading on the landing gears, which is not clearly desirable.

The next major challenge for the landing gear was touch-and-go, followed by high sink rate checks, wherein the aircraft landing gear was subjected to higher and higher loads. Repeated approaches were carried out at the SBTF with gradual sink rate build-up tests. These results were correlated with the simulation carried out and progressively cleared for higher sink rates. These tests are painstaking and need a high level of dedication and concentration from the entire team. A picture of the aircraft performing a high sink rate touch down at the landing area of the SBTF is shown below.

LCA Navy at SBTF, Goa, performing a High Sink Rate Touch and Go

Having successfully completed all the above tests, the landing gear was tested for launch and recovery at the SBTF in Goa prior to embarkation on the aircraft carrier. In this test, the coupling effect of the landing gear and arrester hook was present. At the point of arrestment, the nose landing gear experiences a 'slap-down' force due to the pivot action around the aircraft centre of gravity. The compression of the nose landing gear strut at the point of arrestment is visible in the picture below.

Arrested Recovery of LCA Navy showing the NLG getting loaded

This gave an idea of the type of loads encountered and the structure needed to absorb them. Based on a detailed test matrix that was developed, both launch and recovery tests were carried out and successfully validated. A picture of the LCA Navy performing an arrested recovery is shown below, where the main landing gear struts are compressed and the arrester hook on the aircraft is about to snag the wire at the arresting gear system of the SBTF.

Arrested Recovery of LCA Navy showing the MLG getting loaded

It is to the credit of all the LCA Navy team members across multiple organisations that they came together to successfully accomplish this complex task of designing and developing the landing gear system for the LCA Navy. I would attribute a large part of the credit to the various divisions of HAL for their unstinted support and grit in making this a reality.

In conclusion, landing gear for a deck-based aircraft needs to be significantly larger than its land-based counterpart due to much larger landing loads. In the initial stages it was presumed that the requirement would be met by a mere scaling up of the articulated design LCA landing gear. However, the chapter brings out other constraints, like the interference with the ship's restraining gear, which does not allow the originally envisaged concept. Thus, a new design of a vertical shock strut type of landing gear was evolved. The chapter brings out the development, build, test and integration journey of both the main and nose landing gears of LCA Navy. The nose steering system needs to rotate to a much larger degree to facilitate spot turns on an aircraft carrier, due to limited space on a ship. The chapter also brings out the material development and manufacturing challenges that were encountered. Landing gear development taught us that every challenge, however daunting, can be overcome by sheer perseverance and application.

10

Leading Edge Vortex Control (LEVCON)

It may be recalled that the landing distance on an aircraft carrier is 90 m, with recovery by means of an arrester hook engaging the arresting gear wires on the ship's deck. There is a need to have as low an approach speed of the aircraft as possible for an aircraft carrier landing, so that the engaging speed limits of the ship's arresting gear are not exceeded. Lowering the approach speed also reduces its vertical component, i.e., the sink rate, thereby reducing the loading on the landing gear. This can be achieved by increasing the Coefficient of Lift (C_L) at a given Angle of Attack (AoA or α). This increase in C_L is achieved to some extent by the introduction of a new control surface to the LCA AF wing configuration.

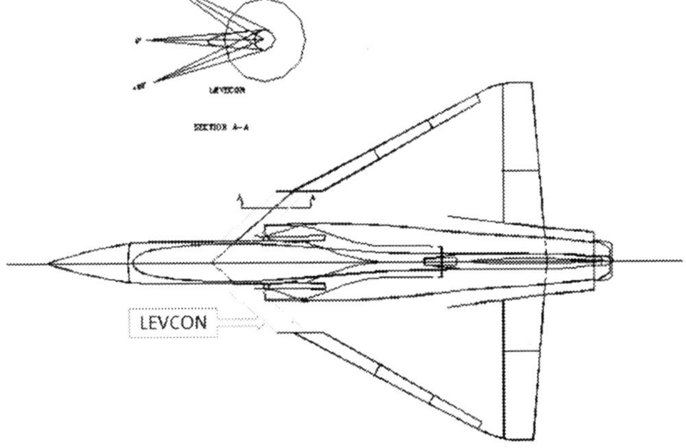

Sketch showing the position of LEVCON in the Wing Apex region

The Leading Edge Vortex CONtroller (LEVCON) is a three-position secondary control surface located at the wing apex region between the fuselage and the wing leading edge kink, which was planned to meet this requirement. It is also used to generate high lift-to-drag ratios at various manoeuvring conditions. The LEVCON may also be used as a scheduled control surface with control law inputs in the flight control system. The figure below shows a general layout sketch of the LCA Navy with the LEVCON surface attached to the wing apex region.

The introduction of LEVCON increases the total wing area by about four per cent, thereby increasing the lift at a given AoA. The LEVCON also changes the vortex patterns over the wing in a favourable way. When deflected upwards by 30 degrees, the LEVCON increases the intensity of leading edge vortices, thereby increasing the C_L. It also anchors vortices at the apex of the wing, which pushes the centre of lift upstream with respect to the Centre of Gravity (C.G), resulting in an increase in the 'pitch up' tendency of the aircraft. A comparison with a pressure flow pattern with and without the LEVCON is shown below.

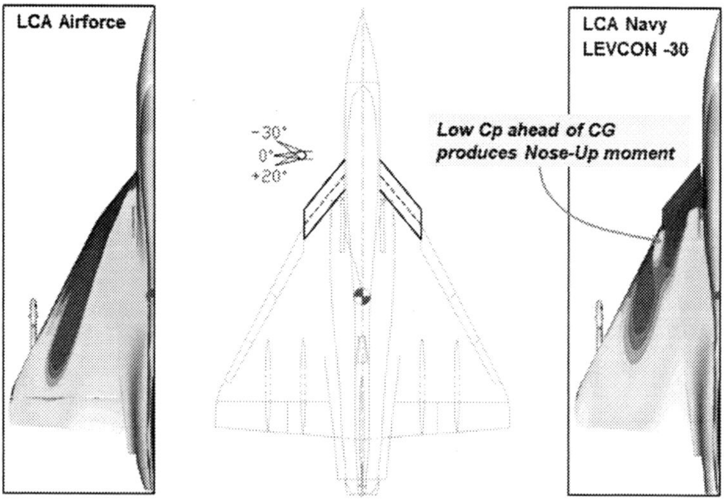

Pressure flow pattern with and without the LEVCON

The LEVCON is used with +20 degree (down) position for improving Lift/Drag (L/D) ratio at subsonic/transonic speeds. It can be deflected to –30 degree (up) position for obtaining nose-up pitching moment, which improves trim C_L for reducing the approach speed during landing. For normal flights, the LEVCON position will be in 0 degrees (neutral) position for minimum drag penalty at all speeds. The LEVCON can also be used as a scheduled control surface driven by the flight control system. The deflection of the LEVCON up by 30 degrees creates a residual nose-up pitching moment which is then trimmed by a balancing moment from the downward deflection of the four elevons, resulting in additional C_L trim at constant AoA to achieve the target value. This is shown in the figure below.

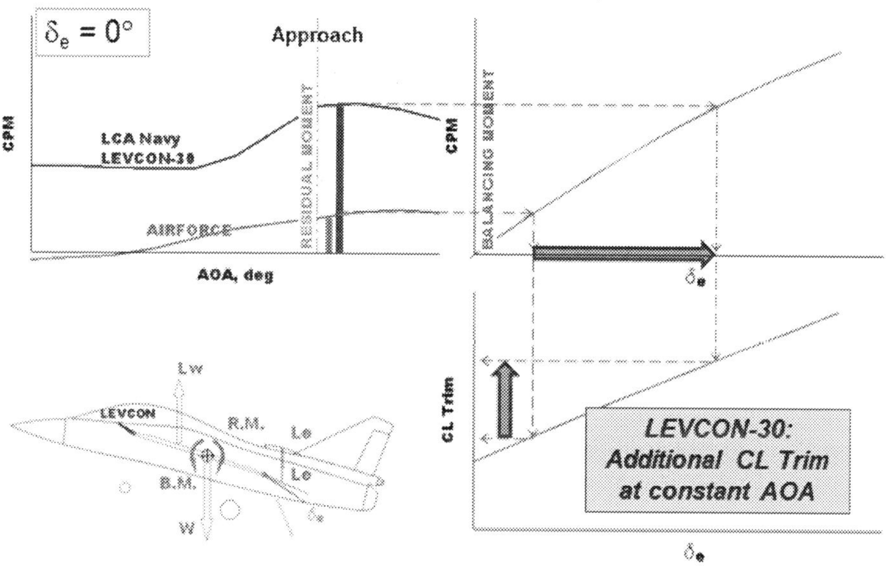

Residual Moment from the LEVCON at -30 Deg

The upward deflection of the LEVCON increases the maximum lift coefficient (C_L Max), while its downward deflection by 20 degrees enhances the lift to drag ratio around the C_L of interest for manoeuvring flight at high subsonic speeds. Improved aircraft manoeuvring performance is particularly advantageous in combat situations. These are shown in the graphs below. The left-hand figure clearly demonstrates that a 30-degree upward deflection of the LEVCON increases the C_L trim at a specific AoA (upper line). Similarly, in the right-hand figure, a 20-degree downward deflection of the LEVCON increases the L/D ratio at a particular AoA (upper line).

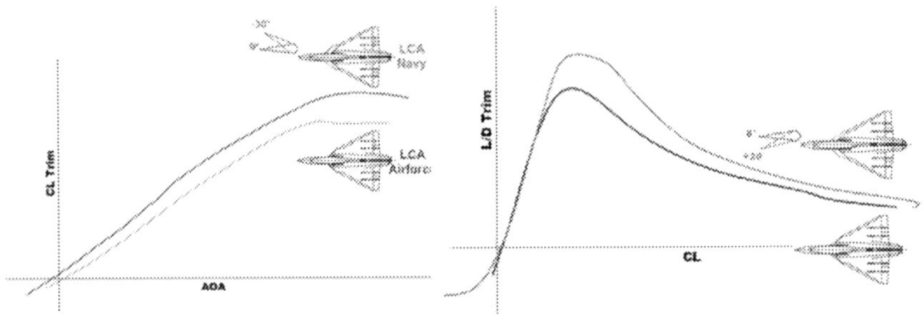

Effect of the LEVCON Deflection

A graphic showing the opportunities to achieve the requisite C_L trim to reach the lower approach speed target is shown below. It indicates that a partial achievement can be made by increasing the angle of attack, with the remainder achieved by using LEVCON deflected up by 30 degrees. The LCA Navy incorporates a higher nose droop by 4 degrees, allowing for an increased angle of attack during aircraft carrier approaches while maintaining adequate over-the-nose vision. This bridges part of the gap in the required trim C_L shown as 'opportunity-1' in the graphic. With the higher angle of attack established, the balance of increased trim C_L is obtained by deflecting the LEVCON up by 30 degrees as shown as 'opportunity-2' in the graphic. As can be seen, by utilising aerodynamic characteristics of both increase in AoA and upward deflection of the LEVCON, we were able to successfully achieve the required objective of reduction in approach speed of the aircraft for carrier recovery.

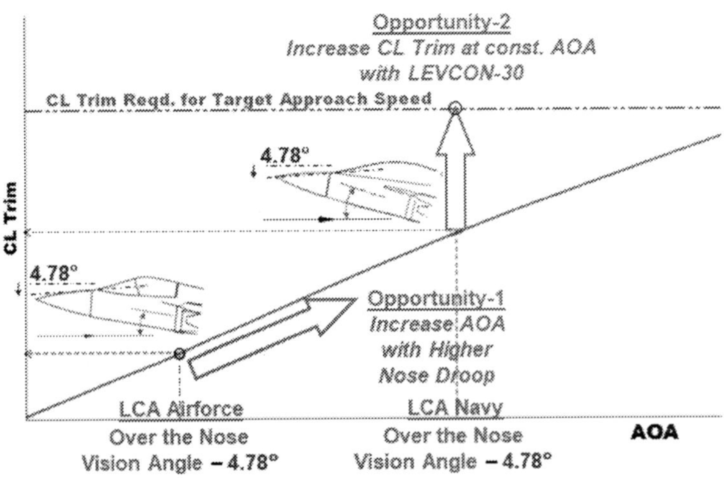

Opportunities for achieving C_L Trim

The LCA Navy aircraft includes two sets of the LEVCON, one for each side of the wing. It was decided to fix the maximum hinge moment for actuator design at 1500 kg-m based on aerodynamic load estimation through CFD and measurements during wind tunnel tests. This parameter is crucial for determining the hardware requirements of the LEVCON actuation system, which controls the movement of the LEVCON flap surface on each wing. Independent Power Drive Units (PDU) will operate both LEVCON flaps, with each PDU controlled by a hydro-mechanical servo-control system. The architecture of the LEVCON system in the flight control system was conceptualised and integrated in such a way that it would act as a secondary control surface.

The LEVCON system is primarily a hydro-mechanical system and includes all the hardware necessary for actuation of the LEVCON flap surface against loads defined herein. Hydraulic power is drawn from the aircraft hydraulic system to provide actuation. On each side of the wing, there are two rotary actuators: one inboard having six slices and the other outboard having four slices. There is one Asymmetry Control Unit (ACU) with Rotary Variable Differential Transformer (RVDT) at the inboard end. There is a PDU comprising of an Angle Gear Box (AGB), a slip clutch, a hydraulic brake, and

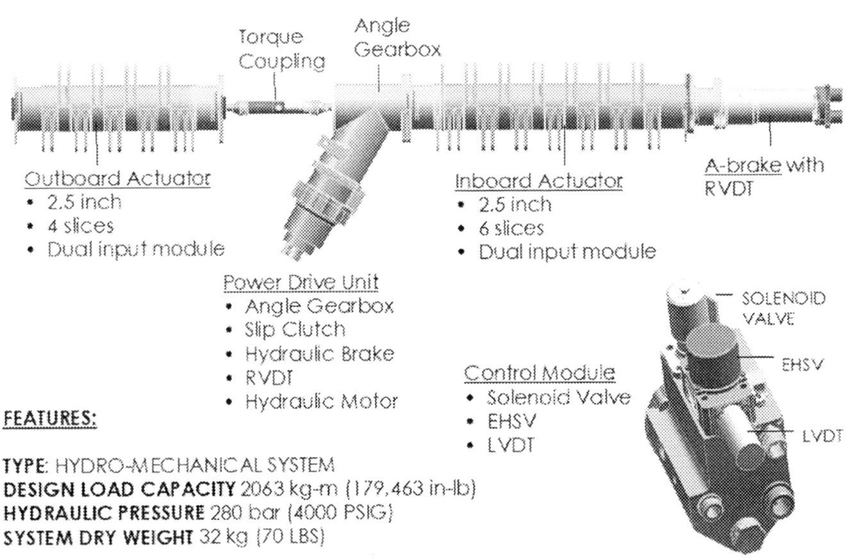

Schematic of the LEVCON Actuating System

a hydraulic motor. A control module is part of the ensemble, consisting of Electro-Hydro Static Valve (EHSV) with Linear Variable Differential Transformer (LVDT), solenoid valve, and manifold with shut-off valve as shown.

The LEVCON Control Computer (LCC), later designated as the LEVCON Air Data Computer (LADC), sends two-channel electrical commands to the servo valve portion of the servo control module. The servo valve responds to the command by sending hydraulic power to the PDU for controlled mechanical output. The output from the PDU is transmitted to the rotary actuators by couplings, passing through the angle gear box and torque shaft as shown. These actuators are connected to the flap panels through pins, driving them to the commanded position. Duplex RVDT feedback signals from the PDU to the LCC close the proportional control loop. Duplex channel signals from RVDTs will be continuously compared to monitor the structural integrity of the drive system. The asymmetry control unit detects differences in the deployment angle between the left and right LEVCONs, sending a signal to the control system for necessary corrective action. All components on both sides of the LEVCON are basically identical, except for the angle gearbox that is handed.

Now let us look at the LEVCON and stub-wing structure that needs to be integrated on the aircraft. The LEVCON is a new control surface introduced in the LCA Navy and will be integrated into the wing apex region towards the root section. Accordingly, the stub-wing required redesigning to accommodate the LEVCON and its actuating system. Further, the interface between the stub-wing and the main wing, fuselage, and, air intake needed to be modified vis-à-vis the LCA AF version.

The LEVCON structure is a conventional all-metal skin stringer, spars, and multi rib construction with a leading edge block that was developed based on strength and stiffness requirements. The LEVCON is interfaced to the stub wing by the rotary actuator, which itself acts as the hinge along with an additional fitting integrated with the inboard spar. Each slice of the actuator is attached to three lugs of the LEVCON spar. A short pin is provided on the outboard side, and a longer pin is provided on the inboard side to function as bolts that transmit the load due to the hinge moment.

Like the LEVCON structure, the Stub Wing Structure also consists of all-metal skin stringer, single spar, and multi rib construction, but with top and bottom skins, interface fittings and diverter skins. Stub wing to wing and fuselage interface is achieved through interchangeability (ICY) points, while interface to air intake and to fuselage is by means of riveted or bolted joints. Provision is made for shimming to accommodate any manufacturing inaccuracies. The stub wing is interfaced to the surrounding structure at various locations as brought out earlier.

New jigs were constructed to assemble the LEVCON and stub wing. The air intake jig was modified to accommodate the interface changes. A picture of the stub wing jig and a close-up view of the LEVCON actuating system installed in the aircraft are shown below.

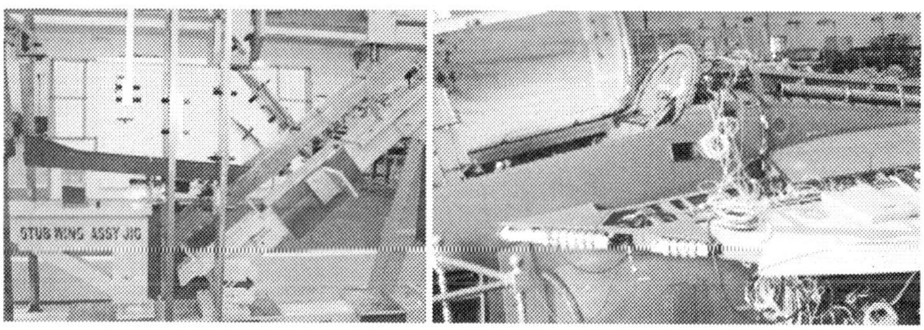

Stub-Wing Jig & View of the LEVCON Actuating System

A dedicated LEVCON structure test rig was designed and built to assess the standalone structural integrity of the LEVCON. The structural elements of the stub wing were integrated into the test rig, allowing for inclusion of various LEVCON system elements during functional checks. Test artefacts like inertia blocks were provided to facilitate loading simulation. A digital version of the test rig is shown below.

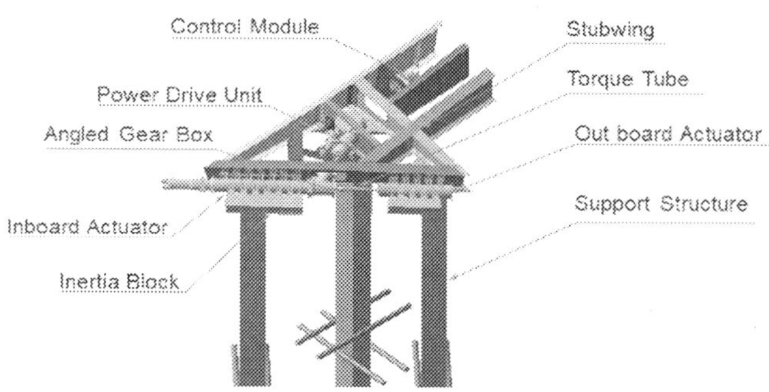

LEVCON Structural Test Rig

As is standard practice, tests were conducted up to 100 per cent loading, namely, limit load. This test proceeded without any failure, and certification agencies will permit loading of the LEVCON structure on the aircraft up to 80 per cent. This implies that the aircraft's flight profile had to be tailored to stay within the approved limits. To obtain full clearance for the aircraft's load, it was necessary to test the LEVCON structure to 150 per cent or ultimate load. Certification requirements entail that when a structure is subjected to ultimate load, there may be yielding in some structural elements, but there should not be a catastrophic failure. However, at about 120 per cent of load, failure was observed, prompting the test to be halted for analysis. A team set up for the purpose revisited the design aspects vis-à-vis the failure observed and came up with a need for a modification in the load path to the stub wing to prevent this failure. With this modification incorporated, the structural test successfully met the design intent and facilitated full structural clearance of the aircraft. This experience highlighted the importance of ground testing and a gradual build-up of the clearance process.

The LEVCON rotated by 30 degrees 'up' for landing is clearly visible in the picture below. Initial flight tests were carried out with the LEVCON set to 30-degree 'up' position on the ground itself, and the entire intended flight profile was executed to validate the analysed aerodynamic behaviour and the structural integrity vis-à-vis simulation and ground tests. Once confidence was gained, the LEVCON was actuated by a pilot from the cockpit during flight to assess transition behaviour from 0 degrees to -30 degrees and +20 degrees. All these characteristics that were captured in flight tests were extremely useful to fine-tuning the control laws of the flight control system.

The LEVCON deflected 'Up' by 30 Degrees for Landing

During the identification of the need for additional control surface, namely LEVCON, its conceptualisation, location identification, interface with aircraft structure, simulation, design, manufacture, testing, etc., significant programme management challenges were encountered. For the first time, a portion of the structure was outsourced and needed to be integrated back in the aircraft Digital Mock Up (DMU). This entailed a detailed definition of interfaces between the LEVCON surface and aircraft structure, which are summarised in a table in the section of tables for additional information at page 237.

To conclude, due to an extremely short landing distance of 90m on a ship's deck, there is a need to reduce approach speed of the aircraft. This is achieved by the introduction of a new control surface, LEVCON. This chapter brings out the aerodynamics involved, the structural integration challenges and the testing that ensued. It also brings out the aircraft performance benefit of deflecting LEVCON down at high subsonic speeds. For the first time, a portion of aircraft structural design was outsourced to a private entity. The challenges faced and how they were overcome has been brought out.

I would like to acknowledge the valuable contributions of the LCA Navy team and, in particular, Mr. RK Jolly for his outstanding work on aerodynamic behaviour studies of the LEVCON. He has also provided some of the sketches and inputs for this section.

11

Other Specialised Test Facilities

An aircraft, its systems, structures, and parts undergo a significant number of tests prior to being certified fit for use. A few system-level and aircraft-level test facilities like the Shore Based Test Facility (SBTF), arrester hook system test rigs, landing gear system rigs, LEVCON structural test rig, etc., were covered in the previous sections. While several other test facilities built for the LCA AF Version were utilised, a few additional test facilities that were specifically built for LCA Navy testing are briefly described in the following paragraphs. It may be noted that one of the most critical tests would be the arrested recovery shock test on all system elements. All equipment installed inside the aircraft undergoes this sudden jerk due to arrested recovery and needs to be structurally sound and also be able to continue its function.

A new Main Airframe Static Test (MAST) rig was conceptualised and built for the structural testing of the LCA Navy. A MAST rig was available for structural testing of the LCA AF Version, which is designed for a typical land-based fighter aircraft subjected to structural loading due to aerodynamic forces and primarily vertical loading during landing on the runway. However, for a carrier-borne fighter aircraft, landing involves both a large vertical loading due to a high sink rate of 7.1 m/s and a significant horizontal load due to arrested recovery. It was not considered feasible to modify the LCA AF MAST rig to meet the loading demands of the LCA Navy, and accordingly, a new MAST rig was conceptualised, as shown in the CAD model below.

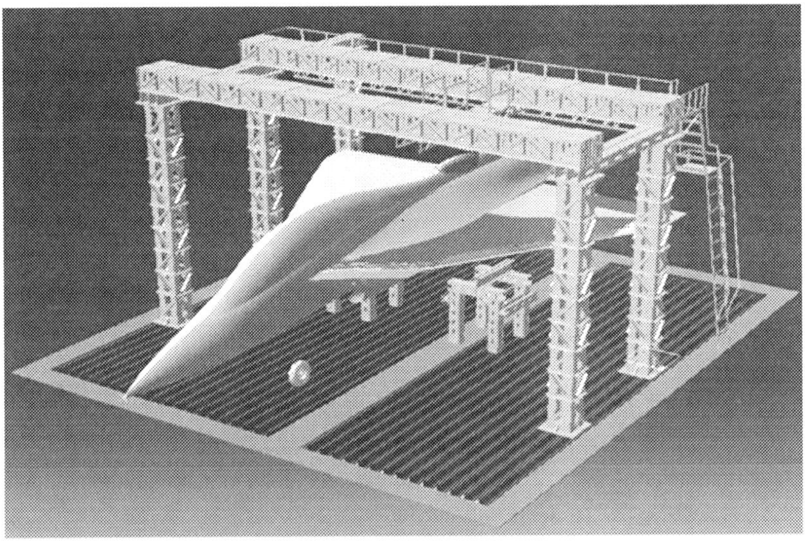

CAD Model of LCA Navy MAST Rig with LCA Navy Model in Rig

The LCA Navy MAST rig was built by HAL in record time with close monitoring by their management. I recall that Mr. Roy, the then General Manager at HAL (AR&DC), took it as a challenge and would go every morning to closely monitor the progress of the test rig build and commissioning. The rig needed to have the capability of imposing flight loads, large vertical loads due to flareless landing on the ship, as well as significant horizontal load due to arrester hook engagement. This entailed foundation strengthening and a vertical backup structure to handle the reaction of the arrester hook load. There was a requirement to build a dedicated LCA Navy standard Structural Test Specimen (STS) that would be subjected to various structural and flight loads likely to be encountered on the aircraft during its lifetime of operations from ship and shore. The STS was also extensively instrumented to capture results of structural loads that would be felt on the aircraft. This would enable correlation with analysis and simulation results that were earlier carried out. A picture of the LCA Navy STS in the MAST rig is shown below.

LCA Navy Structural Test Specimen (STS) in MAST

In the meantime, there was a requirement to prioritise test cases so that aircraft-level clearances for flight tests from SBTF could be progressively accorded. As per specifications, the aircraft needed to be cleared for an envelope of +8 'g', vertical rate of descent (sink rate) of 7.1 m/s, and deceleration of 4.5 'g' due to arrester hook. Priority–1 test cases were developed based on discussions with certification agencies to clear the aircraft for limit load testing of ship landing cases. A limit load test entails testing a structural test specimen to 100 per cent loading. This would allow clearance up to 80 per cent arrester hook load and 5.6 m/s sink rate on the aircraft itself.

The table below shows Priority-1 test cases that focus on landing gear and arrester hook loading, with resulting reactions on the aircraft structure. With clearance accorded by the certification agencies after successful completion of Priority-1 tests, a significant extent of flight testing of the aircraft was feasible to be carried out at the SBTF at the Naval Air Station in Goa.

Sl	*Arrested Landing – Limit Load condition (For 5.6 m/s Sink Rate & 80% Arrester Hook Load*	*Loading*
1	2-Point Main Landing Gear (MLG) Spring Back Load Case (Equivalent of 7.1m/s) – 64T Vertical & 40T Horizontal	Limit
2	3-Point Nose Landing Gear (NLG) Spring Back Load Case	Limit
3	Arrester Hook System (AHS) – 45T	Limit

Priority-1 Test Cases for LCA Navy STS Testing in MAST Rig

Once the STS is placed in the MAST rig, there is extensive preparatory work involved to set up a number of loading actuators on various parts of the aircraft. These actuators are positioned at critical locations based on the results of simulation and analysis that had already been carried out. Loading 'Tree' arrangement is installed on the wings to simulate aerodynamic loads faced by the structure at various 'g' load conditions, using a number of hydraulic jacks controlled by computer programs. For example, structural loads resulting from high sink rate would first affect the landing gears and then transfer through attachment points to the aircraft structure. Therefore, actuators are placed at these attachment locations to simulate landing loads. For the arrester hook, a steel fixture, simulating wire wrap around, is made to impose a horizontal load, reacted by a vertical steel frame structure of the test rig.

At every potential loading location identified by simulation, adequate strain gauges were placed to measure the actual strains during loading of the structure. These measurement results will be used to compare with the analysis results and refine simulation as necessary. The load diffusion path within the aircraft structural elements is identified by readings of the strain gauges. All required loading for testing is imposed through the control system from a remote terminal. Thus, the complex interplay between simulation and actual test results is carefully managed. A picture of the LCA Navy structural test specimen in the region of the arrester hook located in the main airframe static test rig is shown below.

Arrester Hook Installation and Loading Actuators between MAST and STS

Priority-2 test cases primarily involved flight load clearance, with loading done up to the limit condition (100 %). Based on successful testing up to limit loads on the LCA Navy STS in the MAST rig, structural flight envelope clearance would be accorded till +5.4 'g'. The table below shows the primary limit load tests carried out. No surprises were anticipated in the flight load test cases, as the 'up and away' loads were extensively tested on the LCA AF Version.

Sl	*Flight Load Tests (Aircraft Structure)*	*Loading*
4	Maximum –ve 'g' Load Case	Limit
5	Maximum Bending Moment Case	Limit
6	Maximum LEVCON Load Case	Limit
7	Maximum Torque Moment Load Case	Limit

Priority-2 Test Cases for LCA Navy STS Testing in MAST Rig

With Priority 1 and 2 cases completed, limit load cases of both ground and flight loads were finalised. It was a matter of great pride that there were no failures in all these tests. This is a testimony to the design teams at HAL, ADA and other agencies who invested enormous amounts of time and effort in analysis and simulation, with test results correlating well with simulations. The Priority-3 test case was the ultimate load test, during which STS would be subjected to 150 per cent loading. In the ultimate load test, some structural members could yield, but there should be no catastrophic failure. Identifying the most critical load case was crucial, as only one ultimate load test could be conducted. A loading diagram, as shown below, was worked out, and the most critical case identified was the spring back test of the main landing gear. This test was also successfully carried out, and the aircraft was cleared for the full flight and load envelope.

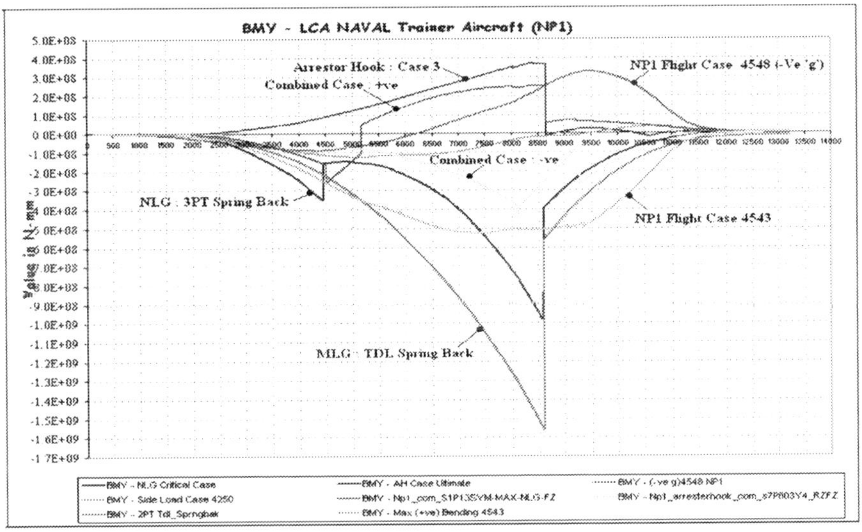

LCA Navy Loading Diagram to identify critical loading case

The next test facility developed was for flight control system tests. As far as the up-and-away flight was concerned, the control law and major elements of the flight control system was largely similar to the LCA AF Version, with aerodynamic changes to account for front fuselage nose droop and the presence of LEVCON. A significant change in the control law of the LCA Navy was made for the ski-jump launch and arrested recovery. At every stage, there were interactions among designers, test pilots, and flight test engineers to enable development of a robust control law. Hence, the flight test crew was part and parcel of the design process and became integral to the development cycle of the aircraft. The broad process followed for development, validation, and testing for ski-jump launch, is shown in a flow diagram below.

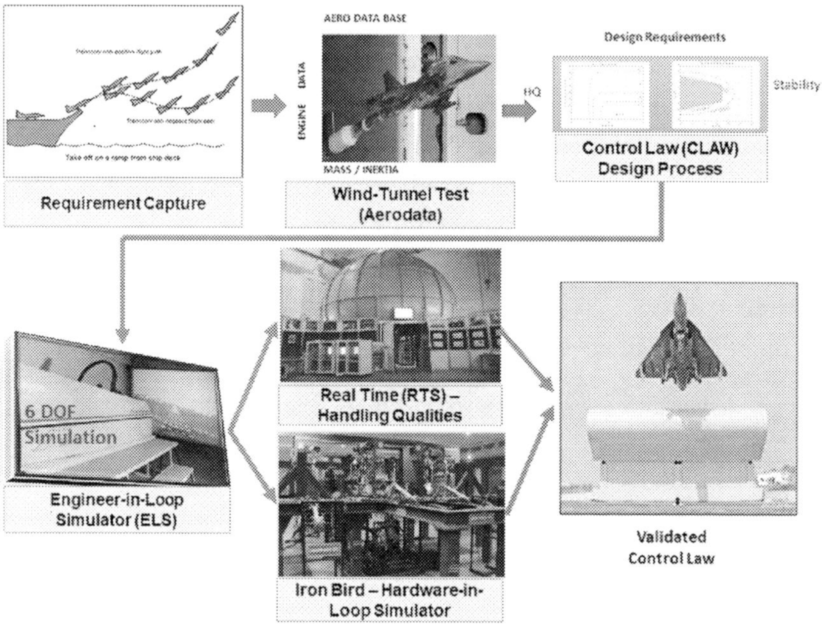

Typical Enablers for Ski Jump Control Law Development

Ship launch and recovery were the most challenging elements in the development of the Flight Control System (FCS). A significant extent of study was required to understand the process, involving brainstorming among designers and flight test crew. This was an important initial step in the development of the control law and the FCS for these critical phases. Once the requirements were understood, the control law algorithm was worked out. An Engineer-in-the-Loop Simulator (ELS) was set up for off-line simulations to understand the behaviour under various conditions such as speed, temperature, altitude, wind effects, aircraft mass, aircraft centre of gravity, etc.

Let us take the example of the ski-jump control law to understand the process as depicted in the process flow above. The first picture indicates requirement capture and depicts take-off profiles after the aircraft leaves the ramp; however, at this time the aircraft is not yet fully wing borne. Due to the forward speed and ramp launch, the aircraft is practically thrown up and forward in a ballistic trajectory. Consequently, the aircraft gains altitude, which represents potential energy. As the aircraft continues to move ahead, there is a gradual decrease in altitude and a corresponding increase in kinetic energy (speed), resulting in a trade-off with potential energy. This continues until the design limiting condition is reached, where the vertical rate of descent or alternately, the rate of climb, reduces to zero. This marks an inflection point where the aircraft starts to climb at an increasing rate. This design curve is shown in the upper profile of the graph. In emergencies, the aircraft may dip with a slight negative rate of climb before pulling up, as depicted in the lower curve. A limiting condition is that the aircraft can descend to the level of the ship's flight deck in emergencies.

This analysis of the requirement is a critical input for the design team to determine the take-off conditions of the aircraft based on ambient conditions. If wind-on-deck is higher, then take-off mass allowed is higher. If ambient temperature is lower, then again, allowable take-off mass is higher. Another significant influencing factor is the allowed angle of attack of the aircraft upon exit, with higher angles permitting for a higher take-off mass. While there are other influencing factors, these three parameters – relative wind-on-deck, ambient temperature, and exit angle of attack – are the major contributors governing the allowable take-off mass of the aircraft. In fact, these factors are crucial in analysing the mission capabilities of the aircraft.

To enable design of the control law, a complete aerodynamic dataset of the chosen configuration (aerodata) is needed. This data is obtained from simulations using computational fluid dynamics and wind tunnel test data. A picture of the LCA Navy 1:20 scale model in a wind tunnel is shown in the second picture above. The aerodata is prepared by a dedicated team and thoroughly checked for accuracy. In addition to this, the complete engine dataset, also known as the engine thrust deck, is required and provided by the engine manufacturer. This dataset includes characteristics that the aircraft experiences throughout its flight profile. The third major element is the aircraft's mass and inertia characteristics, which are computed and assembled by the aircraft design team. These inputs enable the control law design team to compute the potential characteristics and behaviour of the aircraft in various flight regimes.

The preliminary control law that was developed was ported into the ELS, and offline simulations were conducted for various conditions of ambient temperature, wind conditions, varying angles of attack, etc. The design was iteratively improved based on these simulations. Pilots also 'fly' in this simulator and provide their feedback on handling qualities and other experiences, which helped further fine-tune the design. The design intent for a ski-jump launch was to have a 'hands-free' mode of take-off. Also, to enhance engine thrust during the critical phase of a ski-jump launch, it was planned to shut-off engine bleed for 30s, thereby increasing thrust by about 5 to 6 per cent. The output of the design was provided to the software development team for coding and integration into the Digital Flight Control Computer (DFCC).

The special FCS software developed for ski-jump launch (and similarly for the phase of arrested recovery) was validated by an Independent Verification and Validation (IV&V) team, which is a team of software personnel responsible for thorough checks and code walkthroughs. This activity is crucial, especially for an unstable aircraft where safety is paramount. The software was also to be checked for traceability and redundancy. Once these tests were completed and found satisfactory, the software was ready to be ported into the DFCC. One DFCC was made available to the Iron Bird (IB) for engineering tests and the other to the Real Time Simulator (RTS) for handling quality evaluation. The tests could be simultaneously progressed to provide feedback and observations, if any.

The Iron Bird is a test facility that serves as a Hardware-in-the-Loop Simulator (HILS), which replicates the aircraft's flight control system and hydraulics to a large extent. It includes a cockpit to facilitate pilots to fly various profiles and simulate different flight conditions with the DFCC installed in the loop. One of the main objectives is to assess the overall system performance and ensure that the software is 'fault-free'. It may be recalled that in the LCA AF programme, 50 hours of fault-free flying were required for software certification prior to its clearance for the maiden flight of the first technology demonstrator aircraft (TD1) on 4 January 2001. As the name suggests, during the 50-hour period of fault-free testing, no bugs are permitted in the software. In case of any bugs in the software, it needs to be corrected and the test rerun.

Another important aspect is the ability to inject various faults to assess system behaviour and pilot reaction vis-a-vis predictions, which cannot be done during actual flights. Pilots also provide feedback to the design team on any observations made during the course of the tests. These can be suitably incorporated into the software at the appropriate instance, depending on the criticality of observations.

The other DFCC is sent to the RTS, where pilots execute a full-sortie planned profile, including critical phases of ski-jump launch and arrested recovery. In the RTS, handling qualities are evaluated, providing pilots with a realistic feel of how the aircraft would behave. The RTS feature a dome surrounding the cockpit, with visuals designed to be as realistic as possible, creating an immersive experience for the pilot. In fact, standing next to the cockpit within the dome gives a strong sense of immersion. Here also, pilots provide feedback for any necessary improvements.

With FCS software thoroughly checked in the Iron Bird and in the RTS, the stage is set for DFCC to be sent to the aircraft for ground integration tests, followed by flight tests. Prior to aircraft integration, certification and quality assurance teams review all the data and accord their approval. This step is critical to ensure that there are no missing links in the entire process. As can be seen below, the successful ski-jump launch of the first LCA Navy aircraft (NP1) was demonstrated in December 2014 at the shore-based test facility in Goa. It was a magnificent experience to have witnessed this event, although the lead-up to it was quite stressful and anxious.

Maiden Ski-Jump Launch of LCA Navy from SBTF, Goa

The next set of tests were to check for Electro-Magnetic Interference (EMI). Whenever an electromagnetic signal disturbs an electrical or electronic equipment's functional characteristics, then the signal is termed as EMI. Electro-Magnetic Compatibility (EMC) refers to the ability of an electronic system to function properly in its intended electromagnetic environment without causing interference. The Electro-Magnetic Environment (EME) results from the power and time distribution of radiated and/or conducted emission levels across various frequency ranges.

Emission is a phenomenon through which a system emits electro-magnetic energy to its environment. Susceptibility refers to a device's inability to perform its functions without degradation in the presence of unwanted electrical emissions. Vulnerability occurs when performance degradation exceeds acceptable limits due to stress. Degradation refers to the deterioration of a system feature in response to an undesired electromagnetic environment. On many occasions, intermittent malfunction or random failure of an electronic equipment has been experienced by users. These failures were later attributed to EMI and hence, the threat due to EMI is considered 'silent' and has proved dangerous on many occasions. Problems due to EMI are classified as Annoying Effects, such as momentary disturbance in radio and TV reception; Disturbing Effects, such as unwanted reset in computers or digital equipment, and change of status or setting; and Catastrophic Effects, such as loss of data, burnout of electronic components, biological hazards, etc.

The nature of EMI can be classified as transient, intermittent, and continuous. Transient EMI includes switch and relay contacts, motor starters, lightning, electrostatic discharge, etc. Intermittent EMI involves motor speed controllers, welding equipment, wireless transmitters, etc. Continuous EMI includes sliding contacts, communication noise, broadcast transmitters, etc. The EMI test is applicable to determine the performance of equipment installed on aircraft (internal or external to airframe) in the electromagnetic field in which it operates, as listed in the schedule appended in the last section of this book at page 238.

Moving on to EMI requirement of the LCA Navy, MIL-STD-461C was followed for system and sub-system level checks of the LCA Air Force Version, which was deemed adequate for the LCA Navy as well. Additional measurements of RE 101, CE 101, and RS 101, though not mandatory for the LCA Navy, were considered desirable to generate a database. MIL-STD-464 for aircraft-level testing measuring the EMI environment of a ship before carrier operations of the aircraft. With support from the Indian Navy's EMC Centre, the electromagnetic environment of the flight deck of the aircraft carrier was mapped, noting signal strengths with various transmitters active. The Naval EMC Centre team placed receptors at various locations on the flight deck, in the aircraft approach path, and take-off zone. It was observed that the testing levels on the aircraft exceeded those of the actual operating environment. Hence, it was considered safe to operate the LCA Navy from an aircraft carrier.

A specialised portable EMI test facility was developed and available from the LCA AF programme. This set-up was utilised for testing the LCA Navy in a simulated EM environment. The idea was to energise all the systems, especially electronic systems and computers, and ensure there were no disturbances. If disturbances occurred, their location and type needed to be established. The test level was set at 200 volts/m for some test cases. During testing, a few observations were noted, namely, noise enhancement in RT and an isolated case of brake pressure variation within a specific frequency range. However, these observations were not considered significant enough to halt progress; flight testing proceeded while addressing these issues in parallel. An aircraft was flown close to the deck environment and found that there was no distress or observations due to the EM environment of the ship. Based on these findings, the aircraft was authorised for carrier landings and take-offs from an EMI perspective.

We will now see some parts of Integrated Avionics and Weapons System testing. The avionics system of the LCA Navy is largely similar to the LCA AF Version. Changes specified to deck-based requirements for ski-jump take-off and arrested recovery needed thorough testing. ADA has an integrated avionics and weapon system testing environment comprising Systems Design and Evaluation Facility (SDEF), Avionics Integration Rig (AIR), Multi-Mode Radar (MMR) Rig, and Weapons Integration Rig (WIR). These are interconnected to create a comprehensive test and evaluation environment, as shown below.

The SDEF, also known as Cockpit Environment Facility (CEF), is primarily used to develop the Man-Machine Interface (MMI) or Human-Machine Interface (HMI). The cockpit replicates switches, indications, displays, and controls of the aircraft. Pilots can evaluate the software in simulated flights and provide feedback for necessary adjustments. Symbology on the Head-Up Display (HUD) and various Multi-Function Displays (MFD) are checked and fine-tuned based on pilot requirements.

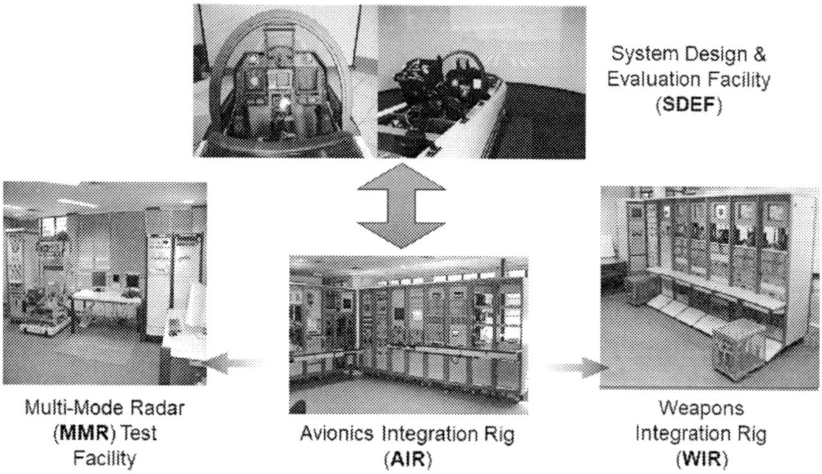

Integrated Avionics and Weapon System Test Facility

The Avionics Integration Rig (AIR) hosts the entire avionics system of the aircraft in a lab environment. In this rig, there could be emulators or actual hardware installed to check system behaviour. Faults can be injected to evaluate their impact on the aircraft. Similarly, the MMR test facility and the weapon integration rig allow comprehensive system checks in a laboratory setup, which helps mitigate surprises during actual aircraft integration tests.

The next test facility is the Telemetry and National Flight Test Centre (NFTC). Integrated flight testing of systems is only feasible on an actual aircraft due to the complex interactions between systems and pilot interfaces necessary to fulfill mission requirements. Adequate replication of flight conditions on ground rigs or through simulation is often not possible. Some discrepancies may exist between actual flight and predicted behaviour. Flight test data is crucial for refining predictive models and simulations validated through ground testing.

An important management decision was to form NFTC pooling talent from the Indian Air Force (IAF), the Indian Navy (IN), Hindustan Aeronautics Ltd. (HAL), Defence Research & Development Organisation (DRDO) and the Aeronautical Development Agency (ADA). Operating under the aegis of ADA, the NFTC integrated the customer into the design, testing, and evaluation teams. To mitigate risks, flight tests were initially in benign regions, gradually expanding to approach the full design envelope. The flight-testing approach in the LCA programme was conservative, starting from scratch in development and wading through uncertainties. Based on experience gained, the validation of CFD codes and calibrated wind tunnel models enabled optimisation of flight test points and more rapid envelope expansion. *Flight testing is not just about flying the aircraft, but actively participating in design and development.*

The prototype aircraft was extensively instrumented with over 10,000 parameters acquired and recorded on board. Approximately 3,000 parameters were acquired and telemetered on L-Band link for real-time monitoring at the telemetry ground station. This included all types of sensors for temperature, pressure, vibration, strain, etc. Specialized instrumentation, like high-speed imaging systems for stores separation trajectory generation were also incorporated. GPS was also used as an aircraft position sensor.

A telemetry facility in Bengaluru was established as part of the National Flight Test Centre (NFTC) for the LCA AF programme. A similar facility had been set up at the SBTF in Goa. The facility included reception antennae installed on the rooftop, receiving and recording equipment, and the monitoring station itself. The monitoring area largely comprised of two segments: the first being the 'test director' station, and the other was the various systems monitoring station. Portable telemetry vans was also configured for flight testing at the outstation. This facility was then connected via optical fibre link to the main telemetry station in Bengaluru. A snapshot of various facets of the telemetry station in Bengaluru is shown below.

Based on design validation and certification requirements, an overall test plan matrix was worked out to enable Initial Operational Clearance (IOC) and subsequently Final Operational Clearance (FOC). For the LCA Navy, a different path was chosen to demonstrate technologies for carrier operation. Therefore, a Carrier Compatibility Test (CCT) matrix was worked out. Notwithstanding the end objectives, the process for every flight test sortie involved preparing a detailed test plan, with the test schedule coordinated by the design, certification, quality assurance, and flight test teams. A detailed sortie briefing was then carried out prior to actual test execution.

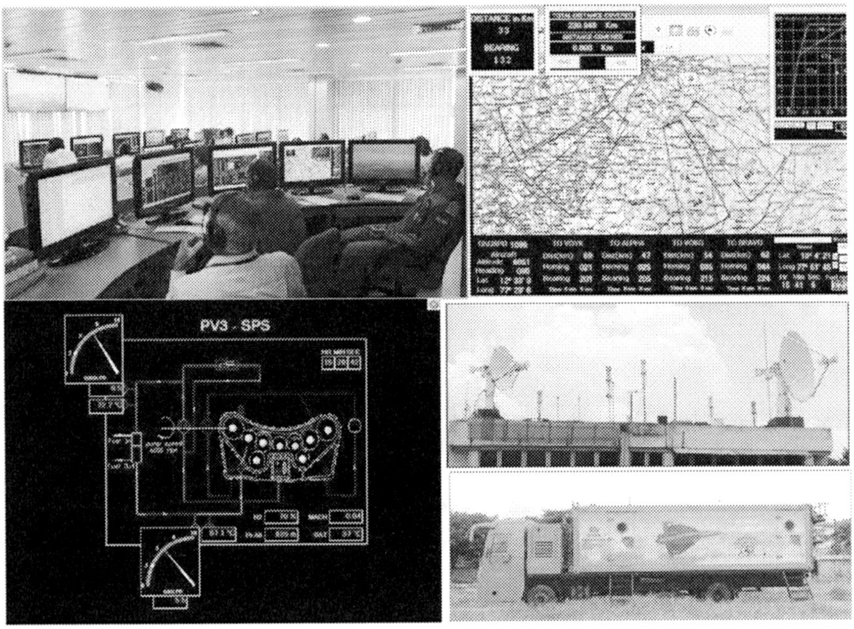

Telemetry Facility at NFTC Bangalore and Portable Telemetry Van

The pilot typically follows instructions given by the test director as per the test schedule during flight. On completion of the sortie, a 'hot-debrief' is carried out based on real-time observations and the pilot's input. This is followed by a more detailed 'data-debrief' after analysing all recorded parameters, where the design teams present their observations. These inputs are carefully noted by the designers, and suitable correction/changes carried out to their respective systems, if necessary.

This chapter has given us a snapshot of various tests and facilities that are so essential for the process of design and development of a typical fighter aircraft. Together with the test facilities discussed in earlier chapters, it highlights the criticality involved in developing a ship-borne fighter aircraft. The bottom line is to diligently test before you fly and the significance of tests during various stages of flight.

12

Carrier Compatibility Test (CCT) or Carrier Suitability Demonstration (CSD)

The LCA Navy aircraft is designed to operate from an aircraft carrier with ski-jump launch and arrested recovery. As per Government of India approval of the LCA Navy programme, a Technology Demonstration (TD) of carrier compatibility was to be carried out. Towards this end, there is a need to carry out tests of the aircraft to demonstrate carrier compatibility. A Shore Based Test Facility (SBTF) replicating an aircraft carrier was built at the Naval Air Station in Goa and has been under active exploitation since January 2014, as was mentioned earlier. In a campaign at Goa for the first LCA Navy prototype (NP1), the maiden ski-jump launch was successfully carried out on 20 December 2014. During this campaign, dummy deck approaches, simulating an aircraft carrier environment, were also carried out on the landing area for preliminary evaluation.

The primary objective of the technology demonstration was sub-divided into TD-Ashore and TD-Afloat. To start with, activities were to be carried out with an objective of demonstrating capabilities in the Operational Clean Configuration (OCC) of the LCA Navy from the SBTF. The OCC is defined as 2*Close Combat Missiles (CCM) + 100 per cent internal fuel. This would complete the TD-Ashore phase. With the availability of the aircraft carrier, the demonstration would be conducted with a defined number of aircraft arrested landings and launches from the carrier in OCC, leading to completion of the TD-Afloat phase. To gain confidence and to validate design in a safe and efficient manner, the first phase of sea trials was planned to be conducted under controlled environmental and operational conditions.

The next set of activities would be focused on demonstrating the enhanced capability of the aircraft by completing the flight test at SBTF with external stores. Two stores were planned for this demonstration: namely, Derby missiles (Beyond Visual Range missile) at the mid-board station and a centre-line fuel drop tank. The objective would be considered met after the second phase of sea trials in which a defined number of arrested landings, aircraft maintenance activities on the carrier, and successful ski-jump take-offs are demonstrated from the carrier in stores configurations.

The final set of activities for a Carrier Suitability Demonstration (CSD) was to operate the aircraft in clean as well as stores configuration from the carrier right up to the limits that the aircraft is designed for. This includes the demonstration of aircraft performance, structural integrity, handling qualities, etc., in severe conditions. There are some concurrent programme activities that are also required to achieve IOC; for example, full flight envelope expansion, demonstration of mission capability, in-flight refuelling capability, avionics integration (radar, data link, self-protection jammer), Derby missile integration, hot refuelling and hot swapping, tests ashore for brake energy, etc.

To start with, there is a need to prove the structural integrity of the aircraft up to defined mass limits during ski-jump launch and arrested recovery operations from the carrier. There is a need to confirm that the aircraft has adequate handling qualities during the ski-jump launch and arrested recovery phases of flight.

The technology demonstration will include validating daytime and fair-weather operational capability of the aircraft. There is also a need to demonstrate Field Carrier Landing Practice (FCLP) sorties by night. The Electro-Magnetic Interference (EMI) behaviour in the aircraft carrier environment, with minimum possible emitters active for initial trials, will be proved as confidence-building measures prior to operations in a full-fledged sea-going environment of the ship. To assess flight and hangar deck compatibility, there is a need to check physical clearances at all Technical Positions (TPs), lashing arrangements that tether the aircraft to the deck of the ship, ground movement on flight and hangar decks, compatibility with aircraft lifts, etc. The development of servicing and maintenance procedures and the demonstration of compatibility with systems onboard Indian Navy aircraft carriers would be carried out. To enhance the safety of flight testing, aircraft in this phase will be operated in an operational clean configuration, with or without CCMs, with partial internal fuel to restrict its mass, and in favourable ambient conditions like moderate Wind on Deck (WoD), restricted crosswinds, low sea states, daytime operations with good visibility, etc.

A flow chart of technology demonstration was worked out, which lists groups of activities that would be carried out to demonstrate the readiness of the aircraft to embark on the carrier for the first time. These would be conducted mainly in the SBTF, but would also include other ground and flight tests, as well as carrier wake survey. The readiness criterion for the parameters/activities is quantified in the table below in terms of achieving target values for each of the control parameters. While a presentation is made in tabular form, in my opinion, it facilitates the appreciation of the entire ground and flight test process better.

No.	*Parameter*	*Target*	*Remarks*
1.	Maximum mass for SBTF launch	-	Clean+2*R73+100% Int. Fuel (no additional pylons)
2.	Maximum value of reference AoA during launch from SBTF	20 deg	RGS launch AoA=20° WoD=0 knots
3.	Maximum/Minimum Head Wind component for launch	+15 knots / -10 knots	
4.	Maximum Cross Wind component for Launch	8 knots	
5.	Maximum mass for arrested landing on SBTF	9,900 kg	Criteria: Engaging speed & Hook Load
6.	Maximum Sink Rate at touchdown for bolter/ arrested landing on SBTF	5.68 m/s	80% of Max Design Sink Rate (7.1 m/s)
7.	Design Hook Load to be achieved during Taxi-in engagement/Arrested Landing	45 t	100% of Design Load
8.	Maximum offset distance for Taxi-in/Arrested Landing engagement	3.0 m	
9.	Maximum offset – pitch – roll – yaw combination for arrested landing	-	As per Structural Demonstration Test points
10.	Maximum Cross Wind component for arrested landing	8 knots	
11.	Maximum EMI levels for aircraft ground tests	As per Standards	

Target Values of Control Parameters during Technology Demonstration

It was ensured that both prototypes of the LCA Navy, namely, NP1 and NP2, identified for participating in the technology demonstration phase afloat (including bolter/wave-offs from carrier as part of TD-Ashore) were tested and certified to EMI levels in excess of the highest level possible at any location on the ship with minimum emitters active. This ensured safety while permitting the progress of testing and establishing other critical activities for the TD-Afloat phase. It may be noted that this EMI level on the ship may be lower than that required in the Mil specifications.

Targets for the technology demonstration block, i.e., declaring readiness of the LCA Navy to embark on the carrier (TD-Ashore) followed by the conduct of the first phase of sea trials (TD-Afloat), were listed in detail. Targets defined for the next two blocks, namely, testing with stores for projecting operational capability and more severe tests for establishing integrity of design, would evolve from experience gained during the technology demonstration block. These would be ratified progressively by design, simulation, and flight test teams in consultation with certification authorities to ensure that adequate safety margins are maintained during tests while achieving adequate severity of tests to validate the models and qualify to progress to the next phase of testing.

Discussions between design, testing, and certification teams were initiated to identify the quantum of flight testing envisaged to complete the technology demonstration phase. Some inputs were also received from the carrier suitability division of the US Navy. Simultaneously, a route-to-certification document was prepared based on phase-wise targets that identified and defined timelines, utilisation of aircraft and other assets to achieve short-term and overall programme objectives. The overall aircraft test strategy was evolved to meet the challenging certification requirements of a typical deck-based aircraft. The landing gear would undergo functional, drop, and strength tests. The arrester hook would be subjected to functional, static strength, and dynamic tests. The LEVCON structure would have control surface tests at sub-system level with associated structure (air intake, stub wing, and linking structure). Ground Vibration Tests (GVT) and Structural Coupling Tests (SCT) would provide necessary inputs to control law design. Aircraft-level structural test specimen testing in the main airframe static test rig would be carried out to check the overall structural integrity. Various equipment of the aircraft or line replacement units would need to be qualified to the arrested recovery shock standard. All in all, it was a great and challenging time for the LCA Navy team.

At the overall aircraft level, various flight tests would be carried out to ensure that the requirements are met. These include flights to estimate the effect of the nose droop of the front fuselage, followed by flights in the basic land-based envelope to assess the effect of LEVCON. Low-speed and high-angle-of-attack handling characteristics would be checked towards validating real-time simulation of ski-jump take-off and arrested recovery. This would be followed by engine bleed shut-off tests and validation of thrust readiness logic prior to take-off. Once these build-up tests were successfully achieved, the stage was set for a ski-jump take-off at the SBTF, 'Taxi-in' engagement at SBTF, followed by flight engagement and finally, arrested recovery and launch from an aircraft carrier.

While some insights were provided in the previous sections, the CCT or CSD of the LCA Navy was divided into different phases to facilitate a stepped approach to test/demonstration. Detailed planning was then carried out to execute these stages in consultation with various stakeholders, including the flight test team, certification agency, quality assurance agency, various design teams, and the Indian Navy. These phases are briefly described in the subsequent paragraphs.

Phase-1: *Ski-jump take-off at SBTF with 40% LG and Structural Loads*: After the first successful ski-jump launch of NP1 on 20 December 2014, there was a need to carry out further launches to explore the full capability of the aircraft with landing gear and structural load limits up to 40 per cent of expected loads. About 15 ski-jump launches were planned during this phase to explore aspects of performance, handling qualities, and loads in a limited envelope. The objective was also to reduce the distance to take-off till the Restraining Gear System (RGS) position located 200 m ahead of the ramp exit. Ramp take-off from the RGS would enable full afterburner thrust to be stabilised prior to aircraft roll. RGS roll-over tests with engine dry thrust were carried out during the December 2014 campaign. The aircraft would be equipped with two outboard pylons and an R73 (CCM) missile launcher. R73 missiles may be installed for later launches based on the results of initial launches. Internal fuel quantities would be determined in the individual sortie test plan.

There are prerequisites to be met, starting with the clearance for up to 40 per cent loads from landing gear and structures perspective. The digital flight control computer software needed to be updated with improvements in the ski-jump mode, based on feedback of the first launch, along with compatible avionics software. Sink rate clearance up to 3.0 m/s for landing gear and aircraft structural loads was another key clearance requirement. The flight control system software was evaluated in a real-time simulator with modified control law. With these done, the certification agency would provide the Certificate of Design (CoD) and Flight Clearance Note (FCN). Having all these, the Safety Review Board (SRB) for aircraft clearance would be convened and clearance accorded after due deliberations.

A ski-jump launch profile with typical parameters is shown in the graphic below. The launch weight is strongly dependent on ambient temperature, wind-on-deck and the permissible exit angle of attack (α). This governs the permissible launch mass from the SBTF / Ship.

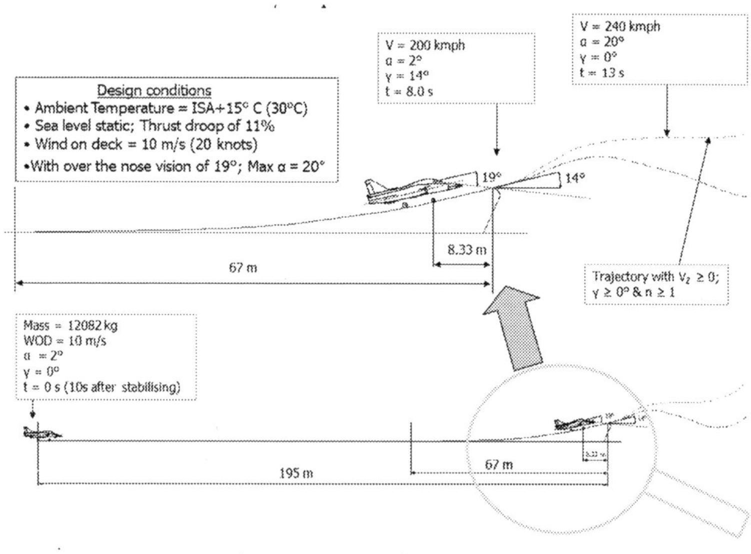

Typical Parameters of Ski-Jump Launch

*Phase-2: Aircraft dummy approaches and "Touch & Go" at SBTF (Up to 4 m/s sink rate)** During the first LCA Navy Prototype (NP1) campaign in December 2014 at the SBTF for ski-jump launch, a few dummy approaches were also carried out for preliminary evaluation of handling qualities of the aircraft.

Based on the feedback of initial approaches that had been carried out at SBTF, the Control Law (CLAW) was suitably updated. The aircraft needed to have the flight clearance to fly with LEVCON deflected to -30 degrees, in addition to LEVCON 0 degree. For this phase of testing, the sink rate clearance was increased to 4.0 m/s, and extensive Real-Time Simulation (RTS) evaluation for approach handling qualities was carried out. Following these, the update of CoD and FCN for LEVCON -30 degrees was obtained from the certification agency.

'Hook-to-Eye' is an important parameter governing the landing approach to an aircraft carrier for a flare-less landing. When the pilot is viewing the Optical Landing System (OLS), the hook must 'see' the arrester wire on the ship. This geometric relationship varies based on the type of aircraft. The OLS has the capability to adjust to this variation in 'Hook-to-Eye' distance depending on the type and size of the aircraft. The LCA Navy 'Hook-to-Eye' diagram is shown below.

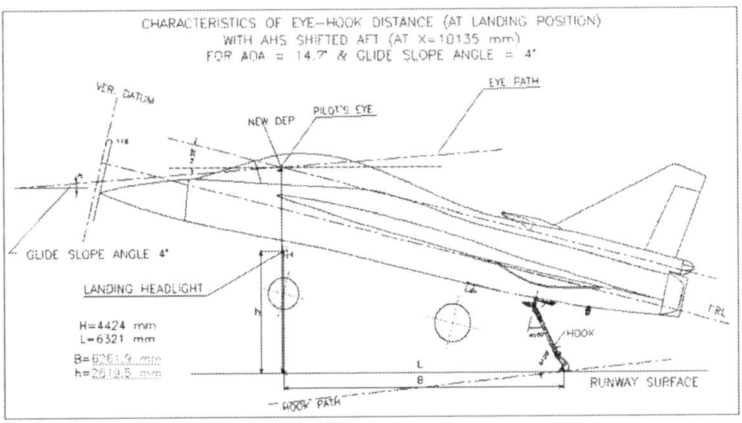

Hook-to-Eye Drawing for the LCA Navy

There are typically three wires on an aircraft carrier (US Navy carriers have four wires). The spacing between each of the wires is 12 m. The intended hook touchdown point (HTDP) is halfway between the first and second wires. If an aircraft is on the correct glide path, then the hook will catch the second wire (middle). If the aircraft is slightly low, the hook will catch the first wire, and similarly, if the aircraft is slightly high, the hook will catch the third wire.

A sketch indicating lateral and angular offsets is shown below. Allowable offsets are dictated by the size of the aircraft carrier. On the *Vikramaditya* class of aircraft carriers, the maximum lateral offset can be 3 m and the maximum angular offset can be 3° to remain within the safe landing zone. However, on the US Navy's Nimitz class of aircraft carriers, the permitted lateral offsets is 6 m, since they are significantly bigger.

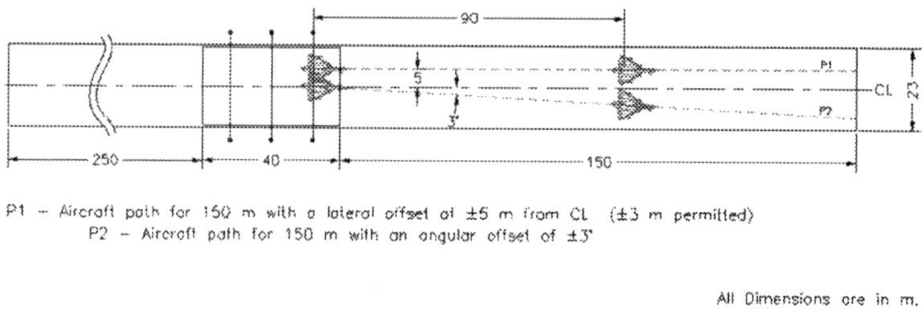

Sketch showing Lateral and Angular Offsets

***Phase-3:** Aircraft dummy approaches and 'Touch and Go' at SBTF (up to 5.68 m/s sink rate)*: Based on the results of Phase-2 tests of carrier approaches and 'touch and go', tests would be continued for higher sink rates of up to 5.68 m/s. During this phase, dummy approaches to the *Vikramaditya* may also be planned to provide a first impression of the aircraft's handling qualities in an actual carrier environment. The aircraft needs to have the flight clearance to fly with LEVCON deflected to –30 degrees, in addition to LEVCON at 0 degrees. The steering actuator ultimate strength test must be completed, and the aircraft structural test specimen must be checked up to limit load. With a sink rate clearance of up to 5.68 m/s, an update of the CoD and flight clearance would be obtained.

***Phase-4:** Ski-jump take-off with Stores (maximum possible take-off mass & loads)*: In Phase-1, initial ski-jump launches were planned with loads restricted to 40 per cent of the allowed loads on the aircraft. This phase continues the testing up to the maximum take-off mass and loads permissible at the SBTF. The aircraft will be equipped with two outboard pylons and R73 missiles, and the Derby missile launcher and missiles will be installed progressively. Based on the allowable mass, it was planned to launch the aircraft with centre-line drop tank. Clearance of the aircraft was necessary for full loads expected from landing gear and structures perspective, up to take-off mass of 12,200kg. Expected loads were evaluated through ADAMS simulation and correlated with the ski-jump Phase-1 tests for satisfactory performance. The aircraft in the air defence configuration would undergo flight testing to carry out Parametric Identification (PID) and flutter tests. The requisite flight control system software will be ported into the DFCC (digital flight control computer), along with compatible avionics software. An aircraft structural test specimen will need to undergo limit load tests of the main and nose landing gears (MLG and NLG). Once these prerequisites are met, the CoD and FCN would be updated, leading to safety review board clearance.

Phase-5: *'Taxi-in' arrested engagement at SBTF (up to 36 tons of arrester hook load)*: In this phase, the aircraft is 'taxied in' to the arresting gear, with the hook extended just short of the arrester wires on the landing area of the SBTF. It commences with lower-energy engagements with lower speeds and masses, gradually progressing to higher energy levels based on the satisfactory performance of the aircraft and data analysis from the structural instrumentation.

Extensive simulations were conducted to establish the required run-up and follow-through for the 'taxi-in' arrested recovery tests at the shore-based test facility in Goa, as outlined in the table below. A picture of the LCA Navy arrestment at SBTF is shown below.

- Accelerate- stop distances for Ac mass of 9500 kg, Sea level, IRA conditions
- Braking factor taken as 0.78
- Thrust factor in accn phase taken as 0.9 to take care of thrust droop effect
- Parachute drag area taken as 11 sq. m

Brake/Chute Deployment	*Target Speed (knots)*	*Dist. to Accelerate (m)*	*Dist. during 3s Dwell (m)*	*Dist. to Decelerate (m)*
Brake only	50	65	79	113
	75	147	119	250
	100	263	158	435
	130	447	206	713
Brake + Chute	50	65	79	108
	75	147	119	217
	100	263	158	342
	130	447	206	497

- For 400m approach distance, engaging speed of 125 knots achievable
- Stopping Distance after touch down with landing mass of 9500 kg:
  - At 150 knots CAS: 855 m
  - At 161 knots CAS: 934 m

Simulation results for 'Taxi-in' Engagement at SBTF

LCA Navy Arresting at SBTF

Based on the notional 'roll-in' or 'taxi-in' matrix discussed with the US Navy, 'Arresting Gear Compatibility and Performance Test Matrix' was derived. A table depicting this matrix can be seen in the section on tables at page 239. This matrix enables validation and aircraft-arresting gear compatibility checks at various engaging speeds and lateral offsets for landing. Based on the results of each test, a simulation model would be compared, and further tests would progress in incremental steps. A detailed structural integrity and handling qualities test matrix was also developed, appended at the end of this book in the section on tables at page 240. This matrix outlines testing conditions with a gradual and graded build-up in a logical sequence to carry out carrier compatibility tests.

The standards of preparation and prerequisites for phase-5 of the CCT for both the LCA Navy prototypes, NP1 and NP2, would be to ensure that the arrester hook is integrated. The limit load test of the arrester hook on the structural test specimen needed to be successfully completed. After the installation of the arrester hook and fairing, the integration of the arrester hook system hydraulics and electrical systems was to be completed. There was a need for modifications to the jet fuel starter exhaust and associated items. Arrested recovery clearance up to 80 per cent of the arrester hook load (36 tons) would be accorded at this stage. With these preparatory activities complete, flights with the arrester hook installed were carried out to check for handling qualities and flutter. In parallel, clearance of LRUs for arrested recovery shock testing would be obtained. As before, the update to CoD and FCN would be completed, leading to safety review board clearance.

Phase-6: *'Taxi-in' arrested engagement at SBTF (up to 45 tons of arrester hook load)*: Based on limit load tests on the arrester hook on the structural test specimen and ADAMS simulations on various loading conditions, the extent of test points that could be covered in phase-5 has been defined above. Full arrested recovery clearance based on the ultimate test of the arrester hook on the structural test specimen would then be accorded. This would be followed by an update to CoD and FCN. This is a very important step as the aircraft would undergo the arrested recovery shocks at higher loads. The safety review board would deliberate on the data gathered so far and grant clearance for this phase of the flight test.

Phase-7: *Flight engagement at SBTF (up to 36 tons of arrester hook load)*: Once handling qualities evaluation and taxi-in tests up to limit loads are carried out at the SBTF, based on the allowed energy levels, initial flight engagements can be initiated. The energy levels of arrested recovery can be increased up to the permitted limit load tests achieved in phase-5 of taxi-in engagement up to 36 tons. The aircraft would already be in the requisite configuration for flight engagement at this stage.

Phase-8: *Flight engagement at SBTF (up to 45 tons of arrester hook load)*: Initial flight engagements would be carried out in Phase-7 as indicated above. Based on the completion of ultimate load tests of the arrester hook on the structural test specimen, higher energy flight engagements would be carried out as per the test matrix developed.

Phase-9: *Arrested recovery and ski-jump take-off on aircraft carrier*: Based on tests completed in the preceding sections, the aircraft would be ready for aircraft carrier demonstration. However, based on the successful handling qualities evaluation phase, dummy approaches and 'touch and go' on the aircraft carrier were planned as an initial step prior to the actual recovery and launch from the ship. Unlike a land-based operating philosophy, the approach involves a flare-less landing, where the aircraft attitude is held steady until touchdown on the ship. The moment the aircraft touches down, the throttle is opened fully so that the aircraft will have adequate thrust to get airborne again and attempt a recovery in case of non-engagement of the hook, in what is loosely called a 'Thump and Bash'. This is called a 'bolter' if the pilot comes in with the intent to arrest on the deck, but misses the wire due to circumstances beyond his control and the aircraft has sufficient thrust to get airborne for another attempt. If there is a successful arrester hook engagement, the aircraft is stopped in 90 m and still has full thrust. Once the flight deck officer on the ship is satisfied with a positive recovery, he asks the pilot to cut the throttle. Due to the release of load, the arrester wire tension is reduced and the aircraft 'walks-back'. The wire releases from the hook and thus, the hook can be retracted to permit the aircraft to taxi on the flight deck away from the landing area.

With sufficient confidence gained in simulation tests at the SBTF, and the effect of the ship's burble and clarity of the EMI environment having been validated, history was made on 11 January 2020 when the LCA Navy successfully carried out an arrested recovery on board the aircraft carrier, INS *Vikramaditya*, followed by a ski-jump launch the very next day on 12 January 2020. A picture of the recovery and launch of the LCA Navy on INS *Vikramaditya* is shown below. It should be noted that during this phase, certain deck movement and handling tests were also carried out to validate the aircraft-to-ship interface. In addition, certain aircraft maintenance activities were carried out in the ship's hangar.

Arrested Recovery and Ski-Jump Launch on INS Vikramaditya

13

Control Law (CLAW) Development

In this chapter, we shall briefly discuss the challenges and lessons learnt during the development of the Control Laws required for LCA Navy. External shaping of LCA Navy has a significant degree of commonality with the Air Force trainer variant of the Light Combat Aircraft (LCA AF Trainer). It has the same primary flight control surfaces – the four elevons and one rudder – and shares the same angular rate, acceleration, and air data sensors as the LCA Air Force fighter variant. Hence, the primary flight control system hardware responsible for stabilisation and control of the aircraft was assumed to be the same as that of the LCA Air Force fighter.

However, since the LCA Navy was intended to be operated from an aircraft carrier, it was necessary to make significant changes to the aircraft in terms of strengthening its landing gear and airframe structure to withstand the strong forces it would experience when landing on the carrier. An arrester hook also had to be installed to recover the aircraft on the ship using its arresting cable. Therefore, the dry empty mass of the aircraft was expected to be significantly higher, resulting in higher landing speeds as well. It was understood fairly early in the design phase that some aerodynamic augmentation would be necessary to reduce the landing speed of the aircraft to be compatible with the arresting gear system of the aircraft carrier.

The aerodynamics team came up with symmetric Leading-Edge Vortex CONtrollers (LEVCON) on either side of the fuselage at the wing leading edge as a solution expected to reduce landing speeds. It was proposed that during landing, LEVCONs would be deflected up by 30 degrees to generate extra lift. Also, since this lift would be created significantly ahead of the centre of gravity of the aircraft, the pitch-up moment created by LEVCONs would need to be compensated by the elevons by rotating downwards to further augment the lift. It was also found that by deflecting LEVCONs downwards, it could improve the lift and reduce the drag at higher speeds, which would improve the overall performance of the aircraft, especially at higher subsonic speeds.

Since LEVCONs were to play an important role in the overall stabilisation and control of the aircraft, it was decided to place them under the purview of the flight control system. The aerodynamics team computed the aerodynamic loads that would act on them across the entire flight envelope. It was decided that sophisticated hinge-line rotary actuators would be installed on the aircraft to handle the strong forces on the LEVCONs, deflect them automatically to optimum angles at different speeds, and smartly handle any failures that may occur by freezing the LEVCONs at the failed position.

Along with the reduction in landing speeds, another important requisite of a naval aircraft is its ability to precisely hold on to a fixed speed during landing. This requires control over the thrust generated by the engine using an auto-throttle system integrated into the engine throttle assembly via a back drive mechanism. Auto-throttle has to be integrated into the FCS as well, and to make it function, new interfaces were therefore necessary between the engine and the throttle lever.

The need to drive the LEVCONs and facilitate the auto throttle, a new onboard flight control computer called the LEVCON Air Data Computer (LADC) was conceptualised. LADCs are augmented versions of the Air Data Computers (ADC) of the fighter and trainer LCAs with significantly enhanced functionality. LADCs, in addition to hosting air data algorithms, contain servo electronics for LEVCON actuators and have the capability to communicate with the Full Authority Digital Engine Controller (FADEC) and with the throttle lever. LADCs also have several new interfaces with cockpit switches and instruments like Angle of Attack (AoA) indexer and AoA lights on the nose undercarriage.

The task of designing control laws for all variants of the LCA was entrusted to the National CLAW team that was formed by picking scientists and engineers with a good background in controls, flight mechanics, and simulation from the National Aerospace Laboratories (NAL), Aeronautical Development Agency (ADA), Centre for Artificial Intelligence & Robotics (CAIR) and Hindustan Aeronautics Ltd. (HAL). Dr. Abdul Kalam created this team in 1992. Some preliminary work on ski-jump take-off control laws was carried out during the feasibility study phase.

The national CLAW team's first introduction to the LCA Navy came about in the 1998-99 time frame when the Indian Navy requested ADA to carry out a feasibility study of modifying the LCA Air Force variant to operate from aircraft carriers. The first big challenge from the controls point of view was to prove that the LCA Navy could perform a ski-jump take-off while carrying sufficient fuel and external payload. The CLAW team put together a team of four scientists to set up a high-fidelity six Degrees of Freedom (6-DoF) simulation platform, carry out performance calculations, and come up with an optimum ski-jump take-off control strategy.

Ski-jump take-off is a challenging control problem because the Air Force variants typically take-off from field runways after a ground run of about 800m, whereas on the carrier the net runway available is only about one fourth (~200m). Typically, aircraft leave the deck at about 100 knots of speed, which is about 40-50 knots short of the wing-borne speed. To aid take-off, carriers are provided with a ski jump in the last about 50 to 60m. This ski-jump forces the aircraft to rotate and to leave the deck at about a 14 degree flight path angle and about 6m higher than the deck height. This change in trajectory allows the aircraft a small time window after leaving the deck to pick up lift and speed to attain wing-borne flight. It is desired that after leaving the deck, the aircraft must maintain a continuous climbing trajectory, which means its rate of climb should always be positive. Flight control laws need to use this time window to generate sufficient lift and ensure a positive rate of climb throughout.

There were two contrasting opinions on whether it is beneficial to pitch the aircraft up quickly to a high angle of attack and generate sufficient lift to balance the aircraft weight or to pitch it up slowly, keeping the aircraft drag low, and allow engine thrust to increase speed to the desired take-off value. The team extensively studied this problem and used mathematical optimisation-based methods and arrived at an optimal strategy that could generate good take-off profiles.

Ski-jump take-off is a dramatic manoeuvre. As the aircraft goes up the ramp, about 3g vertical acceleration and up to 25 deg/s pitch rate is experienced by the pilot for about 1.5 seconds. The moment the aircraft leaves the ramp, all the forces generated by the landing gears instantly drop to zero, reducing vertical acceleration to almost zero until sufficient lift is generated by the wings. All this is happening while the aircraft continues to pitch up to obtain a desired angle of attack. Such pitch rates and large variation in forces could be disorienting to the pilot and he may not be able to take the right actions. So, it was decided to design control laws that would facilitate an automatic, hands-free take-off. A take-off controller was implemented on a Real Time Simulator (RTS), and test pilots evaluated ski-jump take-offs with different aircraft weights and ambient conditions. The automatic and hands-free nature of take-offs was well appreciated by the pilots, and the LCA Navy was found to be a feasible design based on this study. This was one of the critical enhancing features in the LCA Navy aircraft development and led to the start of the ski-jump CLAW design.

The first effort was to integrate the LCA Navy related data into the six degrees of freedom simulation platform. It required the incorporation of validated ski-jump profiles on the SBTF, Indigenous Aircraft Carrier (IAC), and INS *Vikramaditya*. Some of the subsystems that required substantial modelling updates included new models for landing gear, the engine database, arrester hook characteristics, and arresting gear mechanism data.

The Ski-jump take-off mode of the control laws was designed in two phases. In the first phase, the mode designed was called the 'basic' ski-jump take-off mode. This design was initiated by first studying the behaviour of the LCA Navy with the existing LCA Air Force control laws as it was launched from the ski-jump ramp. Simulations showed that the existing CLAW did not produce a good ski-jump take-off behaviour, primarily due to the effect of the ramp on aircraft dynamics. As the aircraft goes up the ramp, it experiences significant pitch rate and normal acceleration. CLAW believed that this was an uncommanded signal and must be counteracted, which it did effectively by generating a large nose-down elevator on the ramp. This nose-down elevator was not effective while the aircraft was on the ramp due to the landing gears generating significant nose-up forces. However, once the aircraft left the ramp, these landing gear forces suddenly disappeared, causing the nose-down elevator to produce a nose-down behaviour, which was clearly undesirable. Ideally, the aircraft's angle of attack should continuously rise to quickly sustain the weight of the aircraft, but the nose-down elevator at the ramp exit did not allow this to happen smoothly.

This problem was addressed by defining a Ski-Jump Take-Off (SJTO) mode, which the pilot could invoke using a newly introduced 'SKI' switch in the cockpit. When the mode was turned on, the pitch rate and normal acceleration feedbacks were clipped to a small positive number until the aircraft left the ramp. This effectively prevented nose-down elevator on the ramp, but this clipping had to be removed as soon as the aircraft entered the air.

The LCA Navy is an unstable aircraft, and the pitch rate is an important stabilising signal. Clipped pitch rate feedback would not allow CLAW to stabilise the aircraft, resulting in uncontrolled pitch-up and eventual departure from controlled flight conditions. After much deliberation, it was decided that the weight-off-wheel signal from the main wheels would be used to detect when the aircraft had left the ramp and to remove clipping of pitch rate and normal acceleration signals.

Another important aspect of the ski-jump was the overall performance of the aircraft. Fighter aircraft need to carry sufficient fuel and weapons to carry out different kinds of missions. The LCA Navy had its own defined weapon loads and fuel configurations that needed to be carried during ski-jump take-offs. The overall take-off weight that could be carried depended upon a number of external environmental factors and internal settings. The external environmental factors included the effect of variables like temperature and atmospheric pressure on engine thrust, and natural winds that determine the total lift on the aircraft. The relevant internal setting mainly was the maximum Angle of Attack (AoA) to which the aircraft should be driven in order to generate the desired lift. It was found through simulation that by changing the trim setting of the elevator, it was possible to drive the aircraft to higher AoA, so the trim setting became another factor in determining ski-jump performance.

During the design and simulation process, it was realised that the SJTO CLAW mode as defined above will have limitations. The design might allow take-offs to happen, but this kind of design would not be sufficient to ensure robustness and guarantee consistent take-off performance in varying circumstances. Hence, it was decided to call this a basic SJTO mode, and work was initiated in parallel to develop an advance SJTO mode that would ensure a more robust design. In this design, the main performance parameter – angle of attack – was actively pulled up to the desired value for take-off and robustly maintained until the aircraft achieved the minimum flight path angle and started climbing. Thereafter, the angle of attack was gently driven down to ensure a smooth fly away and at a gentle climb. The mode was disengaged at about 150 knots, which was higher than the wing-borne speed. This design was more appropriate for ski-jumps because, even if the aerodynamic characteristics or engine thrust or wind conditions changed during take-off, the mode ensured that the desired AoA was always achieved. This design was also completed, implemented and test-flown in several of the ski-jump campaigns that were undertaken subsequently.

Preparing for the first ski-jump was the next major step to be taken in the LCA Navy programme. The national CLAW team played a key role in clearing the LCA Navy for its first ever ski-jump take-off from the SBTF in Goa. This was considered natural, because the safety of flight post a ski-jump was indeed the responsibility of the CLAW design team. Also, since the ski-jump take-off was a very dynamic manoeuvre with aircraft rotation after ski-jump determined by various forces generated by the landing gears and timings of the rise of AoA determined by CLAW, the overall performance of the aircraft could only be determined and predicted using detailed simulation responses. The development of this high-fidelity simulation set-up was a responsibility that was also undertaken up by the CLAW team. In fact, this set-up played a vital role in verification of the CLAW design as well. Hence, validation of the simulator was indeed chosen as the first step towards clearing the aircraft for a ski-jump take-off.

Three subsystems were considered the most important and their modelling and simulation needed to be validated. These were the aerodynamic characteristics, the landing gear characteristics, and the engine thrust. Aerodynamic model validation was carried out using standard parameter estimation and system identification techniques (PID) up to high angles of attack with slats retracted and landing gear extended. Data analysis confirmed that some of the aerodynamic characteristics needed to be updated in the simulator, and these were promptly implemented.

Landing gear modelling update was trickier. The aircraft landing gears could not be subjected to the forces that they would feel on the ramp without the aircraft actually going over it at the high take-off speeds. So, it was decided to focus on validation of only the stiffness and damping characteristics of the three landing gears by running the aircraft over some specific forms of disturbance. A steel plate about 50mm height similar to a speed breaker was bolted onto the taxiway at the HAL airport in Bengaluru. This was extensively used and the aircraft was made to run over it at multiple speeds. The actual responses of the aircraft were compared with the aircraft model going over the same plate modelled in the simulation at matching speeds. The landing gear models were thus validated both by the CLAW and the landing gear teams.

Thrust model validation was also carried out using a number of taxi trials, both in Bengaluru and Goa (~1km altitude and sea-level respectively). These taxi trials up to different speeds helped in understanding the aircraft speed build-up over distances under different temperature and atmospheric pressure conditions, thereby validating the thrust, ground friction, and drag characteristics of the aircraft. Parameter estimation test flights up to expected AoA ranges during ski-jump take-off were also used to characterise fly-away behaviour of the aircraft and the effect of higher AoA on the engine thrust. These were significant confidence-building measures taken one step at a time.

After the validation of these specific aircraft and engine characteristics, an in-depth CLAW evaluation was carried out. Each possible failure envisaged in the system was simulated both in real-time simulation set-up as well as in the hardware-in-the-loop simulator (Iron Bird) to provide pilots with sufficient insight into aircraft's behaviour in case the failures actually occurred during flight. The results were segregated into three categories, with the first being the one that resulted in higher than predicted performance and required minimal pilot intervention, the second resulting in slightly lower performance and necessitating the pilot to intervene using pitch and roll stick inputs to achieve a safe fly-away, and the third category in which the take-off was severely hampered and no safe recovery of the aircraft was possible. The third category, for example, included engine failure or complete flight control system failure, and the simulation provided pilots with an insight into how much time would be available for safely ejecting from the aircraft. All these results were presented to a Safety Review Board (SRB) with experts from all system disciplines and certifying agencies, and clearance for the first ski-jump was accorded.

The idea of 'Free Roll' from an aircraft carrier take-off path was then explored. The LCA Navy had a powerful GE F404-IN20 engine, which had its own dynamics. So, when the pilot commanded a full reheat thrust using the throttle lever in the cockpit, the engine would go up to its max RPM and then, with a small delay, light up the reheat, generating its maximum thrust. Also, the engine had its own internal heating cycle. Its thrust became optimal when the engine heated up. It is desirable that the aircraft remains stationary until this process of thrust build-up is complete, so that when it starts moving, its acceleration is the maximum possible.

The aircraft is normally held in place by the wheel brakes. However, the brakes cannot hold the aircraft when it begins producing such a large thrust. In fact, at around 60–70 per cent thrust level, the brakes cannot hold the aircraft, and the wheels start skidding. This is dangerous because the tyres may burst due to skidding. So, on the ship deck as well as on the SBTF, a restraining gear system or hydraulic chocks were provided to hold the aircraft in place at the main wheels as the pilot warms up the engine and engages reheat. RGS is a hydraulically operated plate-like device that is hinged up from the ground and against which the main tyres rest. Once the engine begins to produce its maximum thrust, the restraining gears are lowered and the aircraft starts to roll.

While the start from RGS is the preferred mode of a ski-jump take-off, if sufficient take-off roll distance is available, it is also possible to perform a free roll, in which the aircraft is placed at any desired distance from the ski-jump ramp and held in place using brakes at whatever max throttle settings the brakes can hold. The pilot then releases the brakes and engages reheat to initiate the take-off run. The advantage of a free roll take-off lies in the flexibility to obtain the desired ramp exit speed. If the RGS-based run does not ensure sufficient exit speed, the free roll can be deployed wherever possible to achieve that. Free rolls can also be used to increase the take-off mass. This additional level of safety was particularly relevant for the first ski-jump launch at the SBTF, as there were a number of uncertainties, including the wind conditions. This step again served as a confidence-building measure in the overall process.

Proper planning for all shipboard take-offs is particularly important, and even more so for ski-jumps, as the only accelerating device is the aircraft's engine. A significant effort was put in by the team to create detailed performance graphs for the LCA Navy. The configuration chosen for the first ski-jump was a clean aircraft without outboard missiles, and with minimum fuel – just enough for taxiing, engine warm up, take-off, followed by landing – to keep the aircraft as light as possible. A free roll take-off was the chosen means for take-off roll, with a take-off distance long enough to handle even emergencies like afterburner flame-out over the ramp. As a result, in the nominal case without failures, the first ski-jump was expected to reach a minimum flight path angle of about 6.5 degrees! Performance charts were created to calculate the free roll distance based on variations of winds, temperature, ambient pressure, and the target angle of attack needed to attain the target ramp exit speed. Headwinds and tailwinds were also accounted for in the simulation and calculation of the free roll distance.

The maiden ski–jump launch of the LCA Navy's first prototype NP1 took place on the morning of 20 December 2014. The day was clear, but the winds were from behind (tailwinds), which was not so good. Tailwinds mean that the aircraft needs to achieve a much higher ground speed to reach the desired fly-away speed. However, this situation was accounted for in the performance graphs, and the aircraft was placed at the appropriate distance away from the ramp. The take-off run was smooth, the aircraft entered and exited the ramp well, but the aircraft pitched up a little more than planned and settled at a slightly higher flight path angle and corresponding trajectory. There was sufficient fuel in the aircraft to perform the planned circuit, and the aircraft landed back safely. The iconic picture of the first LCA Navy prototype, NP1, taking-off over the ski-jump at the SBTF in Goa is shown below.

The Maiden Ski-Jump of NP1 on 20 December 2014

This was a great milestone event, and all the excitement was well captured in a number of news articles and YouTube videos! However, there was much for the CLAW team to introspect on, as the take-off behaviour differed significantly from what had been planned. Data analysis revealed that ramp entry and exit speeds were higher by about 5 knots, the maximum angle of attack was about 3 degrees higher, and the minimum flight path angle was about 5 degrees higher! Behaviour during the ground roll as well as in the air also revealed significantly higher control activity. All these aspects were well captured by extensive instrumentation on the aircraft. They were looked at one by one, and answers were found. The higher speeds were due to two reasons: while placing the aircraft on the take-off position, the CLAW team calculated the position of the aircraft's C.G, whereas in reality, the aircraft nose was placed at that distance, thereby adding a few more extra metres to the run. Secondly, the entire run to the ramp entry had a mild slope downwards, which was not modelled in the simulation. The bigger issue was the extra pitch up.

As mentioned earlier, CLAW clips pitch rate on the ground, and after leaving the ramp, full pitch rate feedback is turned on. The criterion for deciding the ramp exit was the 'weight-off-wheel' switch located on the main landing gears. The criterion looked good on all kinds of simulations, both normal and in failures. However, Weight-off-wheel switch dynamics were not well simulated. The main landing gears for the LCA Navy are significantly longer than the LCA Air Force variants and have a long stroke as well. The weight-off-wheel switch becomes enabled when landing gears are fully extended. On the ramp, due to large loads, the main landing gears compress significantly, and the switch remains in the open condition. As the load is relieved on exit, the main landing gears extend in a damped manner, and at the end of the stroke, the weight-off-wheel signal is received by the flight control system. This process takes close to 1.5s, so during the first ski-jump event, for 1.5s after ramp exit, the FCS did not know that the aircraft had left the ramp and did not use full pitch rate feedback. Hence, the aircraft continued to pitch up for a little extra time with CLAW not responding to its behaviour. After 1.5s, CLAW produced a sharp nose-down elevator command to arrest the pitch up, and the aircraft began to fly away well. Since the peak angle of attack was more than three degrees higher, the lift was significantly higher for a few extra seconds, generating a much higher trajectory. While the extra performance was great, this was in some ways disappointing, but a great learning experience for the whole team. It was decided to defer further ski-jump trials until this issue was thoroughly analysed and effectively fixed.

It became clear that another criterion was necessary to detect ramp exit. There are a few clear signatures that aircraft signals show when it enters and exits the ramp. The pitch angle rises from about 2 degrees to 17 degrees, flight path angle increases to 14 degrees, normal acceleration rises and drops close to zero at the ramp exit, and so on. Normal acceleration and pitch angle were chosen as signals that were most useful to detect ramp entry and exit. All other feedbacks that caused excess control surface activity were toned down on the ground, and the pitch up suppression feedback signals were strengthened. Some typical graphs, including the actual flight test graph (on the right), are shown below.

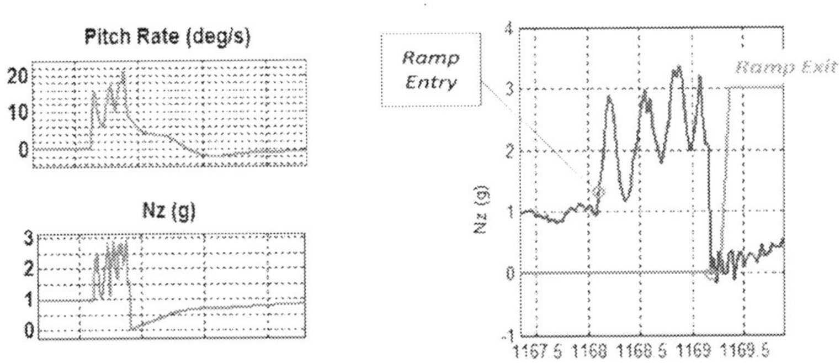

Control Signals for Ramp Entry & Exit

This updated 'basic' mode was then flight tested several times, and aircraft behaviour was found satisfactory and repeatable. There was a good correlation with the simulation model, and, hence, sufficient confidence was built up among the team. The trials included ski-jumps from the restraining gear system, with outboard missiles, and with gradually increasing weight and reduced minimum flight path angle. As can be seen, there was a gradual process of optimising the aircraft ski-jump launch performance, ensuring robustness and repeatability. This gave sufficient confidence to move even further to explore the night launch over the ski-jump. A picture of one of the night launches is shown on page 84, clearly indicating the engine exhaust path as the exit trail over the ski-jump. All these tests helped in validating the simulation model and the performance model. This resulted in the aircraft being declared ready for ski-jump launch from an aircraft carrier.

Let us now look at the CLAW design for landing. If take-off is considered a challenge for naval aircraft, landing back on a moving deck of an aircraft carrier is a much bigger one. Ski-jumps offer a good margin in terms of performance due to the climbing trajectory that leaves the aircraft on, and if the control law design is optimised well, take-off becomes, to a large extent, an automated task. Landing, however, is a different ball game. It is completely a piloted task, and a lot of skill is needed to guide the aircraft down a controlled flight path to the touchdown point accurately and then get arrested. Well-designed control laws for landing can, however, play a significant role in easing the task for the pilots.

The LCA Navy is equipped with an arrester hook mechanism for arrested landing. This hook is lowered by the pilot when he is ready to land the aircraft. The arrester gear mechanism on the ship has cables running across the landing strip that facilitate engagement with the aircraft hook and bring the aircraft to halt in 90m, using the concept of a constant run-out. The characteristics of the ship's arresting gear are adjusted depending upon the weight of the aircraft at landing in order to achieve the same run-out of 90m at all times.

The landing task has three aspects which require the pilot's attention, namely, the horizontal alignment of the aircraft along the centreline of the landing strip (or 'the line-up'), the sink rate of the aircraft at touchdown (determined by the glide slope control), and the speed relative to the carrier that governs the engaging speed. Line-up corrections are normally done by applying a bank angle that helps the aircraft to turn till its heading matches up with the runway direction. Glide slope control requires precision tracking of the approach path right till the touchdown point. The approach needs to be steady with minimal changes in aircraft pitch attitude. Aircraft speed plays an important role in determining the aircraft sink rate at touchdown, which has to be within the acceptable limits as imposed by the aircraft structural design. The arrester gear mechanism on the ship also has restrictions on the maximum speed at which it can allow the incoming aircraft to get arrested – roughly around 140 knots.

Typically, all the three tasks need to be carried out simultaneously by the pilot, and this significantly increases the workload for landing. To add to the complexity, modern naval aircraft need to fly at speeds much lower than the shore runway speeds. The interaction between drag, lift, and thrust at these low speeds becomes more complex. So, any extra help that flight controls can provide to ease the pilot workload is highly desirable.

For the LCA Navy, a unique control law mode for landing was designed and called 'Approach AoA Hold Controller' (AAHC). As the name suggests, the mode holds the angle of attack (AoA) during landing and forces the aircraft speed to be tightly held by moving the elevon (elevator mode). This ensures that the pilot can use the engine throttle to directly control the flight path angle. When the pilot increases throttle, the aircraft speed does not change; it only begins to fly shallower, and likewise, the reduction of throttle causes the approach to become steeper. Damping in the feedback is provided by the aircraft speed.

One issue, however, with this kind of flying is that flight path control tends to be a bit slow. Overall engine thrust dynamics tend to be slower than the aircraft dynamics, and then trading a change in thrust to increase or decrease in the flight path is also a slow process. Besides, feedback on speed makes the whole design prone to wind disturbances close to the landing field. Two versions of this mode were designed. The initial mode, lacking throttle assisted flight path control, was flight tested and deemed inadequate for the speed hold task and was rejected by pilots.

The second and modified mode had a feed through of pilot throttle movements, causing transient variations in the angle of attack. This caused a small reduction or increase in lift transiently, which allowed quicker changes in the flight path angle, while the slower dynamics of thrust and aircraft interaction ensured that speed did not change during the manoeuvre. This design was again extensively tested and fine-tuned in the flight simulator followed by flight testing on the shore-based test facility. The dynamics were found to be adequately fast, and the design concept was well appreciated by the pilots. A picture of the symbology during development testing is shown below.

Landing view with HUD Symbology

Whatever best efforts may be put in by system designers or by pilots, arrestment on the carrier in every attempted landing can never be guaranteed. In fact, pilots are instructed each time they touchdown to open throttle, assuming that their hook is going to miss the arresting cables. This is a safe action to take because if the aircraft gets arrested, this increase in thrust at arrestment makes very little difference, and the aircraft will be stopped within the stipulated distance of about 90m. If, however, arrestment does not happen, the increase in thrust helps the aircraft to accelerate down the landing strip, ensuring a safe flyaway.

While increasing thrust is right, there is another issue that needs addressing.

These unflared touchdowns result in strong nose-down moments, which cause the nose to come down, resulting in the aircraft rolling on all three wheels on the landing strip. At the designed landing speeds, the total time that the aircraft rolls on the carrier is only about 1.5 seconds. To achieve a safe flyaway, the aircraft needs to be pitched up again to generate sufficient lift in this short time. This flyaway manoeuvre in naval parlance is called 'bolter'.

Touchdowns were simulated on a simulator with the hook up, followed by a nose-up pitch stick and the throttle pushed to the maximum rated thrust setting. The result was not very encouraging with classic aircraft control laws. It was seen that the rotation was quite slow, resulting in lower than needed lift of the aircraft by the end of the ship deck roll, causing the aircraft to sink below the level of the deck. It was clear that some significant improvement was required to enable handling of bolters.

The slow response was primarily identified to be due to pitch stick rate limit and filters. These were significantly opened up to allow the pitch stick to quickly command the elevator for rotating the aircraft. In addition, the touchdown event was also linked with an increased pitch trim command automatically. This helped improve rotation, but there was another issue. When the main wheels touchdown, the elevon (elevator mode) moved in the right direction to hold the nose-up, but when the nose wheel touched and rebounded, the elevons moved in the opposite direction, bringing the nose-down. This was clearly undesirable. So, another change in the CLAW was foreseen, as necessary.

The pitch rate feedback was disconnected until the aircraft started rotating nose-up on the deck. This change helped the elevator stay in a position that favoured aircraft nose-up. All these changes were time-limited to close to one second after the touchdown event, and this reconfigured state of control laws were named the bolter mode of CLAW. As with the other designs, this mode was also extensively tested in the simulator and fine-tuned with pilots before actual implementation on the flight control computer, followed by flight testing.

Flight trials and success! Almost 500 landing approach evaluations to the touchdown point on the shore-based test facility were carried out by three different test pilots. During the initial trials, the aircraft was flown fairly close to the touchdown point but waved off before actually contacting the ground. Numerous such approaches established confidence in the test crew that the aircraft could tightly maintain speed, flight path, and pitch attitude despite wind gusts, turbulence, and cross wind conditions. This confidence then led the crew to allow actual 'touch-and-go' manoeuvres on the SBTF. When the landing gear loads on these touchdowns were proven to be adequate, the pilots carried out numerous actual arrestments (traps) on the SBTF.

The next step, of course, was to actually carry out traps and ski-jumps from the carrier, which were successfully done in January 2020, and within a few days, 18 trap and ski-jumps were carried out from INS *Vikramaditya.* The flight control laws played a major role in enabling safe operations from the carrier. This successful demonstration proved the carrier suitability as envisaged by the LCA Navy programme office of ADA.

This chapter clearly brings out the significant differences in control laws of the Naval Version vis-à-vis Air Force Version of LCA. Introduction of LEVCON needed to be handled with a new computer called LADC. Separate control law modes for ski-jump launch and arrested recovery needed to be developed and these were iterated based on feedback from flight test. The culmination of this stupendous effort by the control law team has been the successful launch and recovery from both the SBTF and the aircraft carriers.

I wish to acknowledge the significant contribution by Dr. Amitab Saraf, Project Director at ADA, who served as the nodal point for the LCA Navy control law development and testing. He has provided significant inputs for this chapter as well.

14

LCA NAVY MK2 – AS OF MAR 2017

To meet the mission objectives of the Indian Navy and keeping in view the estimated shortfall in expected performance of the LCA Navy Mk1 (as it was redesignated in 2010), the Government of India approved the programme for the development of an improved variant of the Naval Light Combat Aircraft (LCA Navy Mk2). It was expected that this aircraft, with a higher thrust engine, would enable it to take-off from an aircraft carrier with a heavier payload, resulting in better mission performance. The LCA Navy Mk2 programme is managed by the Aeronautical Development Agency (ADA) with Hindustan Aeronautics Limited (HAL) as its principal partner. The LCA Navy Mk2 is a revised design that uses the single-seat LCA Navy Mk1 fighter (NP2) as a baseline. The objective of this section is to define the features of the LCA Navy Mk2 and its various capabilities, covering a broad description of the systems/equipment that would be installed. It was decided that the LCA Navy Mk2 would have a single seat fighter aircraft variant only. This provides significant flexibility in configuring and shaping the aircraft.

An alternate engine was contracted with a higher thrust both in the dry and afterburner regimes. Based on this, the engine deck details and a 3D CAD model of the engine were made available by the engine manufacturer, which is one of the critical starting points for aircraft design. Concept design activities of the LCA Navy Mk2 were then initiated, and a preliminary 3D CAD model of the LCA Navy Mk2 was generated as shown below.

Requirements for the design of the LCA Navy Mk2 are largely drawn from Naval Air Staff Requirements (NASR) promulgated by the Indian Navy, Air Staff Requirements (ASR) of the Indian Air Force, and other mission

Preliminary CAD Model of the LCA Navy Mk2

definition documents released by the Indian Navy from time to time. While NASR brings out detailed systems requirements for the LCA Navy to achieve carrier compatibility, it also states that all requirements listed for the LCA Air Force fighter in the ASR must be met by the LCA Navy. Accordingly, all-point performance requirements to be met by the LCA Navy are taken from the ASR, albeit it being a heavier platform. There are other requirements like certification, quality assurance, manufacturing, etc., that govern the design of the aircraft. All the requirements are consolidated, and a detailed matrix will be prepared to check the extent of compliance.

Mission performance requirements for the LCA Navy specified by the Indian Navy are used for computation of the air defence Combat Air Patrol (CAP) profile at 20,000 ft, Hi-Lo-Hi profile for the anti-shipping role and Hi-Lo-Hi profile for the ground strike role. The usage pattern of the LCA Navy defines the percentage utilisation of the aircraft on board the carrier and ashore. This is a critical requirement, based on which both aircraft and engine life are defined for design. The usage pattern, showing a breakup of carrier operations and peacetime missions, was revised by the Indian Navy in February 2015. Compliance of the LCA Navy Mk2 with all the above staff requirements and other requirements was documented and provided to the Indian Navy as a part of the System Requirement Review (SRR) held in 2015–2016 timeframes. The compliance status of mission and point performance was prepared and submitted as a separate confidential document.

During the SRR, ADA indicated to the Indian Navy team that some of the performance parameters specified in the ASR would not be met, as they were considered too restrictive. It was also brought out that these parameters may not be met by any known aircraft and accordingly, had requested them to have a relook.

We will now discuss the aircraft configuration evolution of the LCA Navy Mk2 that was planned with the experience gained and lessons learnt from the design and development of the LCA Navy Mk1. It was planned to incorporate a simpler Main Landing Gear (MLG) mechanism. This would create an extra volume within the centre fuselage and allow the new MLG to be mounted and housed. Towards this objective, it was planned to move the existing wings of the LCA Navy Mk1 outboard by 350 mm on each side and redesign a wider stub-wing fuselage fairing. This also increased the planform area of a theoretical wing from 38.4 m^2 for the LCA Navy Mk1 to 44.1 m^2 for the LCA Navy Mk2, which will support increased carrier launch and recovery masses. An increased wing area is typical of deck-based aircraft compared to their land-based versions, as is apparent from other programmes around the world. In the case of the LCA Navy Mk1, there was a marginal increase in the planform area due to the presence of LEVCON.

The existing fin of the LCA Navy Mk1 itself was adequate from the directional stability perspective, due to reduced nose droop. There was a need to redesign the rear fuselage to accommodate the bigger GE-F414-INS6 engine. Due to a higher thrust engine, there was a need to resize air intakes and ducts to match GE-F414-INS6 air volume requirements. Redesigning the front fuselage was carried out to cut down the nose droop angle and the exaggerated canopy shape of the LCA Navy Mk1, while maintaining adequate over-the-nose vision. Fuselage length was planned to be increased by about a metre. It was decided to retain the control surfaces – elevons, rudder, and LE slats – as in the LCA Navy Mk1 version.

A parametric geometry of the aircraft was created as a Computer Aided Design (CAD) model to assist the rapid evolution of different configurations of the aircraft. The primary parameters that varied were the length of the aircraft, wing location and span, cross-sectional area of the fuselage, location and shape of the air intake entry, canopy and spine shapes, Trailing Edge Extensions (TEX), and Küchemann bodies. The advantage of a parametric model is that it enables designers to quickly explore different configurations at a gross level for a first cut understanding.

The wave drag in transonic and supersonic regimes strongly depends on the cross-sectional area distribution of the aircraft. For a given volume and length, there exists an ideal area distribution that would result in the least wave drag. In transonic area ruling, the cross-sections are taken to be normal to the flight direction and compared to the ideal distribution. The closer the match, the lesser the wave drag is expected to be.

A Body of Revolution (BoR) is an axis-symmetric body created with a certain cross-sectional area distribution. A BoR corresponding to an aircraft has the same area distribution, taken normal to the flight direction, and is referred to as derived BoRs. The primary shocks that would appear on an aircraft would also appear on its BoR. Thus, the drag estimated on the BoR through Euler CFD methods is expected to capture the major phenomena that cause wave drag on an actual aircraft. However, the effect of local streamlining and interference effects cannot be captured through BoR analyses. These analyses yielded results about 50 times faster than a full aircraft analysis (Euler) and hence were ideal for studying the sensitivity of wave drag to the parameters described above for a large number of configurations. This analysis was further accelerated by developing scripts for automatic extraction of cross-sectional area distribution for various configurations.

In addition to derived BoRs, bodies whose area distribution did not correspond to any real aircraft were also studied. They are referred to as pure BoRs. Such studies were done prior to the study of derived BoRs. They enabled quantification of drag attainable with an ideal body and helped in understanding the effect of the most important parameters, namely, length, maximum cross-sectional area and its location, as well as local smoothing of the area distribution curve to avoid steep slopes and flats ('balcony' effect). This would also provide ball-park drag values compared to targeted figures. This innovative approach developed by the young team members of the LCA Navy Mk2 was extremely useful in understanding and developing potential configurations of the aircraft in the shortest possible time frame.

Euler CFD methods were used to estimate drag on a few of these configurations, chosen based on BoR analyses. The outcome of the analysis in terms of advantages and main drawbacks was studied in detail. One potential configuration was released to all design groups for detailed analysis at the end of the concept phase. Subsequently, the LEVCON root region was modified to remove span-wise twist, and the local stub wing was also suitably adjusted, which became the final configuration analysed by the aerodynamics group. The effect of this local change in LEVCON and stub wing region was considered for estimating LEVCON hinge moments and the actuation mechanism by the flight controls group.

Let us now look at some of the main features of the LCA Navy Mk2 configuration. Modifications relating to weight optimised landing gear, arrester hook, associated structure and improvement in thrust with the introduction of an alternate engine formed the primary driving factors for the LCA Navy Mk2. In addition, the LCA Navy Mk2 would incorporate an advanced Unified Electronic Warfare Suite (UEWS), On-Board Oxygen Generating System (OBOGS), Active Electronically Scanned Array (AESA) radar and improved systems layout to enhance maintainability. Additionally, fixes based on feedback obtained from development and testing of the LCA Navy Mk1 towards enhanced performance and maintainability would also be incorporated in the LCA Navy Mk2.

The fuselage of the LCA Navy Mk2 is a conventional semi-monocoque structure consisting of bulkhead frames, longerons, shear walls, skin and stringers with aluminium alloy and Carbon-Fibre Composite (CFC) skins. In order to improve accessibility towards enhancing the maintainability of Line Replaceable Units (LRUs), the fuselage has been extended by 1020mm to enable better aerodynamic performance and provide additional volume. The wing is of a compound delta planform configuration and the fin is of co-cured co-bonded construction aiding weight optimisation. As brought out earlier, the wing is a carryover from the 'Tejas', albeit being moved outboard by 350mm on each side.

The leading-edge apex of the wing features an additional control surface, LEVCON (Leading Edge Vortex CONtroller), designed to reduce approach speed during landing on an aircraft carrier. This device is, however, in accordance with the current LCA Navy Mk1 aircraft. The LCA Navy Mk2 variant includes an additional control surface in the wing trailing edge extension region, expected to further assist in reducing carrier approach speeds. This will be explored further to derive maximum performance from the aircraft.

The landing gear of the LCA Navy Mk2 will be made lighter and the provision to use one of the landing gear doors as an airbrake and/or a separate airbrake at the undercarriage area was also under active consideration. It was envisaged to have a direct load transfer to the fuselage structure, without the need for an 'inclined leg' necessitated in the LCA Navy Mk1. The preliminary CAD model of the modified main landing gear is shown below.

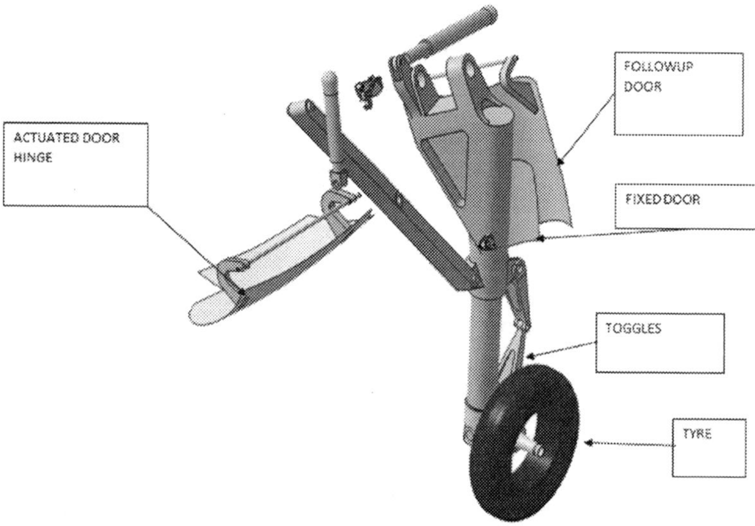

Preliminary CAD model of the LCA Navy Mk2 MLG

The payload take-off capabilities of the aircraft were increased to improve mission performance. External aircraft and engine intake shapes were optimised to enhance point performance capabilities. Higher carrier landing mass was considered for design to bring back expensive stores. The number of store hard points was increased, enabling integration of additional weapons.

The fuel system of the LCA Navy Mk2 will be incorporated with an active fuel transfer system which provides better control on Centre of Gravity (C.G) travel. Internal fuel tanks will also of higher capacity, improving the fuel fraction. The aircraft will also be fitted with a fixed air-to-air refuelling probe.

In short, the modifications required to evolve the LCA Navy Mk1 into the LCA Navy Mk2 are primarily driven by the need to enhance mission performance, survivability, reliability, maintainability and supportability of the aircraft, together with the mandate to incorporate specific systems/LRU's, namely, Ni-Cd battery, UEWS, supersonic fuel drop tank, AESA radar, etc. A preliminary three-view drawing of the LCA Navy Mk2 is shown below.

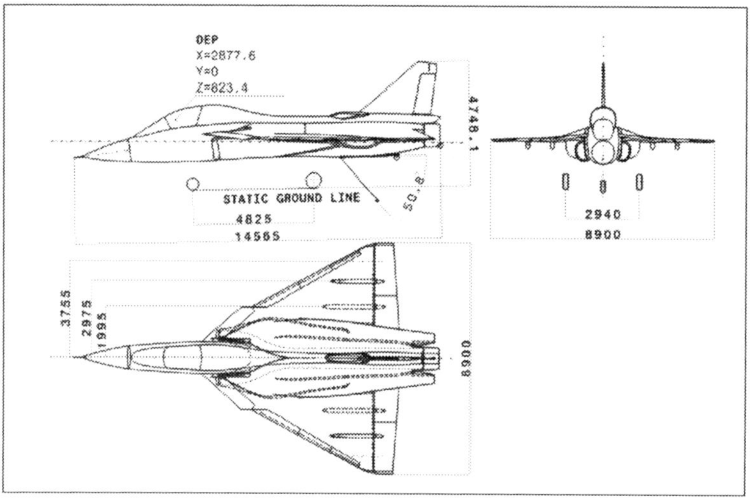

Preliminary 3-View Drawing of LCA Navy Mk2

The aerodynamic configuration and external geometry of the LCA Navy Mk2 are optimised for a single-seat aircraft with features to reduce drag and improve directional stability as compared to NP2. The stretch of the fuselage by about 1.0m would enhance the internal fuel capacity and provide internal volume for better location of equipment, thus enhancing maintainability of the aircraft. Shifting the wing outboard by 350mm on either side has enabled an optimal load transmission path from the main landing gear to the airframe. An additional control surface, a trailing edge extension flap at the rear inboard side of the wing, has been incorporated to enhance recovery characteristics onboard the carrier. Evaluation has confirmed the feasibility of relocating the air brake to the ventral side.

The design of the front fuselage of the LCA Navy Mk2 has augmented space availability for the environmental control system bay, thus improving maintainability of this critical zone. Inboard layout re-optimisation of LRUs has been carried out in order to improve the accessibility and to eliminate/ reduce nose section ballast mass. The main landing gear has been designed with simpler kinematics to improve reliability and reduced mass as compared to the LCA Navy Mk1. The arrester hook is of Y-type with integrated back-up structure in the rear fuselage. A concept of the arrester hook is shown below. The design of the arrester hook includes a pivot in the shank to mitigate lateral loading.

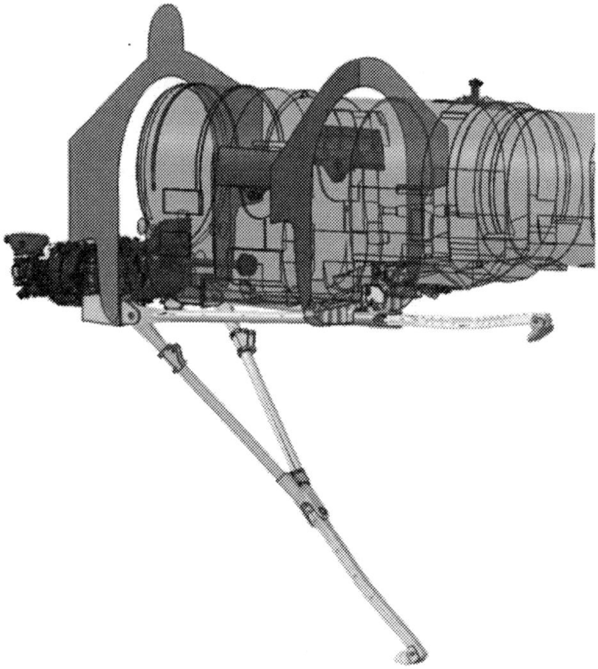

Initial Concept of 'Y' configuration Arrester Hook

The life support system chosen for the LCA Navy Mk2 would be the onboard oxygen generation system, addressing logistics issues of carrying liquid oxygen on ships for carrier operations.

The digital flight control computer would be augmented with a Mark-2 version featuring a power PC architecture that would be capable of handling a higher computation load. This computer would provide more input/output features, thereby improving flight control system performance and catering for long-term supportability.

Avionics upgrade for the LCA Navy Mk2 is evolved with the aim of improving mission management and enhancing display system. An electronic counter measure system with unified electronic warfare suite is another feature considered for the LCA Navy Mk2 avionics. An active electronically scanned array radar as against the mechanically steered radar is planned in the LCA Navy Mk2.

The cockpit display system for the LCA Navy Mk2 would have Smart Multi-Function Displays (SMFD). The LH and RH SMFDs will measure 6"x8", with a central SMFD of 5"x5" will be integrated onto the main instrument panel of the LCA Navy Mk2. Switches and indicators in the At-Hand Control Panel (AHCP) and quarter panels are retained as in the LCA Navy trainer. The LCA Navy Mk2 will be configured with a wider field of vision smart Head-Up-Display, HUD Mk2.

The LCA Navy Mk2 is designed as a single seat multi-role ski-jump take off but arrester recovery class of airplane. Incorporation of state-of-the-art technologies makes the LCA Navy Mk2 relatively lighter, less complex, with high survivability and maintainability. Its design achieves an optimum balance between subsonic and supersonic performances. Further, weight optimisation is targeted, potentially offsetting the mass increase due to an additional ~1.0m fuselage elongation.

The aerodynamic configuration of the LCA Navy Mk2 has been selected considering the critical operational requirements brought out in the naval air staff requirements and the airworthiness requirements laid down in the US Air Force military specifications as guidelines. The front fuselage has been optimised for better aerodynamic performance. Nose droop, which was 9.2° in the NP2, has been reduced to 7.7° that has contributed towards reduction in drag and improvement in directional stability. The droop has been optimised without compromising over-the-nose vision which is one of the essential requirements for aircraft carrier landing.

The air intake is designed for a higher mass flow requirement of the GE-F414-INS6 engine. The design of the lip and cowl has been optimised to improve pressure recovery for better launch performance in heavier configurations. The wing span has been increased from 8.2m to 8.9m. The main objective of this change is to improve main landing gear interface to the airframe thereby enabling a better load transfer path during carrier landing. The effective wing area has been increased from 38.4 sqm to 44 sqm, enabling a higher wing lift.

The structural interface of the main landing gear would be significantly different, avoiding attachment to the fuel tank bottom floor to prevent vulnerabilities for fuel leak. Reduction in fairings of the nose and main landing gear of the LCA Navy Mk1 configuration has been achieved to enhance the aircraft's performance. With the rear fuselage structure designed *ab initio* to accommodate a new engine, the Y-type arrester hook interface to the main structure has been optimised exclusively for the LCA Navy Mk2 requirement.

The integrated flight control system architecture is upgraded with improvements in the computational capability of the digital flight control computer with power PC hardware. Avionics architecture upgrades, including smart displays in the cockpit for improving pilot-vehicle interface, are considered for the LCA Navy Mk2. Weapon systems will have a common hardware for all pylons, with a unified pylon interface computer as an improvement over different hardware for each pylon in the Mk1 configuration.

It was planned to introduce the concept of Design For Manufacture and Assembly (DFMA). The LCA Navy Mk2 design would adopt DFMA principles to reduce development time by addressing all foreseeable manufacturing and assembly issues during the design phase. Structural elements of the aircraft are designed to maximise provision for interchangeable parts. Self-locating features would be incorporated in design, focusing on reducing the number of parts in an assembly, similar to the fin of the aircraft as an example, emphasised in the detail design phase.

The structural parts of the aircraft are mainly made up of readily available aluminium alloys and carbon fibre composites. Special materials are chosen based on the requirements of the operating environment and load conditions. Part design would be carried out based on the standard materials list as defined for use in the LCA programme, particularly for the LCA Navy.

The airframe consists of modular blocks including the front, centre, and rear fuselage, air intake, stub wing, wing, and fin assemblies. Equipment assembly is also carried out in modules, aiding simultaneous assembly and reducing overall lead time. These major assemblies would include sub-assemblies to improve control and handling. Parts, assemblies, material, and design practices are standardised to the maximum extent possible across other aircraft variants of the LCA, without compromising specific requirements of the LCA Navy Mk2. To reduce cycle time of major assemblies like centre and front fuselage, the possibility of splitting them into different stages of assembly would be considered in design. Interfacing with process and tool design is introduced in the concept design phase to incorporate DFMA principles and lessons learnt from other programs.

Digital mock-ups are generated in concurrent design environment to facilitate extensive studies on fitting simulation, ergonomics, and anthropometric studies for pilot-vehicle interface, as well as assembly simulations. In addition, data from tubing and looming of the digital mock up (DMU) would be used for tube bending and preparation of looms for the fabrication activities.

Apart from the above considerations, DFMA would also address other aspects of manufacturing such as testing, procurement, shipping, service, repair, etc. The ultimate objective is to achieve an overall reduction in manufacture cycle time, part count, improved build quality, interchangeability at the part and assembly levels, production costs, overheads, meeting quality, and reliability requirements.

We will now come to some concluding remarks of the LCA Navy Mk2. The concept design of the LCA Navy Mk2 was carried out to meet naval air staff requirements, air staff requirements, and carrier interface requirements provided by the Indian Navy.

The additional thrust available through the alternate power plant (GE-F414-INS6) and aerodynamic optimisation carried out to configure the LCA Navy Mk2 as a single-seat aircraft result in significant improvements in mission performance and point performance compared to the LCA Navy Mk1. System requirement reviews have been conducted by the Indian Navy, and it has been observed that the majority of the requirements have been met.

Weight optimisation of landing gear, with an estimated reduction of around 200 kg despite an increase of ~3 to 3.5 tons in carrier maximum landing mass, and a conformal arrester hook system, represent significant improvements in the LCA Navy Mk2. Further, equipment layout optimisation has led to reduction/elimination of ballast mass.

Extensive aerodynamic studies have been conducted to minimise both subsonic and supersonic drag of the aircraft by effective area ruling and shape optimisation. A new concept of a shelf flap in the trailing edge extension region has been conceptualised to benefit in low-speed handling and reduce approach speed.

The increase in the fuselage volume has improved the equipment layout for the aircraft, which has contributed to better accessibility and maintainability, and has also provided additional internal fuel. The structure is planned to be built on a modular basis that will have the capability of pre-equipping at the sub-assembly level. This will facilitate outsourcing at the module level rather than only at part fabrication level. The concept of DFMA is planned to ensure minimal transition from prototype to production. A robust DMU has been developed that includes piping, tubing, and wire harness.

The fuel system of the LCA Navy Mk2 is based on active fuel flow proportioning to improve flight dynamics by maintaining a narrow band of c.g travel. The baseline configuration of the fuel system would incorporate a fixed air-to-air refuelling (AAR) probe. An alternative to use a retractable AAR would also be explored. Plans include fuel jettison (dump) capabilities similar to those of the LCA Navy Mk1, as well as planning to implement a digital fuel gauging system on the aircraft. The hot-refuelling capability introduced in the LCA Navy Mk1 will be incorporated into the LCA Navy Mk2 also.

An improved system architecture integrating the flight control system and avionics system with state-of-the-art technologies is expected to improve pilot-vehicle interface and address obsolescence issues. Studies have explored the use of LEVCON as an active control surface, which promises to significantly improve the agility and handling qualities of the aircraft.

Studies were carried out for aircraft carrier interface of the LCA Navy Mk2 on the indigenous aircraft carrier, *Vikrant,* for aircraft spotting and movement both on the flight deck and the aircraft hangar. Feasibility assessments for operations and maintenance have also been carried out. A separate report on the aircraft carrier interface was submitted to the Indian Navy, updating initial reports based on discussions held with the Indian Navy's Directorate of Naval Design, the designers of the aircraft carrier.

The status provided in this chapter is as of March 2017, when the author superannuated from the ADA. The design had progressed well, but the Indian Navy decided not to pursue this concept, despite it evolving into an extremely viable platform for operations aboard aircraft carriers. I distinctly remember that Dr. Satheesh Reddy, who was the SA to RM in 2016, extensively reviewed the design, and we presented its benefits to the Indian Navy. However, the Indian Navy has been insisting on a twin-engine configuration, which is now being pursued. Notwithstanding this, a viable design of an optimised LCA Navy Mk2 remains ready to be taken up, if desired. Despite this decision, it has been a wonderful experience for the LCA Navy team to undergo a full design cycle with effective optimisation, providing significant lessons for future developments.

To conclude, two LCA Navy prototypes, NP1 and NP2, were built as part of technology demonstration prototypes of the first programme (LCA Navy Mk1). The requirement as specified by the Indian Navy was that LCA Navy would replace the Sea Harrier aircraft. Mission and point performance analyses showed that the LCA Navy would be better than the Sea Harrier. However, the Indian Navy later opined that they needed an even better performing aircraft and accordingly, in 2010, the CCS approved development of LCA Navy Mk2 with a more powerful engine. This chapter brings out the journey of design and development leading to a viable improved aircraft with a much reduced constraint on commonality. A feasible and improved aircraft design is available in the form of LCA Navy Mk2.

At this stage, the Indian Navy felt that they need deck based aircraft to be twin-engined and thus the LCA Navy has not been pursued beyond the technology demonstration phase, albeit having successfully proved itself in the carrier compatibility demonstration flights on both the aircraft carriers, *Vikramaditya* and *Vikrant*. ADA now is working on the new concept of Twin-Engined Deck Based Fighter (TEDBF) aircraft that would be in the medium weight category (around 25 tons). Design cycle of the LCA Navy Mk2 has shown that due to the technology base and skill sets developed, it was considerably easier than the ab-initio development of LCA Navy Mk1. I am certain that the development of TEDBF will also follow this path and wish the programme all the very best.

15

My Experiences as Director ADA

On superannuation of Mr. PS Subramanyam, Distinguished Scientist, the author was selected to be the next Programme Director (Combat Aircraft) & Director of the Aeronautical Development Agency [PGD (CA) & Director ADA] after a process of deep selection by the Indian Ministry of Defence. It was a pleasant surprise to be given this honour, and it indeed was an emotional moment for my family and me. I took over the reins of the Aeronautical Development Agency (ADA) on 3 July 2015 and continued till 31 March 2017, when I superannuated from service in the grade of a Distinguished Scientist (DS).

I would say it was a short but extremely exciting time in that chair, albeit with its own share of trials and tribulations. It gave me a tremendous sense of satisfaction to have the honour of leading one of the largest and most prestigious fighter aircraft programmes in the country. This satisfaction was particularly enhanced due to the unstinted support of the then Defence Minister of India, the Late Mr. Manohar Parrikar, who was a very hands-on minister. I vividly recall an event when we were having certain issues with the aircraft landing gear. As an engineer, he sat with us, reviewing the drawings to understand the nuances of the problem. He was always available for the programme and actively participated with the team.

During my tenure as PGD (CA) and Director ADA, there were several significant events and achievements, which are enumerated in the following paragraphs.

Bahrain International Air Show (BIAS), 2016

Following an invitation from the Kingdom of Bahrain to the Government of India, the Hon'ble Raksha Mantri, the Defence Minister of India, approved the participation of the LCA 'Tejas' flight display and the exhibition of Defence Research & Development Organisation (DRDO) and Tejas products at the Bahrain International Air Show (BIAS)-2016, held from 21 and 23 January 2016 at Sakhir Airbase, Kingdom of Bahrain. It may be noted that this was the first international exposure of Tejas outside the country. Accordingly, it was planned to ferry two Tejas aircraft to Bahrain, with one aircraft performing the flying display and the second aircraft on ground static display. Hindustan Aeronautics Ltd. (HAL) actively participated in this effort, along with the Indian Air Force (IAF), Indian Navy (IN), certification agencies, quality assurance agencies, and a host of other stakeholders of the Tejas programme.

As would be apparent, a detailed plan was conceptualised and prepared for this mega event, and a snapshot of this plan is shown below. While the graphic is seemingly loaded with information, the objective is to show the meticulous planning that was put in place to ensure a successful mission. While two aircraft would actually proceed and participate in the air show, it was planned that three aircraft were to be prepared and moved from Bengaluru to Jamnagar (Gujarat) for redundancy management. It was envisaged that the flight path for this ferry would be from Jamnagar to Muscat (Oman) and finally to Bahrain. The third aircraft would be on standby at Jamnagar till the date of ferrying from Jamnagar to Muscat. In order to optimise resources and effort, it was planned that the third aircraft would participate in weapon trials after the first two aircraft were ferried out of Jamnagar.

It was proposed to showcase some of the capabilities and technologies of Tejas during BIAS-2016 in the international arena. The Bahrain Air Show is a well-recognised aviation event in the Middle East, known globally in aviation industries around the world, and provides an excellent forum for promoting professional interaction between aircraft designers, air forces, aviators, aircraft industries, and vendors, potentially leading to business opportunities.

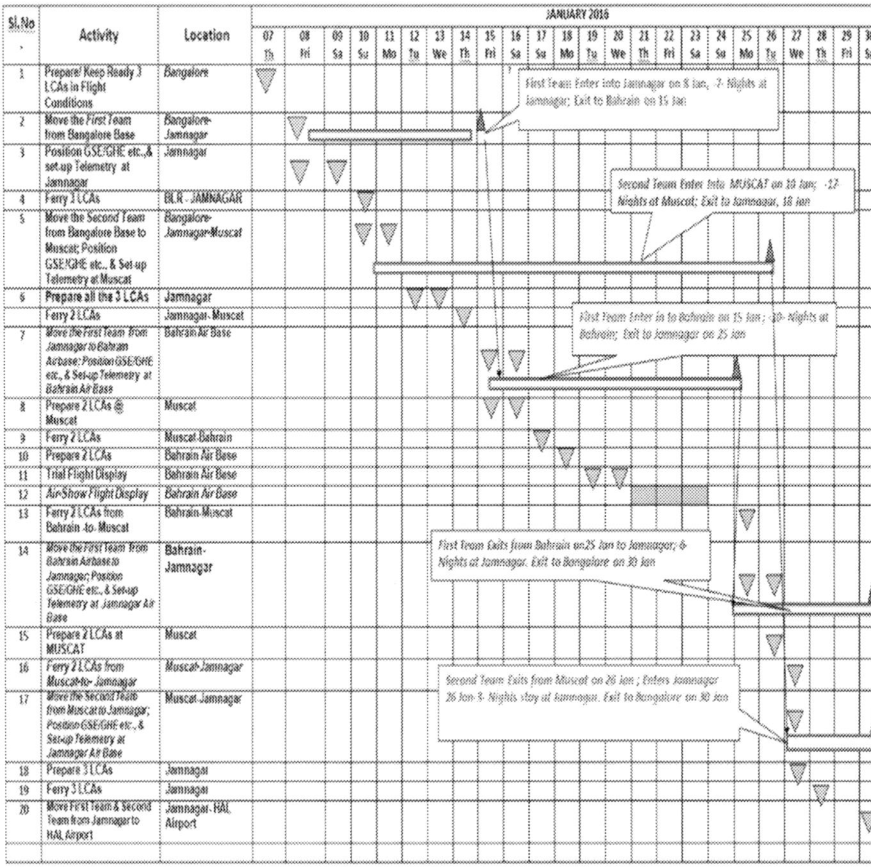

Planning Chart for BIAS 2016

The Aircraft: Ferrying of two Limited Series Production (LSP) Tejas aircraft, LSP4 and LSP7, was undertaken from Jamnagar to Bahrain via Muscat (refuelling stop) on 14 January 2016. The flight from Jamnagar to Muscat was entirely over the sea, marking the first time this long passage over open waters was handled and requiring elaborate planning. The IN was alerted to provide search and rescue (SAR) cover in case of any untoward incidents while the aircraft were transiting over the sea. The IAF assisted with their transport aircraft to position equipment and personnel at both Muscat and Bahrain. The Defence Attaché at Muscat provided outstanding coordination support to the team, which was a significant enabler. In addition, he coordinated arrangements for the detachment in Bahrain.

Nine practice sorties were undertaken from 16 to 19 January 2016 at the Sakhir Airbase (Bahrain), the venue of the Air Show, by the two test pilots of the National Flight Test Centre (NFTC), Cmde. Maolankar and Gp. Capt. Rangachari. This enabled them to familiarise themselves with the local flying area and to fine-tune the display flying profile. Handouts of the actual display flying profile, along with explanatory notes, were prepared to help the audience follow the manoeuvres. In fact, a few international media personnel tracked the Tejas every step of the way, including video coverage. The host team from the air show organisers constantly checked whether we were comfortable and if any support was required. Just for information, the location of the Sakhir Airbase is adjacent to the Bahrain Formula-1 car racing circuit, which is visible in the flying display pictures.

Display flying was undertaken alternately by the two test pilots from 21 to 23 January 2016, with an actual overhead flying time of 10 minutes on each day of the show. This was well-received by the audience, and the country showcased its prowess with the Tejas aircraft's excellent flying capabilities. The aircraft performed manoeuvres up to the boundaries of +8'g' and –2.5'g' flawlessly. A very tight and small radius of turn of 350m was also demonstrated, much to the surprise of discerning experts. A few snapshots taken during the display flying are shown below. The aircraft was carefully checked after each sortie, the data reviewed to ensure there were no failures, and then it was cleared by the certification agency for the next flight.

The Display: A display team of the IAF Sarang, featuring the indigenously designed and built Advanced Light Helicopter (ALH) by Hindustan Aeronautics Ltd., named 'Dhruv', also participated in the air show. Their excellent flying display was also well-received by both the audience and media. The Sarang team's flying displays, accompanied by their signature soul-stopping music, were outstanding. The then External Affairs Minister (EAM), the Late Ms. Sushma Swaraj, witnessed the various flying displays on 23 January 2016, along with the King of Bahrain. The aircraft returned via Muscat to Jamnagar on 24 January 2016. While flying clearances were obtained from the countries Tejas would transit over, there were some heart-stopping moments as information had not percolated down to some of the air traffic controls en route. Hence, while the aircraft was airborne, there was intense coordination

Snapshots of display flying at Bahrain - 2016

to get the clearance across to the ATC, allowing the ferrying continued from Bahrain to Muscat and then to Jamnagar.

The Exhibition: An Indian pavilion was set up with participation from the DRDO, ADA and HAL, displaying various products of relevance and aircraft models to inform the trade and general public. This facilitated showcasing the capabilities already been developed, generating significant interest among potential trade visitors and delegations. This exhibition was well attended and generated substantial interest in the country's developing capabilities. The King of Bahrain visited the Indian pavilion, where mementos were presented to him by the Secretary of the Department of Defence (R&D), Government of India. The EAM of India also visited the Indian pavilion on 23 January 2016, along with the Foreign Minister of Bahrain. The exhibition also provided an opportunity for team members to gain exposure to global advancements in the aviation sector.

The Support: Support for the entire operation was provided to ADA by various organisations and entities, both within and outside the country. The Indian

Ministry of Defence (MoD) accorded approvals for participation in the air show and deputation of key members required to support aircraft operations. The DRDO provided financial sanctions, CEMILAC offered aircraft certification support. HAL played a major role in the preparation of aircraft, and their operations and maintenance at Jamnagar, Muscat and Bahrain. The NFTC of ADA was the backbone for overall planning and flying of the Tejas aircraft. The IAF provided transport aircraft support and support at the staging base at AF Station, Jamnagar and for the ferry locations. The IN provided SAR cover over sea. The Directorate-General Aeronautical Quality Assurance (DGAQA) ensured QA coverage for the aircraft at all operating locations. The embassies of India in Muscat and Bahrain provided unstinted support for local logistics, visa clearances for the team, aircraft operation clearances, etc. Last but not the least, the BIAS, the host organisation, provided support with openness and a wholehearted approach, making the team feel welcome, especially for an aircraft having its first outing outside Indian territory.

The Experience: The entire process provided invaluable experience in planning and execution of a challenging activity, as it was the first time Tejas had been taken out of the country. This outing of Tejas provided an opportunity to plan the logistics required at three different locations, obtaining requisite clearances from various authorities across countries, movement of men and material, route planning and movement of aircraft, etc. The hallmark of the entire show was outstanding teamwork by all stakeholders, ensuring a resounding success. I participated in every step of the process, including in Bahrain, which gave me a tremendous sense of satisfaction. In hindsight, it was the meticulous planning and foresight that enabled successful participation at the Bahrain International Air Show.

Iron Fist 2016

Iron Fist 2016 was the IAF day-night exercise conducted on 18 March 2016 at the Pokhran weapon range in Rajasthan, India to display various operational capabilities. It featured the participation of 181 aircraft, including 103 fighters of the IAF. This exercise also marked the first display of Tejas' firepower, demonstrating its swing role capability. In an impressive show of firepower, the IAF put up a dazzling display of its military prowess during the exercise. A senior official had remarked that the bombs released by Tejas 'hit the target'. A picture of Tejas flying with weapons at the Iron Fist exercise is shown below.

Tejas with Weapons at Iron Fist 2016

The Experience: It was a great experience for Team Tejas to rub shoulders with other operational aircraft and test its capabilities. The results were highly positive in terms of operational capability demonstration and user feedback.

Flight by CAS in 2016

India's Light Combat Aircraft (LCA) programme witnessed another significant event on 17 May 2016, when Air Chief Marshal Arup Raha, the then Chief of Air Staff (CAS), IAF, took to the skies in the indigenously developed Tejas aircraft. The CAS flew in a trainer version of the Tejas aircraft (PV6), which features a tandem seating configuration. HAL and ADA had prepared the Tejas PV6 aircraft for this crucial flight. The sortie lasted for about half an hour, making ACM Arup Raha the first CAS to fly in a Tejas. Upon landing, ACM Arup Raha famously quoted, "*It's a good aircraft to fly and fit to be inducted into our fleet.*" The CAS also stated that the aircraft met the operational needs of the IAF. He has been a staunch supporter of indigenous products and had fully backed the programme. I tend to think that this event was a significant catalyst and a precursor to the formation of the Tejas squadron by the IAF a few months later. A few pictures of his flight activity and post-flight are shown on page 85.

LCA Navy at Def Expo Goa

The 2016 Defence Expo, the ninth edition of the biennial event conducted by the Defence Exhibition Organisation (DEO) of the Ministry of Defence, Government of India, was inaugurated by the then Indian Defence Minister, the Late Mr. Manohar Parrikar. The four-day event, focused on land, naval, and internal homeland security systems, was held for the first time in Goa. The inaugural ceremony featured a live demonstration of India's various land and naval defence systems, including the main battle tank (Arjun), Sarang helicopter aerobatic team, and the Naval Version of the Light Combat Aircraft (LCA Navy) on 28 March 2016. The first LCA Navy prototype, NP1, participated in the demonstration, operating from the Indian Navy's air station, INS Hansa, located at Dabolim, Goa. Pictures of NP1 at the Def Expo are shown on page 85.

Formation of first IAF Squadron of LCA Tejas

Tejas is a fourth-generation fighter aircraft indigenously developed by the ADA after a technology gap of around two decades following the HF Marut development. Its development by the LCA (Tejas) team at the ADA, an autonomous society of the Ministry of Defence, is unique in the light of the fact that there was no infrastructure base and minimal technological base was available in the country for undertaking development of a modern combat aircraft.

Considering the progress of the LCA programme, action for the induction of Tejas into the IAF was initiated, leading to the formation of the first Tejas squadron, the 'Flying Daggers' of the No. 45 Squadron, on 1 July 2016. The IAF had placed an order in 2006 for 20 Tejas aircraft in IOC configuration and another 20 in FOC configuration in 2010. The maiden flight of the first series production (SP1) Tejas aircraft in the initial operational clearance (IOC) configuration took place on 30 September 2014, and it was handed over to the Chief of Air Staff, IAF, by the Indian Defence Minister on 17 January 2015. The maiden flight of the second series production (SP2) Tejas aircraft of IOC configuration was made on 22 March 2016. Subsequent SP aircraft are being delivered progressively by HAL to the IAF for induction. Snapshots of the Tejas Squadron on 1 July 2016 are shown on page 86.

Hot Weather and High-Altitude Test of LCA AF Trainer (PV6)

From August 10 to 26, 2016, the Tejas aircraft underwent rigorous hot-weather and high-altitude performance flight test at Leh, one of the world's highest airfields. The objective of this campaign was to check operations and performance of the Tejas aircraft at high altitudes and corresponding higher temperatures, which would be one of the critical set of conditions for any aircraft. The maximum take-off load would be governed by this ambient condition of 'Hot & High'. The test focused on the Tejas trainer PV6, a two-seater model that represented a more challenging case compared to the single-seat fighter variant. From a performance perspective, the Tejas fighter would be a sub-set of this case. The Tejas aircraft was powered by a GE-F404-IN20 engine. Incidentally, cold-weather trials in Leh were already completed.

The primary objective of the campaign towards a performance flight test was the demonstration of the air staff requirement for take-off operation at 3000m altitude with 1500 kg external disposable load at IRA+5°C (30°C) temperature conditions. The flight segments captured and analysed are take-off, approach, and landing. A few pictures of the Tejas 'PV6' operating in Leh area are shown on page 86.

The take-offs were done at maximum afterburner throttle setting, and the landings (touchdown) were done at flight idle throttle setting. The performance test points were analysed after every sortie. The airfield data was obtained from the air traffic control and listed in the national flight test centre test card. It was observed that there were differences in the wind data obtained from ATC during take-off and landing, compared to the flight data. Therefore, the wind was estimated using flight data. The average value of the wind from 100 KCAS to liftoff calibrated airspeed (CAS) was used in the model for take-off analysis. The small difference in wind magnitude was attributed to the difference in outside air temperature (OAT) in the test card and flight OAT. The flight OAT may not have been correct during take-off roll due to the effect of the anti-icing heater on a temperature probe.

The analysed test points were supported by tables that contained numerical values of relevant parameters captured from flight data. These parameters were used as inputs for the performance model. The analysis table also included performance parameters estimated from the model. The take-off analysis table included takeoff, longitudinal acceleration, rotation speed, rotation rate, liftoff speed, ground roll distance, and take-off distance. The results showed that the aircraft could get airborne with a load of 2400kg as against a requirement of 1500kg, indicating better-than-required performance of the aircraft at the critical condition of high altitude and high temperature. It was a pleasure for me to personally witness this milestone being achieved at the high altitude airfield at Leh in Ladakh.

Participation of Tejas in Republic Day flypast on 26 January 2017

One of the highlights of the Republic Day programme in the Indian national capital is the flypast of various aircraft of the Services, primarily the IAF. These typically consist of formations of multi-engine aircraft, generally not single-engine aircraft. After over two–and-a-half decades, the Government of India decided that Tejas should participate during the Republic Day flypast on 26 January 2017. It was decided that the operations would be carried out from Air Force Station Nal near Bikaner, Rajasthan, with the aircraft going in for the formation at the designated slot over Rajpath in New Delhi.

I participated in the rehearsal taking place from Nal and was in Delhi on Republic Day itself to proudly see Tejas flying overhead.

Extensive planning was done with wholehearted participation of all the stakeholders, as it involved a mix of both prototypes and IAF Tejas squadron aircraft. The modalities for participation of the Tejas were discussed, and a detailed task directive was issued to inform all stakeholders of the plan, so that preparatory activities could commence immediately. Some of the salient features are highlighted in the subsequent paragraphs.

Three Tejas aircraft participated in the flypast, with one aircraft on standby in the air and one on ground standby. Hence, a total of five aircraft operated as a detachment consisting of SP1, SP2, and SP3 of 45 Sqn of the IAF and PV6 & LSP7 as the main aircraft, with LSP3 as standby. All the aircraft were in operational clean configuration (OCC) + 2x1200 ltr drop tank configuration. As noted, we had taken six aircraft to Nal in Bikaner.

The aircraft detachment, comprising personnel from the IAF's 45 Squadron, HAL, ADA, NFTC, certification agencies, quality assurance agencies, and others, operated from the Indian Air Force Base Nal near Bikaner in Rajasthan. The aircraft staged through Ozhar (Nashik) en route ferry to Nal and on return as well. The detachment period at Nal was from 13 to 28 January 2017.

Since 45 Sqn of the IAF would also operate a detachment at Nal and Ozhar, optimum pooling of resources in terms of Ground Handling Equipment and Ground Support Equipment (GHE/GSE) was planned to economise on the requirements of air and ground transport. All designers and coordinators were requested to ensure that an adequate number of spare line replaceable units (LRUs), including aircraft batteries, wheel assemblies, brake parachutes, LOX converters, etc., were available at the detachment location. Despite carrying various spares, one of the aircraft developed a fuel system snag, and the spare was not available at the detached location. However, the team members were able to mobilise the spare from Bengaluru at very short notice and recover the aircraft to the flight line.

Preparatory work and responsibilities were chalked out for successful operations to achieve a three-aircraft flypast over Rajpath among various agencies. HAL (LCA-Tejas Division) was overall responsible for aircraft preparation and operations at Nal, Bikaner, including provisioning of adequate spares and LRUs. HAL (ARDC) was overall responsible for aircraft preparation at Ozhar, Nashik, as the staging base to ensure successful ferrying of aircraft from Bengaluru to Nal via Nashik. IAF (PMT) was requested to facilitate heavy transport aircraft (C-17) for induction and de-induction of the detachment. They also took care of security clearance of non-IAF personnel to operate from the Nal IAF base. NFTC arranged positioning of a mobile telemetry station both at Nal and Ozhar for flying of Tejas aircraft. A recce team had earlier visited the IAF base Nal to coordinate various administrative and logistical requirements at the base.

The Tejas participated in the Republic Day flypast for the first time since its inception, especially as a single-engine aircraft. This being a national event, all the stakeholders put their best foot forward and extended wholehearted support to make it a great success. A few pictures of the aircraft parked at Nal and the three-aircraft formation flight are shown on page 87. It was truly a sight to behold and gave a tremendous sense of pride to look at our own fighter aircraft participating in this prestigious event.

Aero India 2017

The Biennial Aero-India 2017 International Air Show was held at the Indian Air Force Station, Yelahanka, Bengaluru, from 14 to 18 February 2017. The theme of the air show, declared by the Ministry of Defence, Government of India, was 'National Security through Technological Self-Reliance'. ADA coordinated the exhibition and air show display efforts for both the DRDO and ADA. A large exhibition area was set up on the air show premises. Another interesting feature was the inclusion of Customer Demonstration Flights (CDF) in the two LCA trainers, PV5 and PV6, to showcase the performance capabilities of the Tejas aircraft.

A major crowd-puller at the ADA indoor exhibition included various aircraft scale models, namely the LCA AF Mk1, LCA Navy Mk1, LCA AF Mk2, LCA Navy Mk2, and Advanced Medium Combat Aircraft (AMCA). Another significant draw from the indoor exhibition perspective was the aircraft simulator and the virtual reality facility. The exhibits displayed also included aircraft system themes with models, actual hardware, super graphics, and video panels. Adequate brochures and literature were made available to the public. The outdoor exhibits, including both the LCA AF and Naval Versions, also drew significant crowds. A few pictures of the exhibits are shown on page 87.

With a view to showcasing the light combat aircraft, the fighter variant actively participated in display flying. Two LCA trainer variant aircraft (PV5 and PV6) were flown during the air show for Customer Demonstration Flights (CDF), showcasing LCA's air experience to selected personnel from friendly countries and other dignitaries. The CDFs were undertaken by Mr. Jayant Sinha, the then Minister of State for Civil Aviation, senior members of the IAF, and some members of the media. The flights were well appreciated by all of them, who remarked that the aircraft handled well.

The LCA trainer was flown from the front seat by test pilots of the NFTC of ADA. The flight profiles were planned and tailor-made for each occupant of the rear seat by the NFTC. The flying profile ranged from, depending on the occupant's exposure to fighter flying, basic aircraft manoeuvring capability, cockpit displays while flying, circuit flying including take-off and landing (for all occupants), to more involved avionics functionality and simulated weapon attack with sensors (onboard radar and laser designation pod) for customer demonstration.

During the opening ceremony, a Tejas formation with three aircraft participated in the flypast. Tejas participated in both the morning and afternoon sessions on all days with its excellent display flying. The aircraft carried out enthralling manoeuvres and were well appreciated by the audience attending the air show. A few pictures are shown below.

Tejas at Aero India 2017; Trainers in a Pair Take-off with Media Personnel in both the Rear Seats

Other Highlights

There were other major highlights during my tenure as Director ADA, a few of which are enumerated above. Approval for the procurement of 83 aircraft in an improved version of Tejas, namely the LCA Mk1A, was granted by the Defence Acquisition Council (DAC) of the Government of India, chaired by the late Mr. Manohar Parrikar, the Indian Defence Minister, in 2016. This paved the way for detailed discussions and finalisation of proposals between the IAF and HAL, with formal orders placed in 2020. This is considered one of the largest orders placed by the IAF and a significant boost for self-reliance in the country towards fighter aircraft development.

A project for undertaking major technology 'lead-in' aspects for Ghatak was sanctioned. This would facilitate the study of advanced technology activities involved in this complex vehicle. Approval for the Project Definition Phase (PDP) of the Advanced Medium Combat Aircraft (AMCA) was accorded, enabling the exploration of technology challenges and mitigation strategies of this complex air vehicle.

The integration and firing of the Derby Beyond Visual Range (BVR) missile were successfully carried out, paving the way for a significant confidence boost in advanced weapon integration capabilities in the country. The integration and flight testing of 'Quartz' Radome was a great enabler for minimising losses in radar transmission. Integration of the air-to-air refuelling probe on LSP8 was completed, pending flight testing. Integration of 23mm Gsh gun on LSP7 was also carried out. One significant capability enhancer was the 'Hot-Refuelling' demonstration on the LCA Navy. This facilitated multiple sorties in a single flight, thus providing efficient flight testing capabilities. The 'in-flight fuel jettison' demonstration on the LCA Navy was also completed. Further, as brought out in the preceding chapter, the concept design of the LCA Navy Mk2 was completed. In addition, the Chief of Air Force of Turkmenistan, the Indian Minister of State for Civil Aviation, and various journalists flew in the Tejas trainer to get a feel of the aircraft's prowess.

My Flights in PV6 and NP1

The personal highlights of my tenure as Programme Director (CA) and Director ADA were the two flights I undertook. When I proposed the idea, there was a moment of total silence, as nobody had anticipated it and did not know how to react. This had never happened before; until then, only pilots had flown in the aircraft. The flight on PV6 preceded customer demonstration flights during Aero India 2017. However, after a series of discussions, it was decided that I could fly in the aircraft to gain a first-hand feel, having been part of the design and development process.

The first of these flights was on 29 December 2016, with me in the rear seat of the LCA AF trainer PV6, flown by Gp. Capt. Raj Tyagi (Retd.). The sortie was preceded by a detailed brief on procedures and emergencies, followed by a medical examination. The briefing was conducted by the test director and the test pilot on the planned profile and the intended test points to be carried out. The briefing was attended by the Project Director (Flight Test). The sortie commenced with aircraft start-up, followed by taxiing, line-up, take-off, and moving to the sector. Certain standard test points were executed, and for some time, I was given control of the aircraft to experience the wonderful machine.

After all the test points were executed, Gp. Capt. Tyagi carried out 'g' manoeuvres, taking the aircraft up to 4 'g'. I could feel the inflation of the 'g' suit during the process. I was comfortable throughout the sortie, and it was a real pleasure to be in the aircraft. The Head Up Display (HUD) repeater visuals on the rear Multi-Function Display (MFD), which shows the feed from the HUD camera, were quite clear. Upon completion, we returned to base. A few visuals of the experience, from the briefing to strapping up, flight (HUD picture at take-off), and after the flight, are displayed on page 88.

While I had flown in the LCA AF trainer in December 2016, I also wanted to fly a sortie in the Naval Version, as it has been very close to my heart. Three days before my superannuation from the post of Director ADA, on 28 March 2017, Cmde. Jaideep Maolankar, the Chief Test Pilot, took me up for the sortie on the LCA Navy trainer, NP1. This was indeed very emotional, as it was the aircraft that I was a part of taking through from '*Paper to Flight*', the theme of this book. With this sortie, I was able to complete my tenure at the ADA on a high note on 31 March 2017. A few pictures of the sortie are shown on page 88.

16

Conclusions & Lessons Learnt

In the preceding chapters of the book, we have briefly read about the genesis and development of the Air Force Version of the Light Combat Aircraft (LCA) or 'Tejas'. History was made on 04 January 2001 when the first technology demonstrator underwent its maiden flight. This section summarised the design and development process, starting from the establishment of the Aeronautical Development Agency (ADA) to the test and development phases of the aircraft. We have also seen the Tejas being accorded the Initial Operational Clearance (IOC), Final Operational Clearance (FOC), and induction into the Indian Air Force (IAF).

We have seen in more detail the design and development of the Naval Version of the Light Combat Aircraft (LCA Navy) that would operate from an aircraft carrier, which has the capability of Ski-jump Take-off But Arrested Recovery (STOBAR). We have seen some of the major challenges during the first-time development of this complex aircraft and how they were successfully surmounted. We have also seen the various test facilities and infrastructure that were built during the process, and which have become assets for future aircraft development, testing, and training.

The preceding chapter highlighted the significant events and occurrences during my period as Director ADA, including participation for the first time in the Bahrain International Air Show (BIAS-2106), participation in IAF's Iron Fist, DefExpo-2016, Aero India-2017, and hot weather trials at Leh, etc. In early 2016, the then Chief of Air Staff, Air Chief Marshal Arup Raha, flew in the LCA AF trainer, and praised it as 'a great aircraft'. Another historic moment occurred on 1 July 2016, when the first Tejas squadron was formally set up by the IAF, namely, 45 Sqn – The Flying Daggers. Personal highlights included my flights in both the Air Force and Naval Versions of the LCA, with which I superannuated at a high point.

In this chapter, we will look at some of the lessons learnt and takeaways for the future. ADA was established as an autonomous body under the Indian Ministry of Defence to enable efficient programme management. This singular and bold step heralded quick and efficient decision-making, bringing together various stakeholders, attracting talent, creating infrastructure, setting up various test facilities, involving academia, utilising consultants both in the country and abroad, and a host of others. Hindustan Aeronautics Ltd. was the principal partner in the development journey; the Aircraft Research & Design Centre of HAL was co-located with ADA, with only a wall separating the two organisations. There were a host of others who formed the team from the Defence Research & Development Organisation (DRDO), National Aerospace Laboratory (NAL), Bharat Electronics Ltd. (BEL), other public and private sector agencies, academic institutions, quality assurance and certification agencies. These entities were located across all parts of the country, and it presented a classic challenge and lesson in programme management to orchestrate the development of the aircraft.

In the journey from 'Paper to Flight,', the first step is the 'Paper', namely, the Note to the Cabinet Committee on Security (CCS Note). The CCS serves as the highest decision-making body for matters pertaining to defence and national security, chaired by the Prime Minister of India. As per the guidelines, the note should be around 5 to 6 pages typed in double space. It is essential to meticulously narrate the story to ensure it outlines the entire rationale for seeking approval, facilitating consideration by the CCS. Any errors could result in rejection. The note also specifies the deliverables and financial sanctions for the entire programme.

As mentioned earlier, the design and development of a typical product starts with a thorough and robust requirement capture. For this step, assembling a core team to prepare the requirements document and follow through various steps is essential. I cannot emphasise enough the importance of this step; detailed requirements and a clear understanding are crucial for effective product development. In the case of the LCA Navy, the aircraft itself is the top-level product. However, all assemblies and equipment involved also qualify as products and undergo the same process. Once the requirements are documented, compliance is verified through analysis and simulation, identifying any non-compliance. It is necessary to discuss these non-compliances with the originator of the requirement to either modify them or grant concessions. Neglecting this step could lead to challenges in product acceptance when developed.

A team for design and development needs to be built up, both within the organisation and with teams identified from other stakeholders who would work on the programme. This is a critical need to enable a collaborative approach and would aid in programme management. This team needs to formulate a detailed work plan (work breakdown structure) of various activities and use any of the standard programme management tools for tracking physical and financial progress. We have seen in the development journey of the LCA Navy that there is a close correlation between physical progress and the corresponding financial outlay.

Based on the product, associated technologies need to be identified and the current Technology Readiness Levels (TRLs) of each of these need to be understood. Based on the TRLs, technology development in those areas is to be launched in parallel with product development. As an example of the LCA Navy aircraft as a product at the macro level, the technology for an arrester hook system needed to be developed. There were other similar products developed.

Analysis and simulation are key areas in the concept design phase and subsequently, during the testing phase. In the initial stages, they help in gaining an understanding of the potential outcome of the product and making suitable iterations to the design itself. In the later stage of the testing phase, simulation results are correlated with the test results to check how close the match is. If there is a variation, then the simulation model is checked and attempts are made to get close to the actual test results. Once confidence is built up with the simulation model, actual tests can be minimised. As an example of this process, we discussed the load diffusion within the longeron of the LCA Navy aircraft structure due to arrested recovery loads. The process followed was structural load simulation, ground test on a full-fledged structural test specimen with instrumentation, taxi-in arrested recovery with aircraft instrumented under increasing energy levels, and finally flight engagement.

Identification and Build-up of Test Facilities and Augmentation of Existing Test Facilities for Product development. For example, in the development testing of the LCA Navy, there was a need to replicate an aircraft carrier ashore having capability of ski-jump launch and arrested recovery, along with telemetry facilities for prototype testing. Accordingly, a Shore Based Test Facility (SBTF) was established at the Navy Air Station in Goa. One forward-thinking highlight was that the specifications were drawn up with the objective accommodating testing of larger aircraft in the future. Also, the facility proved beneficial for the initial and ongoing training of Indian Navy pilots on MiG-29K's.

Sourcing of raw materials and establishing lead time for their supply is another important activity to enable timely availability for fabrication and build. Necessary tooling, jigs, fixtures, and assembly lines need to be established concurrently with the design and development process. Potential partners in both public and private sectors need to be identified, partnerships established, and products realised. Thus, there would be a build-up of an entire aviation eco-system.

Ground and flight testing are extremely important steps in the development journey of an aircraft. Tests are conducted from the component level to the subsystem and system levels. Environmental tests, conducted according to relevant standards, need to be carried out and checked for compliance. Structural tests on the airframe provide confidence in the integrity and robustness of design. Flight tests represent the ultimate step in proving the veracity of the design and confirming that all requirements would be met. Detailed test plans and an execution matrix must be developed and coordinated by the certification agency for all these activities.

The development of the product, in this case, the LCA, should be the ultimate objective. As is apparent, the aircraft is an assemblage of various structural and system elements. There may be some aggregates/equipment that are not readily available, or the country may not currently have the technological capability. These can be bought outright from sources available anywhere in the world, and the aircraft should not be held hostage due to non-availability from indigenous sources. One of the examples is the engine that was not immediately available within the country. This has been sourced from General Electric (GE), USA, which is one of the leading specialised engine manufacturers in the world. The engine chosen for the LCA, the GE-F404 family, is in use by the US Navy on the F-18s, the SAAB Gripen (licence built by them), and the Korean fighter programme. Similarly, Martin Baker of the UK is one of the major suppliers of aircraft ejection seats, with Zvezda from Russia being another. The seat for our programme has been sourced from Martin Baker, UK.

Institute a robust review mechanism at various levels and defined frequencies during the development journey. For the LCA Navy development, there would be daily reviews by the LCA Navy Project Director with design teams to discuss any challenges or concerns, followed by daily reviews in the hangar during the build of the aircraft and test facilities. Weekly reviews were held at programme coordination team meetings at ADA with the Programme Director (Combat Aircraft) & Director ADA in the chair. This was an occasion to de-conflict any clashes of priorities between the LCA AF and Navy programmes. Monthly reviews were held by the Deputy Chief of Air Staff for both the programmes, with participation from the Asst. Chief of Naval Staff (Air). Quarterly reviews were held by the Chief of Air Staff, with participation from the Deputy Chief of Naval Staff. Half-yearly reviews were held by the Governing Body of ADA, chaired by the Secretary, Dept. of Defence (R&D), and annual review by the General Body of ADA, chaired by the Indian Defence Minister, the President of ADA Society.

All in all, we have seen glimpses of the exciting journey of design and development of a deck based fighter aircraft in the country from 'paper to flight'!

In Gratitude

I humbly start by thanking the Indian Navy for giving me the opportunity to gain experience on a deck-based aircraft operating onboard the earlier avatar of the *Vikrant* and also for deputing me to pursue a Master's degree in Aerospace Engineering at the prestigious Indian Institute of Science (IISc) in Bengaluru. In my opinion, this background probably served as a catalyst for my deputation to the ADA, ably supported by Admiral Arun Prakash. I wish to thank him for writing the foreword for this book.

My sincere thanks to Dr. TG Pai, who, as the Project Director (Technology Development) at ADA, led the LCA Navy programme in the initial stages of feasibility, pre-project studies, and the approval process of the CCS note, as well as the initial concept stages of the development process. I would like to thank Dr. Kota Harinarayana, the then Programme Director (Combat Aircraft), for accepting me on deputation at ADA and giving me the opportunity to take an active part in the LCA Navy development, followed by the late Mr. MB Verma and Mr. PS Subramanyam. I also express my gratitude to Dr. Girish Deodhare and Mr. Jitendra Jadhav for their whole hearted support.

I would like to express my gratitude to DRDO, HAL, NAL, ISRO, BEL, CEMILAC, DGAQA and several industrial partners from the public and private sector with whom I interacted extensively while spearheading the LCA Navy programme. I wish to acknowledge the unstinting support and encouragement provided by the Indian Air Force during the development of the aircraft and throughout various review meetings.

I would like to thank my family for encouraging me to write this monograph to document the entire journey from 'Paper to Flight'. I wish to thank Mr. RK Jolly, Dr. Amitab Saraf, and Mr. Vinod Kumar for their inputs for this book. I wish to thank the National Flight Test Centre (NFTC) team for providing me the opportunity to fly in the aircraft and gain firsthand experience, as well as for some of the photographs in this book. In particular, I would like to thank Mr. Deb Rana and Mr. Sanjay Simha for the outstanding pictures. I thank Cmde. Jaideep Maolankar and his team, who stood together with the design teams to realise the carrier-borne fighter aircraft. The Indian Air Force was also very supportive of the LCA Navy programme and, at times, helped de-conflict activity clashes between multiple programmes.

I thank Mr. Shiv Aroor, Mr. Jagan Pillarisetti, and Mr. Angad Singh for encouraging me to write the book and giving valuable inputs on the very first draft. I also thank Mr. Vyas Sivanand, Assistant Editor with *The New Indian Express*, Bengaluru, for shaping this book with his final editing. I thank Ms. Sonali K Balaji, my daughter-in-law, for giving wonderful ideas for the cover of the book and its design.

I also thank leading aerospace and defence journalist and Editor-in-Chief of Tarmak Media House, Dr. Anantha Krishnan M., for reposing faith in this work and introducing me to Mr. Rajan Arya of Pentagon Press LLP, who agreed to publish the monograph. Dr. Anantha Krishnan also acted as a catalyst in putting in place a perfect and inspiring flight path for this book, which was very crucial.

I thank the editorial team of Pentagon Press for providing me with feedback to modify the book and to refine and format it.

SECTION ON REFERENCE TABLES

Technology Readiness Levels (TRL)

TRL No.	*TRL Details*
0	Idea. Unproven Concept, No testing has been performed
1	Basic Research. Principles postulated and observed but no experimental proof of concept available
2	Technology Formulation. Concept and application have been formulated
3	Applied Research: First Laboratory test completed; Proof of Concept (PoC)
4	Small Scale Prototype built in a laboratory environment ("Ugly" Prototype)
5	Large Scale Prototype tested in intended environment
6	Prototype System tested in intended environment close to expected performance
7	Demonstration System operating in operational environment at pre-commercial scale
8	First of kind commercial system. Manufacturing issues resolved
9	Full Commercial application: Technology available for consumers

Aircraft Technical Specification for SBTF Design

Sl	*Description*	*LCA (Navy)*	*MiG-29K*
1	Maximum take-off weight, kg	12,500	22,400
2	Nominal take-off weight, kg	9500	18,550
3	Maximum speed at breaking off ski-jump, kmph	200	250
4	Nominal speed at breaking off ski-jump, kmph	180	160
5	Maximum landing weight, kg	9500	16,300
6	Minimum landing weight, kg	7000	13,500
7	Maximum true air speed at landing, kmph	278	268 (at 15°C)
8	Minimum true air speed at landing, kmph	240	240
9	Maximum vertical sink rate, m/s	7.1	7.1
10	Maximum engine thrust during arrestment (ISA), kN	50	88.40
11	Wing span, mm	8200	11,992/7460
12	Maximum deceleration during arrestment	4.5 g	4.5 g
13	Nominal glide slope angle	4°	4°
14(a)	Eye Hook distance, h (vertical), mm	4424	4468
14(b)	Eye Hook distance, L (horizontal), mm	6321	10,084
15	Maximum load on main LG, kN	326	550
16	Size of main tyres imprint at max load when landing (mm x mm)	200 x 380	300 x 500
17	Wheel track, mm	3010 (Static) 3100 (Free)	3120

SBTF Work Share Matrix

SI	*Content*	*Detail Des*	*Doc*	*Mfr./Sup*	*Inst*	*Test/Accept*
1	Ski-jump metal structure	R	R	I	I	R,I
2	Ski-jump foundation with support & drainage	R	R	I	I	R,I
3	RGS Site housing (metal structure)	R	R	I	I	R,I
4	RGS foundation pit	R	R	I	I	R,I
5	Restraining Gear supply	R	R	R	R	R,I
6	AGS Site housing (metal structure)	R	R	I	I	RJ
7	AGS foundation pit	R	R	I	I	R,I
8	Arresting gear supply	R	R	R	R	R,I
9	Hydraulic system for AG	R	R	R	R	R,I
10	Compressed air system for AG	R	R	I	R	R,I
11	Auxiliary facilities for AG (Hoisting, etc.)	R	R	I	R	R,I
12	Electrical power supply system	R	R	I	I	R,I
13	Air conditioning	R	R	I	I	R,I
14	Lighting	R	R	I	I	R,I
15	Fire fighting	R	R	I	I	R,I
16	Optical landing system	R	R	R	R	R,I
17	Landing monitoring TV system	R	R	R	R	R,I
18	Light signaling system	R	R	R	R	R.I
19	Offices, insulation and outfitting	R	R	I	I	R,I
20	AGS Internal communication	R	R	I	I	R,I
21	Radio and external communication	I	I	I	I	I
22	Services / auxiliary equipment external	R,]	R,I	I	I	R,I

Note: 'R' indicates Russian Agencies; T indicates Indian Entities

Programme Management Challenges during LEVCON System Development

Item	*Challenge*
LEVCON & Stub-Wing Structure	• Outsourced to a Private Sector Entity • Interface definition was done by ADA • Monitoring work progress, clarifying doubts raised and integrating back the digital sub-module into the overall Digital Mock Up (DMU) of the aircraft was the task of ADA • Test & Certification requirement document jointly developed
LEVCON Actuating Mechanism	• Extensive worldwide market survey to identify potential sources of customisation and supply • Integrating with overall Flight Control System (FCS) • Software development
Manufacturing	• Fabrication of complex spars on both the stub-wing and LEVCON sides with close manufacturing tolerances • Leading edge member to interface with the LEVCON Rotary Geared Actuator (RGA) with 'gun-drilling' concept • Fabrication of lengthy connecting pins
Simulation & Testing	• Extensive CFD simulations of different positions of LEVCON to understand the flow patterns • Wind tunnel testing and corelate with the CFD simulations and also obtain the hinge moments • FCS simulation on Real Time Simulator (RTS) and the 'Iron-Bird' • Conceptualisation and fabrication of ground test rig • The structural test – failure and redesign • Aircraft integration and functional testing on ground • Flight testing

EMI Test Schedule

Sl	*Test Method*	*Test Description*	*Frequency Range*
1*	CE 01	Conducted Emission, Power and Interconnecting Leads (Narrowband & Broadband)	30Hz – 15 kHz
2	CE 03	Conducted Emission, Power and Interconnecting Leads	15 kHz - 50 MHz
3	CE06	Conducted Emission, Antenna Terminals	10 kHz to 26 GHz
4	CE 07	Conducted Emissions, Transients, Spikes, Time Domain	—
5*	RE 01	Radiated Emission, Magnetic Field	30Hz – 50 kHz
6	RE 02	Radiated Emission, Electric Field (NB&BB)	14 kHz - 10 GHz
7	RE03	Radiated Emissions, Spurious and Harmonics, Radiated Technique	—
8*	CS 01	Conducted Susceptibility, Power Leads	30Hz – 50 kHz
9	CS 02	Conducted Susceptibility, Power & Interconnecting Control Leads	0.05 MHz - 400 MHz
10	CS 03	Inter modulation	15 kHz to 10 G Hz
11	CS 04	Rejection of Undesired Signal	30 Hz to 20 G Hz
12	CS 05	Cross Modulation	30 Hz to 20 G Hz
13	CS 06	Conducted Susceptibility, Spikes, Power Leads	200 V/m peak
14	CS 07	Conducted Susceptibility, Squelch Circuit	—
15	CS 09	Conducted Susceptibility, Structure (Common Mode) Current	60 Hz to 100 k Hz
16*	RS 01	Radiated Susceptibility, Magnetic Field	30Hz – 50 kHz
17	RS 02	Radiated Susceptibility, Magnetic & Electrical Fields, Spikes, and Power Frequency	Power Frequency of operation
18	RS 03	Radiated Susceptibility, Electric Field	20 V/m, 40 V/m, 200 V/m#

Note: Tests marked * they are though desirable for LCA Navy, they are not of mandatory requirement; # For Flight critical system only.

Arresting Gear Compatibility and Performance Test Matrix

Test Point No.	*Ac weight (kg)*[1]	*Fwd. Speed (Knots)*	*Offset (m)*	*Remarks*
1	9000	100	0	Lowest possible Ac weight
2	9900	100	0	Arresting gear and Aircraft loads build up
3	9900	110	0	Arresting gear setting verification
4	9900	110	0	
5	9900	110	0	
6	9900	115	0	Build up to limit condition (hook load or arresting gear)
7	9900	120	0	
8	9900	125	0	
9	9900	130	0	
10	9900	135	0	
11	9000	135[2]	0	Light weight at limit speed
12	9900	110	1.5	Off centre build up to limit condition
13	9900	115	1.5	
14	9900	120	1.5	
15	9900	125	1.5	
16	9900	130	1.5	
17	9900	135	1.5	
18	9900	110	3.0	
19	9900	115	3.0	
20	9900	120	3.0	
21	9900	125	3.0	
22	9900	130	3.0	
23	9900	135	3.0	

Notes:

a) Gross Weight (GW) range: –200kg to +45kg
b) Limit engaging speed (for whichever limit parameter occurs first, aircraft or arresting gear)
c) Test point tolerances assumed:
   i) Hook load: ± 2.0% at limit condition
   ii) Off-centre distance: Not to exceed 3.0m
d) Off centre conditions will be reduced based on 'on-centre' conditions
e) Assume MIL power ground run until arrestment complete

Arrested Landings – Structural Demonstration – Test Point Conditions

Test Point Number	*Manoeuvre*	*Gross Weight (kg)*	*Sink Speed (m/s)*	*Touchdown Attitude*			*Hook Load*	*Off center (m)*	*Comments (kN)*
				Pitch (deg)	*Roll (deg)*	*Yaw (deg)*			
AL-001	Arrestment - Mean Pitch High Sink	10,000 (+226/681)	3.23	-	-	-	-	-	10.6fps
AL-002	Arrestment - Mean Pitch High Sink	10,000 (+226/681)	3.84	-	-	-	-	-	12.6fps
AL-003	Arrestment - Mean Pitch High Sink	10,000 (+226/681)	4.45	10.2	-	-	-	-	14.6fps (Mean pitch at 14.2AOA-4GS = 10.2
AL-004	Arrestment - Mean Pitch High Sink	10,000 (+226/681)	5.06	10.2	-	-	-	-	16.6fps
AL-005	Arrestment - Mean Pitch High Sink	10,000 (+226/681)	5.37	10.2	-	-	-	-	17.6fps
AL-006*	Arrestment - Mean Pitch High Sink	10,000 (+226/454)	≥ 5.68	10.2 (± 1.5)	-	-	-	-	80% Vv design=7.1mps (5.68mps/18.6fps), 5.0° GS based on Ve=241kph
AL-007*	Arrestment - Mean Pitch High Sink	10,000 (+226/454)	≥ 5.68	10.2 (± 1.5)	-	-	-	-	1 of AL-006 – AL-008 must be with MLG deck obstruction
AL-008*	Arrestment - Mean Pitch High Sink	10,000 (+226/454)	≥ 5.68	10.2 (± 1.5)	-	-	-	-	
AL-009	Arrestment - Nose Down High Sink	10,000 (+226/681)	3.84	-	-	-	-	-	10.3° AOA.

AL-010	Arrestment - Nose Down High Sink	10,000 (+226/681)	4.45	-	-	-	-	-	10.3° AOA.
AL-011	Arrestment - Nose Down High Sink	10,000 (+226/681)	5.06	-	-	-	-	-	10.3° AOA.
AL-012	Arrestment - Nose Down High Sink	10,000 (+226/681)	5.37	-	-	-	-	-	10.3° AOA.
AL-013*	Arrestment - Nose Down High Sink	10,000 (+226/454)	≥ 5.68	≤ 5.7	-	-	-	-	10.3° AOA. 4.75° GS based on Ve=250kph
AL-014*	Arrestment - Nose Down High Sink	10,000 (+226/454)	≥ 5.68	≤ 5.7	-	-	-	-	10.3° AOA. 1 of AL-013 – AL-015 must be with NLG deck obstruction
AL-015*	Arrestment - Nose Down High Sink	10,000 (+226/454)	≥ 5.68	≤ 5.7	-	-	-	-	10.3° AOA.
AL-016	Arrestment - Tail Down High Sink	10,000 (+226/681)	3.84	-	-	-	-	-	17.4° AOA.
AL-017	Arrestment - Tail Down High Sink	10,000 (+226/681)	4.45	-	-	-	-	-	17.4° AOA.
AL-018	Arrestment - Tail Down v	10,000 (+226/681)	5.06	-	-	-	-	-	17.4° AOA.
AL-019	Arrestment - Tail Down High Sink	10,000 (+226/681)	5.37	-	-	-	-	-	17.4° AOA.
AL-020*	Arrestment - Tail Down High Sink	10,000 (+226/454)	≥ 5.68	≥ 12.0	-	-	-	-	~17.4° AOA./5.25° GS based on Ve=222kph
AL-021*	Arrestment - Tail Down v	10,000 (+226/454)	≥ 5.68	≥ 12.0	-	-	-	-	~17.4° AOA. 1 of AL-020 – AL-022 must be with MLG deck obstruction

Test Point Number	*Manoeuvre*	*Gross Weight (kg)*	*Sink Speed (m/s)*	*Touchdown Attitude*			*Hook Load*	*Off center (m)*	*Comments (kN)*
				Pitch (deg)	*Roll (deg)*	*Yaw (deg)*			
AL-022*	Arrestment - Tail Down High Sink	10,000 (+226/454)	≥ 5.68	≥ 12.0	-	-	-	-	~17.4° AOA.
AL-023	Arrestment - Rolled	10,000 (+226/681)	4.33	-	≥ 5.0			-	Mean Vv = 4.33mps/14.2fps Roll only
AL-024	Arrestment - Yawed	10,000 (+226/681)	4.33	-		≥ 5.0	-	-	Yaw only
AL-025*	Arrestment - Rolled-Yawed	10,000 (+226/454)	4.33	-	≤ 5.0	≥ 5.0	-	-	Roll/yaw opposite.
AL-026*	Arrestment - Rolled-Yawed	10,000 (+226/454)	4.33	-	≥ 5.0	≤ 5.0	-	-	Roll/yaw opposite.
AL-027*	Arrestment - Rolled-Yawed	10,000 (+226/454)	4.33	-	≥ 5.0	≥ 5.0	-	-	Roll/yaw same.
AL-028*	Arrestment - Rolled-Yawed	10,000 (+226/454)	4.33	-	≤ 5.0	≤ 5.0	-	-	Roll/yaw same.
AL-029	Arrestment - Free Flight	10,000 (+226/681)	3.78	-	-	-	-	-	~15.3°AOA. Touch and go landing
AL-030	Arrestment - Free Flight	10,000 (+226/681)	3.17	-	-	-	-	-	~15.3°AOA. Touch and go landing. Vpa for Ve ≥ 85% hook load
AL-031	Arrestment - Free Flight	10,000 (+226/681)	2.56	-	-	-	-	-	~15.3°AOA. Touch and go landing. Vpa for Ve ≥ 85% hook load
AL-032*	Arrestment - Free Flight	10,000 (+226/454)	≤ 2.25	≥ 13.0	-	-	≥ 374	-	~15.3°AOA. Vpa for Ve ≥ 85% hook load. 2.0GS based on Ve=232kph

AL-033*	Arrestment - Free Flight	10,000 (+226/454)	≤ 2.25	≥ 13.0	-	-	≥ 374	-	~15.3°AOA. Vpa for Ve > 85% hook load. 2.0GS based on Ve=232kph
AL-034*	Arrestment - Free Flight	10,000 (+226/454)	≤ 2.25	≥ 13.0	-	-	≥ 374	-	~15.3°AOA. Vpa for Ve > 85% hook load. 2.0GS based on Ve=232kph
AL-035	Arrestment - On Center	10,000 (+226/681)	4.33	-	-	-	374	-	Ve for 85% hook load.
AL-036	Arrestment - On Center	10,000 (+226/454)	4.33	-	-	-	396	-	Ve for 90% hook load.
AL-037	Arrestment - On Center	10,000 (+226/454)	4.33	-	-	-	418	-	Ve for 95% hook load.
AL-038*	Arrestment - On Center	10,000 (+226/454)	4.33	-	-	-	≥ 440	-	Ve for ≥ 100% hook load.
AL-039	Arrestment - Rolled	10,000 (+226/681)	4.33	-	≥ 6.0		-	-	Mean Vv = 4.33mps/14.2fps
AL-040	Arrestment - Rolled	10,000 (+226/681)	4.33	-	≤ 6.0	-	-	-	
AL-041*	Arrestment - Rolled	10,000 (+226/454)	4.33	10.2 (± 1.0)	≥ 6.0		≥ 440	-	Ve for ≥ 100% hook load
AL-042*	Arrestment - Rolled	10,000 (+226/454)	4.33	10.2 (± 1.0)	≥ -6.0		≥ 440	-	Ve for ≥ 100% hook load
AL-043	Arrestment - Off Center	10,000 (+226/681)	4.33	-	-	-	≤ 418	3.1	Mean Vv = 4.33mps/14.2fps Ve for ≤95% hook load Off-center to short side purchase cable
AL-044	Arrestment - Off Center	10,000 (+226/681)	4.33	-	-	-	≤ 418	4.58	Same side as AL043.
AL-045	Arrestment - Off Center	10,000 (+226/454)	4.33	-	-	-	≤ 440	4.88	Same side as AL043.
AL-046*	Arrestment - Off Center	10,000 (+226/454)	4.33	-	-	-	≥ 440	4.88 (-0.3/+0.61)	Ve for ≥100% hook load. Same side as AL043.

AL-047*	Arrestment - Off Center	10,000 (+226/454)	4.33	-	-	-	≥ 440	-4.88 (-0.3/+0.61)	Ve for ≥ 100% hook load. Opposite side to AL-046.

Table-12.4: LCA-Navy Arrested Landing Test Matrix

Notes:

1. *Denotes endpoint condition. Not all conditions need to be conducted for the various test loadings. Test points for mis-serviced landing gear/tires would have to be determined, but typically just the high sink points are done.
2. All conditions are notional and based on previous briefing notes. Vpa for AOA vs. GW unknown. Arresting gear performance estimating 135kt Ve, 10000kg GW, 440kN HL, -4.5g Nx.
3. All test points are negotiated based on loads analysis and aircraft FQ.
4. Assumed a 907kg GW range for build-up points and 680kg GW range for end points.
5. Test point tolerances assumed:
   a. Sink speed: ≥ (target – 0.3 m/s) for build-up conditions and ≥ target for end points.
   b. Pitch: ± 1.5 deg for mean pitch (10.2 deg) conditions, ≤ 5.7 deg for nose down, and ≥ 12.0 deg for tail down.
   c. Hook load: ± 2.0% unless stated otherwise.
   d. Off-center distance: > (target – 0.3 m) and not to exceed 5.5 m at endpoint.
6. An arrested landing is required whenever the target sink speed > 5.06 m/s or the glideslope ≥ 5.0 deg. Touch and go landing may be used when test conditions preclude an arrested landing within limits of the aircraft or arresting gear. However, no more than three touch and go landings (typical) may be performed prior to a flared full stop landing and subsequent aircraft inspections.
7. Deck obstruction is typically the cable (but could be something else). Obstruction is hit with ≥75% load on the MLG/NLG for the test point if all conditions are met.
8. A touch and go table should be generated for build-up purposes for each type of arrested landing endpoint conditions.

GLOSSARY

Term	*Description*
AAHC	Approach AoA Hold Controller - Control law mode specially designed for LCA Navy deck recovery to be an aid to ease pilot workload
AAGE	Advanced Arresting Gear Engine - Newly installed on US Navy aircraft carriers for arrested recovery of aircraft
AAID	Auxiliary Air Intake Door - To improve pressure recovery and thereby engine static thrust and hence, improves overall aircraft performance
AAR	Air-to-Air Refuelling
ACU	Asymmetry Control Unit - Part of LEVCON system that can detect mismatch between left and right systems and facilitate corrective action
ADA	Aeronautical Development Agency - Autonomous Body of Ministry of Defence, Government of India and was set up specifically for development of fighter aircraft in the country
ADC	Air Data Computer - Part of flight control system of aircraft to provide sensory information to the Digital Flight Control Computer (DFCC)
ADE	Aeronautical Development Establishment - DRDO facility that was largely supporting the FCS software development and had developed and built the Real Time Simulator (RTS)
ADS	Air Defence Ship - Designation given by the Directorate of Naval Design of the Indian Navy for Indigenous aircraft carrier in development phase

Aerodata	Aerodynamic Data Set - Based on CFD and wind-tunnel tests and is one of the key parameters for the Control Law of the flight control system
AESA	Active Electronically Scanned Array Radar - no complex mechanical parts as in conventional Radars
AGB	Angle Gear Box - Part of LEVCON system that conncets the drive system to the leading edge hinge elements
AGS	Arresting Gear System - Installation on aircraft carrier to facilitate aircraft landing on ship
AHCP	At-Hand Control Panel - in the aircraft cockpit
AHS	Arrester Hook System - Installed on aircraft to facilitate snagging of arrester wire on ship for landing
Aileron	Control surfaces mounted on wing trailing edge at outboard section acting in opposite sense for roll control of aircraft
AIR	Avionics Integration Rig that brings together all elements of the avionics system to facilitate extensive testing. Can have actual aircraft equipment or emulators to complete the system for testing
ALRB	Aircraft Launch and Recovery Bulletin
AMAGB	Aircraft Mounted Accessory Gear Box
AMCA	Advanced Medium Combat Aircraft
AoA	Angle of Attack
AR&DB	Aircraft Research and Design Board - An entity within DRDO
ARDC	Aircraft Research & Design Centre of HAL
ASM	Anti-Shipping Missile
ASR	Air Staff Requirements promulgated by the Indian Air Force (IAF) giving detailed requirements that the aircraft should meet, provide mission and performance goals and other supportability needs
ATC	Air Traffic Control
ATP	Acceptance Test Procedure - document that gives the criteria that equipment/systems need to meet. Will be the benchmark against which the quality assurance team clears the equipment/system

ATR	Attained Turn Rate - point performance value of the aircraft specified in ASR
AuW	All up Weight - maximum allowed take-off mass of the aircraft
BEL	Bharat Electronics Limited - Public Sector Undertaking of Indian Ministry of Defence
BIT	Built-In Test
BoI	Bought-out Item - include fasteners, cables, electrical connectors, pipelines, fluid connectors, equipment trays, etc.
BoM	Bill of Material
BoR	Body of Revolution - A digital tool mimicking an aircraft concept to enable faster configuration checks
BVR	Beyond Visual Range - Missile
C.G	Centre of Gravity
CAD	Computer Aided Design
CAE	Computer Aided Engineering
CAM	Computer Aided Manufacturing
CAP	Combat Air Patrol - Type of aircraft mission
CAS	Chief of Air Staff
CATOBAR	Catapult Take-Off But Arrested Recovery - Type of aircraft carrier
CCE(R&D)	Chief Construction Engineer (Research & Development) - Construction wing of DRDO
CCM	Close Combat Missile
CCS	Cabinet Committee on Security of the Government of India, chaired by the Hon'ble Prime Minister
CCT	Carrier Compatibility Test
CDF	Customer Demonstration Flights
CDR	Critical Design Review - Stage for giving a go-ahead for aircraft build
CEF	Cockpit Environment Facility - To facilitate Man-Machine Interface
CEMILAC	Centre for Military Airworthiness and Certification
CFC	Carbon-Fibre Composite

CFD	Computational Fluid Dynamics
CLAW	Control Law - Algorithm for flight control system
CMTI	Central Machine Tool Institute
CNC	Computer Numerical Control
CNS	Chief of the Naval Staff
CoD	Certificate of Design - provided by CEMILAC
CROV	Constant Runout Valve - Installed in ship's arresting gear with adjustment for aircraft mass
CSD	Carrier Suitability Demonstration
CVRDE	Combat Vehicles Research and Development Establishment, DRDO
DAC	Defence Acquistion Council - Chaired by the Indian Defence Minister
DFCC	Digital Flight Control Computer
DFMA	Design For Manufacture and Assembly - combination of two methodologies; design for manufacture, which means the design for ease of manufacture of the parts that will form a product, and design for assembly, which means the design of the product for ease of assembly deriving creative ideas at the same time
DGAQA	Director General Aeronautical Quality Assurance
DMU	Digital Mock-Up
DRDO	Defence Research and Development Organisation - Indian Ministry of Defence
ECS	Environmental Control System - basically is the airconditioning and cooling system on the aircraft
EGR	Engine Ground Run
EHSV	Electro-Hydro Static Valve
Elevator	Control surfaces mounted on tailplane trailing edge acting in same sense for pitch control of aircraft
Elevon	Combination of Elevator and Aileron used in tailess aircraft - like in the LCA
ELS	Engineer-in-Loop Simulator - Used for development testing of Control Law Algoritms

EMALS	Electro-Magnetic Aircraft Launch System - Installed on recent US Navy aircraft carriers
EMC	Electromagnetic Compatibility
EME	Electromagnetic Environment
EMI	Electromagnetic Interference
Ergonomics	Ergonomics, also known as human factors, is the scientific discipline that seeks to understand and improve human interactions with products, equipment, environments and systems
FADEC	Full Authority Digital Engine Control
FAT	Factory Acceptance Test
FCLP	Field Carrier Landing Practice
FCN	Flight Clearance Note - provided by CEMILAC
FCS	Flight Control System
FE	Foreign Exchange
FEM	Finite Element Methods - Aircraft strucural simulation methodology
Flap	Control surface loacated on the wing inboard section trailing edge - actuated downwards to increase lift especially during landing
FMEA	Failure Mode and Effectiveness Analysis - study by quality assurance team
FOC	Final Operational Clearance - Final certification standard with the build as per specifications
FSED	Full Scale Engineering Development
Fuel Dump	Also called fuel jettison - capability in a typical deck based aircraft to release some quantity of fuel from the aircraft to bring it to a safe landing mass for emergency deck recovery
GE	General Electric
GHE / GSE	Ground Handling Equipment / Ground Support Equipment
GSI	Geological Survey of India
GSL	Goa Shipyard Limited - Public Sector Undertaking of the Indian Ministry of Defence

GTRE	Gas Turbine Research Establishment of DRDO - Engine development organisation (Kaveri engine)
HAL	Hindustan Aeronautics Limited - Public Sector Undertaking of the Indian Ministry of Defence
HF	Hindustan Fighter
HMI	Human-Machine Interface
HSTT	High Speed Taxi Test
HTDP	Hook Touch Down Point - Intended hook strike point on ships deck between first and second wires
HUD	Head-Up Display - provides pilot visual display of key parameters during ground roll and flight
IAC	Indigenous Aircraft Carrier
IAF	Indian Air Force
IFLOLS	Improved Fresnel Lens Optical Landing System - Used on US Navy Aircraft Carriers for providing glide slope information to pilots as a landing aid
IFR	In-Flight Refuelling - taking in fuel when aircraft is flying from a tanker aircraft to enhance range/endurance and thus will be a significant capability booster
IISc	Indian Institute of Science, Bangalore
IN	Indian Navy
INS	Indian Naval Ship
IOC	Initial Operational Clearance - An interim certification standard of release to service for aircraft exploitation and obtaining user feedback
Iron Bird	Hardware-in-loop Simulator
ISRO	Indian Space Research Organisation
IV&V	Independent Verification and Validation - Software quality
JBD	Jet Blast Deflector - installed on large aircraft carriers
LADC	LEVCON Air Data Computer
LCA	Light Combat Aircraft (Air Force Version)
LCA Navy	Light Combat Aircraft (Naval Version)

LCN	Load Classification Number - A system of classification of the supporting capacity of pavements, indicating their ability to support loads without cracking or becoming permanently deformed.
LCP	Landing Control Post - near arresting gear of ship / SBTF
LEVCON	Leading Edge Vortex Controller - Additional control surface in LCA Navy to enable reduction in aircraft approach speed
LG	Landing Gear
LGB	Laser Guided Bomb
LRU	Line Replaceable Unit - equipment/aggregate for various aircraft systems
LSO	Landing Safety Officer / Landing Signalling Officer - individual who controls the landing of the aircraft on to the ship
LSP	Limited Series Production
LSS	Light Signalling System - aids for take-off and landing on board an aircraft carrier
LSTT	Low Speed Taxi Test
LVDT	Linear Variable Differential Transformer
MAST	Main Airframe Static Test Rig - used for testing a Structual Test Specimen (STS) upto ultimate loads (150%)
MFD	Multi-Function Display - digital display surfaces installed in the cockpit to provide information to pilot
MLG	Main Landing Gear
MMHFH	Maintenance Man-Hours per Flight Hour
MMI	Man-Machine Interface
MMR	Multi-Mode Radar
MRM	Medium Range Missile
NAL	National Aerospace Laboratories - CSIR laboratory and has provided support for Control Law, composites, wind tunnel, etc.
NASR	Naval Air Staff Requirements - requirements given by Naval Headquarters
NDB	Nevskoye Design Bureau, St. Petersburg, Russia - design house for the Russian aircraft carrier, inputs for SBTF and the IAC

NDT	Non-Destructive Test
NFTC	National Flight Test Centre - coordinates entire flight test activities for the programmes of ADA
NHQ	Naval Headquarters
NLG	Nose Landing Gear
NMG	Numerical Master Geometry - Defines the shape of the aircraft also called the outer mold line
NP	Naval Prototype of LCA Navy
OAC	Open Architecture Computer - Mission computer of the aircraft
OAT	Outside Air Temperature
OBOGS	On-Board Oxygen Generating System - eliminates need to carry liquid oxygen on ships
OCC	Operational Clean Configuration
OLS	Optical Landing System - Installed on aircraft carrier to provide glide slope information for landing
PDP	Project Definition Phase
PDR	Preliminary Design Review - clears concept design and allows detail design to commence
PDU	Power Drive Unit - Part of LEVCON system that is the prime-mover
PERT	Program Evaluation and Review Technique - Programme Management tool
PID	Parametric Identification
PLM	Product Lifecycle Management
PMT	Project Monitoring Team
PPP	Pre-Project Phase
PSU	Public Sector Undertaking
PV	Prototype Vehicles
QA	Quality Assurance
QT	Qualification Test
R&DE(E)	Research & Development Engineers (Establishment) of DRDO
RAC-MiG	Russian Aircraft Corporation - MiG

RGS	Restraining Gear System - Installed on aircraft carrier to hold aircraft at take-off point
RTS	Real Time Simulator - Flight simulator designed for LCA and its variants
Rudder	Control surface mounted on the vertical tail used for yaw control
RVDT	Rotary Variable Differential Transformer
SBTF	Shore Based Test Facility - Replicates aircraft carrier at a shore base having capability of ski-jump for take-off and arresting gear for landing
SDEF	System Design and Evaluation Facility - also called the Cockpit Environment Facility (CEF)
SJTO	Ski-Jump Take-Off
SP	Series Production
SPS	Secondary Power System
SPV	Special Purpose Vehicle
SRB	Safety Review Board - consists of relevant expert who review specific aspects as defined to them and accord clearance, if satisfied
SRR	System Requirement Review - comprehensive review and creation of a compliance matrix to check extent of meeting requirements
STOBAR	Ski-jump Take-Off But Arrested Recovery
STOVL	Ski-jump Take-Off and Vertical Landing
STR	Sustained Turn Rate - aircraft point performance parameter as specified in ASR
STS	Structural Test Specimen - a full-fledged instrumented aircraft structure used in the Main Airframe Static Test (MAST) rig to check structural integrity
TD	Technology Demonstrators
TEDBF	Twin-Engined Deck Based Fighter Aircraft - under development for the Indian Navy
ToCP	Take-off Control Post - for controling take-off on board aircraft carriers or in the SBTF

TP	Technical Position - located at parking spots of aircraft and would normally contain aircraft securing devices (lashing), power supply, fuel, hydraulics, etc.
TRL	Technology Readiness Level
UAV	Unmanned Aerial Vehicle
UEWS	Unified Electronic Warfare Suite - Internally located in aircraft'
Wave Drag	Component of the aerodynamic drag on aircraft wings and fuselage, propeller blade tips and projectiles moving at transonic and supersonic speeds, due to the presence of shock waves
WIR	Weapon Integration Rig
6-DoF	Six Degrees of Freedom - Three rotary being Roll, Pitch and Yaw; Three linear being longitudinal (fore & aft), lateral (side to side) and vertical (up & down)

INDEX

2D Computer-Aided Design (CAD), 58-59, 67
3D CAD, 58, 65, 67, 100, 199

Aatre, Dr. VK, 2, 69
Acceptance Test Procedure (ATP), 122
Active Electronically Scanned Array (AESA) radar, 203, 205
ADAMS, 178, 181
Admiral Gorshkov, 33, 98
Admiral Kuznetsov, 33, 98
Advanced Arresting Gear Engine, 36
Advanced Light Helicopter (ALH), 215
Advanced Medium Combat Aircraft (AMCA), 223-24
Aero India 2017, 223, 227
Aerodata Set, 63
Aeronautical Development Agency (ADA), 2, 4-5, 7, 10-12, 14, 17, 19-21, 28, 31, 37-38, 95, 98, 103, 110, 122, 130, 167-69, 185, 198-99, 212, 216, 218, 221, 223, 227-28
AF Mk-1A aircraft, 12
Air Data Computer (ADC), 55, 184
Air Defence Ship (ADS), 28
Air Force Version, 13-14, 22, 25, 29
Air Staff Requirements (ASR), 2, 199
Air Traffic Control (ATC), 95
Aircraft Build Process Flow, 68
Aircraft Mounted Accessories Gear Box (AMAGB), 52
Aircraft Mounted Accessory Gear Box (AMAGB), 27
Air-to-air Refuelling (AAR), 210
Alize Aircraft, 37, 95, 97, 101, 113, 115
Alize Squadron, 35
All up Weight (AuW), 53
Angle Gear Box (AGB), 151
Angle of Attack (AoA), 14, 147, 149, 184, 187, 195
Anti-Shipping Missile (ASM), 27
Antony, Shri AK, the then Indian Defence Minister, 19, 75
Approach AoA Hold Controller, 195
Arrakonam, 95
Arrested Recovery, 27
Arrester Hook System (AHS), 19, 43, 113, 121, 125
Arresting Gear System (AGS), 18, 101, 107
Arunachalam, Dr. VS, 2
Asymmetry Control Unit (ACU), 151
At-Hand Control Panel (AHCP), 207
Attained Turn Rate (ATR), 24
Autoclave, 49
Auxiliary Air Intake Door (AAID), 17, 50, 52
    free-floats, 51
    Auxiliary Air Intake Door, 43
Avionics and Cockpit Controls, 55
Avionics Integration Rig (AIR), 167, 168

Bahrain, 213-15, 217
Bahrain International Air Show (BIAS), 213, 217, 227
Baker, Martin, 54
Balaji, Lt Cdr. CD (later Commodore), 13

Bengaluru, 18, 169, 189, 213, 222-23
 2017 Aero India International Air Show, 129
Biennial Aero-India 2017 International Air Show, 223
Bill of Material (BoM), 67, 124
Body of Revolution (BoR), 202
Boeing's Super Hornet, 43
Bought out Items (BoI), 69
Brake Parachute, 54
Built-in-Test (BIT), 78

Cabinet Committee on Security (CCS), 6-7, 14, 29, 38, 41, 57, 38
Calibrated Airspeed (CAS), 220
Cameras, 105
Carbon-Fibre Composite (CFC) skins, 203
Carrier Compatibility Test (CCT), 99, 169, 171, 175
Carrier Suitability Demonstration (CSD), 171-72, 175
Catapult Take-off But Arrested Recovery (CATOBAR or CV), 35-36, 41
CCE, 96, 110
Central Machine Tool Institute (CMTI), 18
Centre for Artificial Intelligence & Robotics (CAIR), 185
Centre for Military Airworthiness and Certification (CEMILAC), 122
Centre Fuselage, 46
 Jig, 71
Centre of Gravity (C.G), 63-64, 122, 148, 192, 204
Certificate of Design (CoD), 176-81
Certification (CEMILAC), 60, 75, 77, 79
Chetak, 37
Chief Construction Engineers (R&D), the civil engineering arm of the DRDO (CCE R&D), 99, 103-4
China, 35, 41
Close Combat Missiles (CCM), 27, 171
Cochin Shipyard Ltd., 33
Cockpit Environment Facility (CEF), 27, 167
Coefficient of Lift (C_L), 147, 149-50
Combat Air Patrol (CAP), 24, 200
Computational Fluid Dynamics (CFD), 23-24, 39, 63-65, 129, 151, 169
Computer Aided Design (CAD), 5, 65, 127, 137, 141, 201, 204
Computer Aided Engineering (CAE), 5
Computer Aided Manufacturing (CAM), 5
Computer Numerical Control (CNC) machines, 70-71
Concept Design, 62
Constant Run-Out Arresting Gear, 97
Constant Run-Out Valve (CROV), 97, 121
Continuity and Meggar Checks, 75
Control Law (CLAW), 3, 25, 64, 177, 187-89, 192-94, 197
 Development, 183
Correlation, 65
Critical Design Review (CDR), 62, 68
CSIR, 10, 20-21
CSIR Labs, 75
Customer Demonstration Flights (CDF), 223
CVRDE, 52

Dassault Aviation's Rafale Aircraft, 43
Dawson, Adm. OS , former Chief of the Naval Staff, 75
Defence Acquisition Council (DAC), 224
Defence Exhibition Organisation (DEO), 219
Defence Research & Development Organisation (DRDO), 2, 3, 5, 20-21, 26, 28, 52, 75, 99, 103, 168, 213, 216-17, 223
Derby Beyond Visual Range (BVR), 225
Derby Missiles, 172
 Launcher, 178

Design and Ergonomics, 65
Design For Manufacture and Assembly (DFMA), 208-10
Design Liaison, 62
Design Stage Process Flow, 61
DFCC (Digital Flight Control Computer), 164-65, 179
Dhruv, 215
Digital Flight Control Computer (DFCC), 76, 164
Digital Mock Up (DMU), 59, 67-68, 73-74, 155, 209-10
Digital Twin, 72
Directorate General Aeronautical Quality Assurance (DGAQA), 123, 217

Ejection Seat, 54
Electrical Harness Design & Installation, 66
Electrical System, 55
Electro-Hydro Static Valve (EHSV), 152
Electro-Magnetic Aircraft Launch System (EMALS), 36
Electro-Magnetic Compatibility (EMC), 22, 165
Electro-Magnetic Environment (EME), 166
Electro-Magnetic Interference (EMI), 22, 51, 165-67, 172, 174, 182
Emeritus Scientists, 11
Engine(s), 51-52
 GE-F404-IN20, 7, 27, 51, 54, 62, 190, 220
 GE-F414-INS6, 52, 201, 207, 209
 Kaveri, 7, 24, 26-27, 51, 62
Engine Ground Run (EGR), 77-78
Engineer-in-the-Loop Simulator (ELS), 162
Environmental Control System (ECS), 27, 45, 54
Equipping and Integration, 73
ESCO Systems (Zodiac), 98

Eugene Ely, 90
Euler CFD methods, 202
Europe, 90

Factory Acceptance Tests (FAT), 107
Failure Mode and Effectiveness Analysis (FMEA), 28
Falkland War, 34
Field Carrier Landing Practice (FCLP), 91, 172
Final Operational Clearance (FOC), 6, 10, 12, 169, 227
Finite Element Methods (FEM), 65
First Technology Demonstrator Aircraft (TD1), 164
Flight Clearance Note (FCN), 176-77, 179-81
Flight Control System (FCS), 4, 45, 55, 76, 162, 164, 193
Flight Control System (FCS), 54
Flying Daggers, 219
FNS Foch, 90-91
Foreign Exchange (FE), 7
France, 1, 35, 41
Free Roll, 190
French, 97, 125
 Navy, 90
Front Fuselage Jig, 71
Front Fuselage, 44
Fuel System, 52
Full Authority Digital Engine Controller (FADEC), 184
Full Scale Engineering Development (FSED), 6-8, 10, 14, 20-21, 37-41
Full-Scale Engineering Development for a Naval Version of the Light Combat Aircraft (FSED LCA Navy), 14, 29-30, 57, 90

Gas Turbine Research Establishment (GTRE), 26
General Electric (GE), 231

Geological Survey of India (GSI), 95-96
Goa, 18-19, 95-96, 98-99, 103, 107, 110, 143-44, 169, 171, 179, 188-89, 191, 219
  Dabolim Airport, 94
  Indian Naval Air Station, 59, 158, 230
Goa Shipyard Ltd. (GSL), 99, 103, 106, 110
Government of India, 6, 14, 17, 21, 37, 41, 90, 213, 216, 219, 223-24
GPS, 169
Ground Handling Equipment and Ground Support Equipment (GHE/GSE), 222
Ground Vibration Tests (GVT), 174
Gujarat, 213

Hamara Tejas, 8
Hard Gate, 62
Hardware-in-the-Loop Simulator (HILS), 76, 164
Harinarayana, Dr. Kota, former Programme Director of ADA, 3, 8, 13, 75
Head Up Display (HUD), 55, 167, 226
HF-24 (Marut), 1, 5
High-Speed Taxi Test (HSTT), 78-79
Hi-Lo-Hi Profile, 200
Hindustan Aeronautics Ltd. (HAL), 1, 3, 5, 10, 14-15, 17-21, 23, 38, 46, 122, 137, 146, 168, 185, 189, 199, 213, 215-18, 221-22, 224
  Foundry and Forge, 137
HMS *Hermes*, 34
Hook Point Design Features, 118
Hook Shoe, 118-19
Hook Touchdown Point (HTDP), 177
Hook-to-Eye, 177
Hot & High, 220
Hot Refuelling, 53, 225
Human-Machine Interface (HMI), 167
Hyderabad, 137
Hydraulic System, 53

Improved Fresnel Lens Optical Landing System (IFLOLS), 101
Independent Verification and Validation (IV&V) team, 4, 164
India, 33, 35, 41, 95
Indian Air Force (IAF), 1-3, 7, 10, 15, 20, 40, 53, 75, 168, 199, 213-14, 217, 221024, 227
Indian Navy (IN), 1, 3, 7, 13, 15, 21-22, 30-31, 33-35, 37-38, 40-41, 60, 75, 97-99, 101, 110-11, 125-26, 168, 175, 185, 199-200, 209, 211, 213, 217
Indian Navy's Directorate of Naval Design, 210
Indian Registry of Shipping (IRS), 107, 109
Indian Space Research Organisation (ISRO), 3, 10
Indigenous Aircraft Carrier (IAC), 186
In-flight Refuelling (IFR), 33, 62
Initial Operational Clearance (IOC), 6, 10, 169, 172, 227
INS *Dega*, 95
INS *Garuda*, 95
INS *Hansa*, 13, 95
INS *Rajali*, 95
INS *Vikramaditya*, 15, 19, 33-34, 37, 98, 111, 121, 131, 142, 178, 182, 186, 198, 211
INS *Vikrant*, 15, 28, 34-35, 37, 41, 97-98, 101, 107, 113, 210-11, 121
INS *Viraat*, 15, 34, 144
Integrated Life Support System (ILSS), 27
Interchangeability (ICY) Points, 153
Iron Bird (IB), 40, 76, 125, 164
Iron Fist, DefExpo-2016, 217, 227

Jamnagar, 52, 213, 217
Jet blast deflector (JBD), 92
Joint Strike Fighter (JSF), 34, 98
Jolly, Mr. RK, 155

Kalam, Dr. APJ Abdul, 2, 185
Kandru, Lt Cdr. Vijay (later Commodore), 13
Kochi, 94
Kotiyal, Wg. Cdr. Rajeev, 8
Krishnan, Mr. Anantha, 8
Kumar, Mr. TV Vinod, 14

Lakehurst, 90-91
Landing Control Post (LCP), 101, 105, 121
Landing Gear (LG), 133-46
Landing Monitoring TV System, 102
Landing Safety Officer (LSO), 102, 140
Laser Guided Bombs (LGBs), 27
Leading Edge Vortex CONtroller (LEVCON), 16, 18-19, 22-24, 27-28, 40, 43, 49, 50, 53, 55-57, 62, 147-56, 161, 174-75, 177-78, 183-84, 198, 201, 203, 210
    Jig, 71
    Structural Test Rig, 153
LEVCON Air Data Computer (LADC), 55, 152, 184
LEVCON Control Computer (LCC), 152
Licence Build, 6
Lift/Drag (L/D) Ratio, 148
Light Combat Aircraft (LCA), 1, 20, 29, 58, 218, 227
    Air Force, 20, 27-28, 37-40, 44-47, 49, 51-55, 75, 77, 79, 133-34, 166, 187, 192
        Fighter, 70, 183
        Trainer, 70, 183, 220, 225-27
    Navy, 1-8, 10-11, 13, 15-18, 20-29, 31-32, 35, 37-40, 42, 44-47, 50-53, 55-57, 60, 67-71, 74, 76-77, 79-80, 89, 91, 94, 103, 105-7, 110, 112-13, 121, 126-27, 129-30, 133-36, 139, 142, 145-46, 148, 150-52, 156-57, 159, 161, 163, 165-67, 169, 171, 174-75, 180, 182-83, 185-88, 190-92, 194-95, 200, 208, 219, 225, 227-29
        CCS, 21
        Fighter, 17, 43, 45-47, 70
        Fighter Prototype (NP2), 14, 17
        Mk1, 52, 199, 201, 203-5, 208-11, 223
        Mk2, 52, 62, 199-211, 223, 225
        PDP, 21
        Team, 75, 80, 131, 145, 155, 175, 211
        Trainer, 39, 43, 45, 70, 207, 226
Light Signalling System (LSS), 108
Limited Series Production (LSP), 10, 21
Line Replaceable Units (LRUs), 39, 46, 48, 67, 73-74, 203, 205, 222
Linear Variable Differential Transformer (LVDT), 152
Lockheed Martin's Joint Strike Fighter, 43
Low Speed Taxi Tests (LSTT), 78-79
LOX converters, 222

M/s Proletarsky Zavod, 108
Mac Taggart Scott, 98
Main Airframe Static Test (MAST), 125, 128, 156-60
Main Landing Gear (MLG) mechanism, 46, 114, 116, 134-38, 145, 161, 179, 201, 204-5, 207-8
Maintenance Man Hours per Flight Hour (MMHFH), 28
Man-Machine Interface (MMI), 167
Maolankar, Cmde. Jaideep, the Chief Test Pilot, 19, 215, 226
Maryland, 90
Maximum Lift Coefficient (C_L Max), 149
Meat Ball, 101
MIDHANI, 17, 137
MiG-21s, 20
MiG 29K, 15, 107, 109
MiG-29K Aircraft, 33, 43, 99, 109-10, 125-26, 134-36, 230

MiG-29Ks, 95, 110
MiL-A-18717C, 116
MIL-A-8860 series, 116
MIL-L-6730, 119
MIL-STD-203G, 119
MIL-STD-461C, 166
MIL-STD-464, 166
Ministry of Defence (MoD), 14, 40-41, 217, 219, 223
Ministry of Finance, 41
Mk-1A aircraft, 10
Model-D Curtiss bi-plane, 90
Moscow, 110
Mr. Roy, the then General Manager at HAL (AR&DC), 157
Ms. Chitra, 14
Multi-Function Display (MFD), 55, 167, 226
Multi-Mode Radar (MMR) Rig, 167-68
Muscat, 213-14, 217

Nal IAF base, 221-22
Nasik, 17
National Aerospace Laboratories (NAL), 23, 49, 64, 185
National CLAW team, 184-85
National Flight Test Centre (NFTC), 7, 75, 80, 106, 168-69, 215, 221-22
National Security through Technological Self-Reliance, 223
Naval Air Staff Requirements (NASR), 13, 21, 37, 60, 199-200
Naval EMC Centre team, 167
Naval Head Quarters (NHQ), 13, 21, 28
Naval Prototype (NP), 43
Naval Structural Test Specimen (STS-N), 14
Navy Project Definition Phase (PDP-Navy), 13
Nayak, Mr. Ashok, Chairman HAL, 75
Nevskoye Design Bureau (NDB), 92, 98-99, 110
New Jersey, 90
Ni-Cd battery, 205
NITKA Complex, 92
Non-Destructive Test (NDT) methods, 119
Nose Landing Gears (NLG), 179
Nose Wheel Steering (NWS) test, 142
Note to the Cabinet Committee on Security (CCS Note), 41, 228
Numerical Master Geometry (NMG), 39, 63-64, 67

OEMs, 110
Oman, 213
On-Board Oxygen Generating System (OBOGS), 203
One-side Connectorisation, 73
Open Architecture Computer (OAC), 4
Operational Clean Configuration (OCC), 171
Optical Landing System (OLS), 44, 101, 105, 177
Outer Mold Line, 63
Outside Air Temperature (OAT), 220

Pai, Dr. TG, 14, 21
Parametric Identification (PID), 179, 188
Parrikar, Mr. Manohar the then Defence Minister of India, 212, 224
Patuxent River (Pax River), 90
Piping and Tubing, 67
Power Drive Units (PDU), 151-52
Preliminary Design Review (PDR), 61-62, 68, 125
Pre-Project Phase (PPP), 28-29
Product Lifecycle Management (PLM), 70
Programme Evaluation and Review Technique (PERT), 69
Programme Management Challenges, 57
Project Assistants, 11
Project Definition Phase (PDP), 6, 21, 23, 26, 28-29, 37, 42, 62, 224

for LCA Navy, 21-28
Project Engineers, 11
Proletarsky Zavod, 98
Prototype Vehicle (PV), 7, 43
Public Sector Undertakings, 10, 103
Pune, 99, 103

Qualification Test (QT), 122
Quality Assurance (QA), 60, 75, 77, 79, 217
Quartz, 225

R&D, 11, 40, 75, 96, 99, 103-4, 110, 216, 231
Rafale Marine (Rafale M) aircraft, 90-92
Raha, Air Chief Marshal Arup , the then Chief of Air Staff (CAS), IAF, 218, 227
Rail-launched Medium Range Missiles (MRMs), 27
Rajkumar, Air Marshal Philip, 8
Rajasthan, 217, 221-22
Rangachari, Gp. Capt., 215
Real Time Simulator (RTS), 79, 164-65, 177, 186
Rear Fuselage, 48
Restraining Gear System (RGS), 16, 105, 108-9, 134, 175, 190
Roll-in, 180
Rotary Variable Differential Transformer (RVDT), 151-52
Russia, 1, 41, 92, 98, 108, 110
Nevskoye Design Bureau (NDB), 107
Zvezda, 231
Russian, 97, 125
Russian Aircraft Corporation, MiG (RAC-MiG), 99, 104, 110-11, 125-26
Russian OLS, 102
Russian SU33, 93

SAAB Gripen, 231
Safety Review Board (SRB), 176, 190
Saraf, Dr. Amitab, Project Director at ADA, 198
Scotland, 98
Sea Harrier Aircraft, 15, 24, 30, 34, 41, 95, 98, 211
Sea Harrier Squadron, 97
Sea Hawk(s), 35, 37, 41, 94, 101
Sea King, 37
Sea-Eagle Class, 27
Search and Rescue (SAR), 214
Secondary Power System (SPS), 27
Shore Based Test Facility (SBTF), 15, 18-19, 59, 89-90, 95-96, 98, 102-3, 106-8, 110-11, 125, 128-30, 134, 143-45, 156, 158, 169, 171-72, 175-77, 179, 181-82, 188, 191, 198, 230
Simulation, 65
Capabilities, 66
Sinha, Cdr. Shekar (later Vice-Admiral), 13
Six Degrees of Freedom (6 DoF), 185
Ski-Jump Take-Off (SJTO), 27-28, 185-88, 190
Ski-jump Take-Off and Vertical Landing (STOVL), 15, 35-36, 41, 98
Ski-jump Take-off But Arrested Recovery (STOBAR), 14-16, 30, 34, 36, 41, 99, 227
Smart Multi-Function Displays, 207
Soft Gate, 61
Special Purpose Vehicle (SPV), 4
St. Petersburg, 92, 98
Structural Coupling Tests (SCT), 174
Structural Test Specimen (STS), 125, 128, 157-61
Structural Test Specimen in Navy standard (STS-N), 37
Stub Wing Jig, 71
Stub Wing Structure, 153
Subramanyam, Mr. PS, Distinguished Scientist, PGD (CA) & Director ADA, 212

Sukhoi, SU33 Programme, 92
Sustained Turn Rate (STR), 24
Swaraj, Late Ms. Sushma, the then External Affairs Minister, 215
System Requirement Review (SRR), 200
Systems Design and Evaluation Facility (SDEF), 167
Systems Requirement Review (SRR), 61

Take-off Control Post (ToCP), 100, 108
Tarmak Media House Networks, 8
Taxi Tests, 78
Taxi-In, 19, 91, 100, 109-10, 125, 128-30, 175, 179-81, 230
TD-Afloat, 171, 174
TD-Ashore, 171, 174
Technical Positions (TPs), 172
Technology Demonstrators (TD), 7-8, 20-21, 164, 171
Technology Readiness Levels (TRLs), 2, 20, 229
Tejas, 8, 10, 12, 21, 67, 203, 213-15, 217-25, 227
Telemetry, 168
Thangavel, Mr. P, 14
The Times of India, 8
Thump and Bash, 181
Tip of the iceberg, 96
Touch and Go, 144, 178, 181, 198
Trailing Edge Extensions (TEX), 201
Turbotech, 122
Twin-Engined Deck Based Fighter (TEDBF) aircraft, 211
Tyagi, Gp. Capt. Raj (Retd.), 225-26
Typical bomb drop trajectory, 65

UK, 1, 34, 35, 54, 90, 96-98
  Martin Baker, 231
  Royal Navy, 34
Ukraine, 15
  Saki, 89, 92
Unified Electronic Warfare Suite (UEWS), 203, 205
Unmanned Air Vehicles (UAVs), 1
US/USA, 1, 7, 35, 41, 97-98, 125, 231
  Lakehurst and Patuxent River, 89
  T-45A Goshawk, 91, 93
US Military Spec. MiL-A-18717C, 113
US Navy, 15-16, 35-36, 51, 89-91, 98, 101, 174, 177-78, 231
  'Arresting Gear Compatibility and Performance Test Matrix', 180
  F-18 Super Hornet, 119
USS *Birmingham*, 90
USS *Pennsylvania*, 90

Verma, Admiral Nirmal, 19
Visakhapatnam, 95

Wave-off, 27
Weapons, 55
Weapons Integration Rig (WIR), 167
Weight-off-wheel Switch, 192
Wind on Deck (WoD), 24, 53, 163, 173, 176
Wind Shield and Canopy, 46
Wind Tunnel Model Test, 64
Wing, 43, 49-50
Work Package Personnel, 11